Sandakan Brothel No. 8

Publication of this book was generously supported by
a grant from the Japan Foundation.

Sandakan Brothel No. 8

an episode in the
history of lower-class
Japanese women

Yamazaki Tomoko

Translated by
Karen Colligan-Taylor

 AN EAST GATE BOOK

M.E. Sharpe
Armonk, New York
London, England

AN EAST GATE BOOK

Photographs courtesy of Yamazaki Tomoko.

Library of Congress Cataloging-in-Publication Data

Yamazaki, Tomoko, 1932–
[Sandakan hachiban shōkan. English]
Sandakan brothel no. 8 : an episode in the history of lower-class Japanese women / by
Yamazaki Tomoko ; translated by Karen Colligan-Taylor.
p. cm.
"An East Gate book."
Includes index.
ISBN 0-7656-0353-5 (alk. paper). ISBN 0-7656-0354-3 (pbk. :alk. paper)
1. Prostitutes, Japanese—Asia, Southeastern. I. Colligan-Taylor, Karen. II. Title.
HQ232.A5Y31613   1998
306.74'2'095953—dc21
98-18941
CIP

Printed in the United States of America

The paper used in this publication meets the minimum requirements of
American National Standard for Information Sciences—
Permanence of Paper for Printed Library Materials,
ANSI Z 39.48-1984.

MV (c) 10 9 8 7 6 5 4 3 2 1
MV (p) 10 9 8 7 6 5 4 3 2 1

For Sumi

Contents

Translator's Preface and Acknowledgments

Sandakan Brothel No. 8, by Yamazaki Tomoko, reveals a neglected dimension of Japanese history and contributes to our documentation of the history of lower-class women. In her book Yamazaki records the oral history of a Japanese woman who was born at the turn of the century and sold at age ten into prostitution in North Borneo. The central issues addressed in *Sandakan Brothel No. 8* continue to confront us today: the trafficking of women and the interrelated causes of this traffic, including poverty, gender inequality, famine, war, and the development strategies of certain governments. Poor families may sell daughters to a trafficker, who will buy the girl outright or provide a loan which the girl must pay off through prostitution. In some cases girls are simply kidnapped and placed in the sex industry. Women in search of work may migrate from the countryside to the city or from one nation to another, where, separated from support networks, they are especially vulnerable to deception, exploitation, and abuse. They become easy prey for traffickers.

Human rights advocates today recognize the trafficking of women of all ages as a violent criminal act, which must be countered through the cooperation of the United Nations, all governments, and nongovernmental organizations at the international, national, and local levels. Community volunteer groups that provide safe living accommodations, medical care, and counseling are increasing. However, only a small fraction of captive women manage to escape and find such assistance.[1]

The New York–based Women's Environment and Development Organization (WEDO) reports that of 1.3 billion people living in poverty today, 70 percent are women.[2] Because women's labor is undervalued, their wages may be insufficient to support themselves, let alone contribute to the support of families who do not have a place in the new economic order. As the global economy evolves, our objectives and processes should be subject to constant reassessment. It is critical that we define the benefits and costs of economic globalization, identifying those who profit the most and those who bear the greatest burden. Special consideration should be given to those whose positions are often ignored: women, children, and the land that sustains us all.

Sandakan Brothel No. 8 will provide a historical context for and a human face to some of these issues. The translator's introduction examines further an evolving pattern in the traffic of women between Japan and other Asian countries.

I would like to express my deepest gratitude to my husband, Mike Taylor, for the hours he spent reading the manuscript in its many phases and making suggestions for improvement. I appreciate the advice and encouragement offered by my colleagues at the University of Alaska, historians Carol Gold and Peter Cornwall; my friend Yumi Fujiwara, a sensitive reader of women's literature; and my sister, Sumi Colligan, professor of cultural anthropology. Student assistants Reuben Loewen, Katie Raychel, and Heather Zimba freed my time for completion of the project.

The author, Yamazaki Tomoko, worked closely with me throughout the translation process, responding in detail to the many questions I faxed her and providing me with supplementary sources. It has been a pleasure to work with someone who has contributed so much to cross-cultural understanding among Asian women. Hayakawa Yoshihide, manager of the Rights Department at Bungei Shunju, facilitated negotiations between the various parties concerned in the project, and offered his support throughout the process.

To all of you: *kokoro kara no kansha o moshiagemasu.*

Karen Colligan-Taylor
Fairbanks, Alaska
March 1998

Notes

1. Some women's rights organizations define prostitution as work, clearly separating it from the issue of trafficking. Respecting the rights and human dig-

nity of the prostitute, these organizations aim to provide standards of protection for women in the sex industry, in terms of health and work conditions, as well as wages. Prostitutes do not constitute a homogeneous group; nor do the victims of traffickers today always come from the lower economic classes. The reader is encouraged to contact the Global Alliance Against Traffic in Women (GAATW) for further information on human rights platforms regarding prostitution and trafficking, particularly in the Asia Pacific region.

   2. *Christian Science Monitor,* March 13, 1998, p. 7.

Translator's Introduction

Sandakan Brothel No. 8 is a pioneer work on *karayuki-san,* impoverished Japanese women sold into overseas prostitution between the 1860s and 1930s.[1] The author, Yamazaki Tomoko (1932–), has recorded the oral testimony of one such *karayuki-san,* whose identity she protects by giving her the fictitious name Yamakawa Saki (1900?-1984).[2] The narrative follows the life of Osaki,[3] who is persuaded as a child of ten to accept cleaning work in Sandakan, North Borneo, then forced to work as a prostitute in a Japanese brothel, one of many such houses of assignation established throughout Asia in conjunction with the expansion of Japanese business interests.

While Osaki's story depicts a time long past, its relevance for the present day is startling. In an ironic reversal, the economic and social factors that a century ago drove poor, desperate women like Osaki to lives of prostitution in Southeast Asia now impel their Asian sisters of similar circumstances to sell themselves to Japanese customers in brothels from Thailand to Japan. Moreover, through Yamazaki's work, we see how the same discrimination against class and gender that promoted the traffic of Japanese women overseas in the Meiji and Taisho periods (1868–1926) would later justify the large-scale abduction of other Asian women as military "comfort women" along the Japanese front lines prior to and during World War II. In Osaki's life Yamazaki has discovered a window into the lives of women who have existed at the lowest tier of the socioeconomic hierarchy. As the century turns anew, how many modern-day lives will be illuminated by the same window?

In the following pages we will explore the roots of *karayuki-san* in geography, history, social relations, and economic conditions. We will look at the role played by *karayuki-san* in colonial expansion, and the model provided by the *karayuki* system for the large-scale recruitment of women for the Japanese military. A study of the past provides a basis for understanding the contemporary commodification of women by Japanese men at home and abroad. Finally, we will become acquainted with the author, Yamazaki Tomoko, and her efforts to present another facet of modern Japanese history through a study of the exchange of lower-class women between Asian countries since the 1860s.

Karayuki-san of Northwestern Kyushu: Geographical and Historical Origins

The term *karayuki* (literally, going to Kara, that is, China, or abroad) was initially coined by the people of northern Kyushu to refer to those who sought work overseas. Later, *karayuki* came to refer primarily to impoverished women who sought work in China, Southeast Asia, or Siberia during the Meiji (1868–1912) and Taisho (1912–1926) periods. These women, more often than not, were lured abroad through coercion, deception, or abduction, expecting to find jobs in the service industry, only to be thrust into prostitution.

Karayuki-san came initially and principally from the Shimabara Peninsula and the Amakusa Islands of northwestern Kyushu. Most of these women left their homeland from the port of Nagasaki. The city of Nagasaki, west of the Shimabara Peninsula across Tachibana Bay, was a major center of international exchange during the premodern period. Yamazaki's final chapter provides a detailed analysis of the geographical and historical reasons for a mass exodus of the lower-class population from this region following the collapse of the Tokugawa shogunate in the 1860s. Here we will provide a backdrop for Yamazaki's discussion, beginning with related events in the sixteenth century.

In 1562 the daimyo of Omura converted to Christianity and in 1571 this feudal lord established Nagasaki as the chief port of call for Portuguese ships. In 1579 he gave control of the community to the Jesuits. This act was rescinded in 1587 by Toyotomi Hideyoshi (1536–1598), one of three powerful generals who unified the country after two and a half centuries of civil war. Hideyoshi feared that Christianity would disturb the established social order and become a political threat. In 1600 the reins of power were seized by Tokugawa Ieyasu (1542–1616), who established the Tokugawa *bakufu*, or shogunate, a political regime that was to govern the country until the restoration of imperial power in 1868. By 1615 there were close to five hundred thousand Christians in Japan.[4] Ieyasu followed Hideyoshi's policy of suppressing Christian influence, and his successor, Hidetada, escalated the persecution, which culminated in 1638 in the slaughter of more than twenty thousand peasants. This incident, known as the Shimabara–Amakusa Rebellion, began as an uprising over oppressive taxation and misgovernment, but soon developed into a Christian revolt. With this mass slaughter of the peasants in Shimabara and Amakusa, the Christian movement in Japan was virtually extinguished.

Hidetada instituted a policy of seclusion which severed trade and cultural relations with other countries for two centuries. In laws passed between 1633 and 1639, Japanese were prohibited from traveling abroad. Should anyone leave and attempt to return, they would face the death penalty. As another means to prevent Christians or Christian thought from entering the country, the Portuguese were expelled, and the Dutch were permitted entry only to Dejima, a small island in Nagasaki harbor. Chinese merchants were restricted to Nagasaki.

During the Genroku period (1688–1704), Chinese merchants involved in trade with Japan established a flourishing residential district in Nagasaki known as Tojin Yashiki ("residence of Chinese"). It was common for these Chinese to hire Japanese women as maids (called, derogatorily, *toohi,* "maidservant or slut of a Chinese"), and a number of them traveled to China when their masters returned home. Among those Japanese who moved to China were some who earned money doing only housework and returned safely to Japan, but most of the women were deceived by the Chinese and sold to brothels. In addition to these maidservants, there were Japanese women who entered the Tojin Yashiki district of their own accord as prostitutes. It is with these two groups of women—those who followed their masters to China and those who entered the Chinese district to sell their favors, that we find the origin of the term *karayuki-san.*[5] *Karayuki* is a contraction of the earlier terms *karabitoyuki,* "going with/to Chinese people," and *karankuniyuki,* "going to the country of China."

From the end of the Tokugawa period through the first few years of Meiji, around 1850 through 1870, the term *karayuki-san* came to be used for those women who went abroad as prostitutes, regardless of their destination. The law forbidding travel abroad—largely ignored as the shogunate had weakened—was officially rescinded in 1866. As the Tokugawa period came to a close, more and more women from different regions of Japan were sold into prostitution and sent by various routes to China and Southeast Asia.

Karayuki-san as an Outgrowth of Organized Prostitution

The export to foreign countries of prostitution services from northwestern Kyushu and other regions of Japan was the natural extension of a long history of officially condoned prostitution at home. For centuries girls from impoverished rural areas were abducted and sold to brothels in cities and along trade routes throughout the country.

During the Kamakura period (1185–1333), travel between the imperial capital of Kyoto and the first military capital of Kamakura, just south of present-day Tokyo, increased, bringing a flourishing business to inns along this route. A loosely organized system of prostitution grew to serve travelers. Along the great highway linking the western and eastern capitals, prostitutes were controlled locally by specific procurers. During the Muromachi period (1378–1573), the political capital was again centered in Kyoto. Prostitution boomed with urban growth and gained official recognition and regulation. Under the shogun Yoshiharu (in office 1521–1546), a bureau of prostitution was established, and a tax was levied on all prostitutes.

As Toyotomi Hideyoshi amassed power in the 1580s, he chose Osaka as the site for his principal castle. Here in this city one of Hideyoshi's vassals created the first walled-in "pleasure quarter" in Japan. Following the unification of the country in 1600, many *ronin* (masterless or unemployed samurai) opened brothels or sections of towns designated as "pleasure quarters." The most famous of these red-light districts was the Yoshiwara, established in 1618. Located in Edo (present-day Tokyo), headquarters of the Tokugawa shogunate, the Yoshiwara was a large walled-in district with a hierarchy of brothels and teahouses.

Though highly glamorized by the woodblock prints and erotic literature of the Tokugawa period, the Yoshiwara kept in its confines girls and young women sold into sexual servitude by parents desperate for cash.[6] Many older daughters left willingly to help their families, though they had only the vaguest notion of the world they were to enter. Theoretically women could pay off their contracts, but the expenses they incurred made this almost impossible. As a prostitute aged, her prospects became ever more bitter and degrading. Nevertheless, prostitution was apparently accepted by the employed as a means of livelihood, and by the employer as a social necessity, considered "no more immoral than offering a glass of water to a thirsty man."[7] The "recruitment" of rural girls to work in urban brothels continued into the nineteenth and twentieth centuries, particularly in response to the rapid growth of the male labor force. If public brothels were abolished, it was argued, the wives and daughters of "refined families" would be victimized by frustrated men.[8]

Whatever rationalizations may have been voiced for the maintenance of licensed prostitution and whatever euphemisms may have been used to disguise human traffic as temporary contractual employment, Japan's longtime approbation of the flesh trade came under international scrutiny in June 1872 when a Peruvian vessel, the *Maria Luz,* entered Yokohama harbor for repairs. On board were a group of Chinese slaves under transport from Macao to Peru. One of the coolies jumped ship and was rescued by the crew of an English battleship. The resident charge d'affairs of the British Empire investigated the incident, contacting the Japanese minister of foreign affairs about the mistreatment of some 230 Chinese "passengers," among whom were thirteen children. Under close scrutiny from many foreign legations, the Japanese government declared the Chinese coolies to be free and condemned the Peruvians for running a slave trade. The Peruvians strongly objected, pointing out that the Japanese themselves sold girls and young women to brothels. Much concerned about adopting, at least superficially, Western political and social values, Meiji policymakers issued in October 1872 an act of emancipation, prohibiting the buying and selling of persons for any type of service, and freeing those in bondage from their current contracts.[9] The law, designed only for cosmetic purposes, did not bring about significant social change. Later, those women who had no alternative but to continue their work as prostitutes were issued a license by the government.

By closing many establishments in the water trade without making any attempt to provide job training or other assistance, the Meiji government had left women stranded.[10] The day after the edict was issued, for example, seventy women released in Yokohama found themselves without a means to survive. A Chinese man arranged their transport to Hong Kong, Singapore, and other destinations where they were again sold into prostitution. Of course, not only women from the water trade went overseas, but also men and women who had no other way to overcome their poverty.

Whereas many *karayuki-san* had heretofore gone abroad of their own accord, by 1877 a system emerged to systematically gather them up and send them abroad. Prostitutes were deemed necessary for European and, later, Japanese colonies in Asia, where the proportion of men constituting the colonizing elite and imported labor was far higher than the women available to serve them. When Japanese men working abroad realized that they could profit by making arrangements for *karayuki-san* to be sold into such services, they returned to Japan to collect women, sending them in groups to China and Southeast Asia.[11] Government statistics show that by 1910 there were close to twenty thousand Japanese women registered as overseas prostitutes.[12] By comparison, there were 47,541 women registered as prostitutes in public brothels within Japan.[13]

Patriarchy, Poverty, and the Lower-Class Female Work Force

Yamazaki views her informant, Osaki, as the embodiment of the suffering experienced by all Japanese women who have long been oppressed under the dual yoke of gender and class. At the root of this oppression is the Confucian system of patriarchy, introduced to Japan from China in the seventh century. Confucian thought exerted its greatest influence on social structure from the seventeenth century, when it became the framework of all social relations under the Tokugawa shogunate (1600–1868). The Neo-Confucian concepts adopted by the Tokugawa regime emphasized fulfilling one's social duty in terms of five basic relationships: lord/subject; father/son; husband/wife; elder brother/younger brother; friend/friend. All siblings deferred to the eldest brother, who was expected in most cases to become the family heir. Women were told to obey first their fathers, then their husbands, and later in life, their sons. The social superiority of the male within this system permitted the exploitation of women financially, physically, sexually, and emotionally.[14]

The economic causes for the exploitation of women can be found in agrarian poverty and in the government's inability or unwillingness to introduce measures to aid the peasantry. Although improvements in agriculture during the Meiji period (1868–1912) brought about a certain degree of rural prosperity, this rise in living standards was distributed unevenly. Northwestern Kyushu and the "underdeveloped" regions of northern Japan in particular tended to be sacrificed for the urban growth of central Honshu. Taxation rates for tenant farmers were the equivalent of 60 percent of their yield, and, especially during times of famine, starving peasants felt compelled to sell their daughters in order to save the rest of the family.

In the peasant household, where economic survival was the most important consideration, marriage was a way of recruiting a permanent member of the family workforce.[15] The essential prerequisites for a wife were her capacity for hard labor and her ability to bear children. Because one was expected to make personal sacrifices for the economic survival of the family and village, it was not uncommon for the most dispensable members of the family, young girls, to take jobs as maids or baby-sitters in nearby towns or coal mines, or to be sold out of the region to work in brothels or geisha houses, farms or factories.[16] These transactions were conducted by traffickers, or procurers (*zegen*), victims of the same rural poverty who then exploited their own class.

The type of work available to young rural women with little or no education in late-nineteenth- and early-twentieth-century Japan was temporary in nature, with positions in constant flux. Most frequently the girl would have to leave home to find employment in a more highly developed region. Many found work as factory operatives in spinning, silk reeling, or textile weaving mills, where the manufacturer's profits in the international market were attributable to the skillful fingers, long working hours, and pitiful wages of their female employees. Old records of interviews held with factory women as well as an analysis of the songs these semiliterate and illiterate girls made up to describe their working conditions and to express their feelings have become an important source for writing their history.

In her article, "Yet to Be Heard, the Voices of Meiji Factory Women," Patricia Tsurumi suggests that in spite of the long working hours, very poor living conditions, and harsh treatment, including sexual harassment, to which these women were subjected, they, like their counterparts in other lower-class professions, may not have seen themselves as victims, but rather as proud contributors to family and village economy.[17] On the other hand, the number of suicides and runaways, not to mention the multitudes who died of malnutrition, overwork, and tuberculosis, suggests that whether or not the girls viewed themselves as victims, they were certainly abused. And, if their situation at home was little better than conditions at work, the role of the government, which did nothing to alleviate the misery of either, should be brought into question. In her article about factory women, Professor Tsurumi makes a point equally relevant to our discussion of *karayuki-san*: "Questions about the Meiji state as victimizer are what historians of modern Japan should put to one another and perhaps to the Japanese people today. Such questions are extremely relevant in Japan today, where we witness harsh exploitation of foreign workers that looks suspiciously like the treatment of female factory women during Japan's early industrialization."[18]

According to a survey taken in 1921, there were as many women working as maids in Japan as there were factory women. No distinction was made between their work time and free time; their job descriptions and salaries were vague; and in the case where relatives were employed, there was not even an opportunity to retire. Because these maids were confined within one household, they found themselves isolated from society and could not unite as did factory workers to improve their conditions. They were psychologically lonely as well, separated as they were from their own home and family. Before World War II, maids were not only asked to do all the housework, but to serve as sexual playthings for the amusement of the father or eldest son in the household.[19]

Promotion of an Overseas Flesh Trade by Local Traffickers and National Leaders

Going to an urban center or even venturing abroad to find work and send money home was not uncommon among other cultures in the nineteenth century. In the 1870s, at the same time that young women from northwestern Kyushu were going abroad to seek work, young Irish women were finding positions as maids in the eastern United States. One-third of all money sent home to Ireland at this time came from its women. Whereas the Irish sold only their labor, however, their Japanese counterparts did not fare as well. Promised higher-paying jobs abroad than they could find at home, they became ensnared in the flesh trade.

The primary objective of the Meiji government was to catch up with the advanced capitalism of America and Europe. At the foundation of this effort lay the miserable lot of the rural peasant and urban laborer.

Because the government did not wish to show the underside of society, there are few records of transactions in white slavery. In 1960, however, the nature of this trade was brought to light by the publication of *Muraoka Iheiji jiden* [The Autobiography of Muraoka Iheiji], discussed by Yamazaki in chapter 1. We learn from this work that the majority of Japanese traffickers, like the women they sold, were born into agrarian poverty, usually the second or third sons of peasant families. Whether working as a procurer or his agent, the wages these men earned in the flesh trade were far greater than they could expect as tenant farmers or mine workers at home. Many of these men already had criminal records; they were either fleeing from the law or seeking easy money after release from prison. In 1890 Muraoka's extensive network of traffickers included gamblers, thieves, pickpockets, rapists, and embezzlers. Muraoka justified his activities on the ground that *karayuki-san* would establish a foothold for Japan in Southeast Asia, making it easier for merchants and soldiers to follow.[20] The familiarity of these traffickers with their merchandise made the girls easy prey.

In an October 1967 article, *"Ikiteiru karayukisan"* [Living *Karayuki-san*], written for the journal *20 seiki* [20th Century], agrarian writer Shima Kazuharu describes a conversation he had with a former *karayuki-san* born in 1886. At the time of the interview she was eighty-two. She told him that she had left Amakusa at age sixteen to work in Nagasaki as a maid. She had to work very hard from early morning to late at night. One day a man approached her and asked her in a kind voice where she was from and whether she found her present job difficult. Then he told her about an opening for a shop clerk at a wool yarn factory. The salary would be 40 yen per month, he said, so wouldn't she consider it? As the young woman worked day in and day out without a single holiday for only fifty sen (1 sen = 1/100 yen) per month, the offer was very tempting. The next day the man returned and gave the young woman a box of cosmetics and a flannel kimono. Thus baited, she walked away from her master's home right then and there, and followed the man, only to be sold into prostitution.[21]

Many other young women in Kyushu who had left home to work as maids or shop attendants were baited in the same manner, gathered together at such ports as Nagasaki or Moji, and stowed away on ships bound for China or Southeast Asia. These ships were generally freighters, so the women were put in boxes, loaded onto small boats, lifted up onto the ship, and placed down in the holds. The average meal was two small balls of rice, one pickle, and one cup of water. If the freighters expected to encounter strict customs surveillance, the women might be stowed in coal bunkers or beneath the toilets.[22]

As the Meiji period progressed, *karayuki-san* came to play an integral, if not clearly articulated, role in national policies of expansion. The amount of foreign currency sent back to Japan was enormous. The Nagasaki post office alone reported handling over two hundred thousand yen a year remitted by *karayuki-san* working in Southeast Asia.[23] Acknowledging their contribution to the economy, a leading statesman, Fukuzawa Yukichi (1834–1901), encouraged the emigration of women as prostitutes, particularly to regions undergoing rapid economic development. Their presence was influential, he asserted, in forging a modern free enterprise economy.[24] On March 16, 1885, *Jiji shimpo* published an editorial by Fukuzawa in which he states that Japan cannot wait for its neighboring countries to modernize; Japan must cut itself free from its "bad companions" in Asia, and align itself with the civilized nations of the West. Japan should deal with China and Korea, Fukuzawa advocated, in the same way that Westerners do.[25] This treatise, known as *Datsua-ron,* "Abandoning Asia," set the tone for Japanese attitudes and policies toward Asia—attitudes of contempt and policies of aggression that made use of lower-class women as if the national interest, devoid of social justice, were all that mattered.

Karayuki-san and Japanese Expansion

The total number of women who traveled overseas as *karayuki-san* is unclear, but estimates for the year 1910, the height of *karayuki-san* engaged in prostitution, ranges from twenty thousand to thirty thousand. The table on the next page illustrates the number of Japanese women engaged in prostitution who registered as foreign residents for the years 1910, 1916, 1926, and 1935. In order to avoid the social stigma attached to prostitution, women often reported other occupations. Therefore, data collected by offices of the Foreign Ministry probably underrepresent women involved in prostitution. It should be noted that Taiwan and Korea, also major centers of *karayuki-san* activity, are not represented in this table since, by 1910, they were colonies of Japan. The *karayuki* presence in Southeast Asia peaked in 1916, dropping off rapidly with changes in Western colonial policies and concomitant pressure to eliminate the Japanese flesh trade. Fluctuations in the numbers of prosti-

Japanese Women Registered as Foreign Residents, 1910–1935, Who Reported Prostitution as Their Primary Occupation

Region	1910	1916	1926	1935
Siberia	631	870	22	0
Manchuria	4,275	2,839	2,114	10,735
Kwantung	7,928	1,461	—	—
Mainland China	1,420	997	1,327	2,063
South Asia	3,745	3,938	789	193
North America	1,033	350	179	182
South America	34	5	24	5
Europe	29	0	0	0
Oceania	2	0	3	0
Africa	—	—	8	0
Totals	19,097	10,460	4,466	13,178

Adapted from: Kurahashi Masanao, *Kita no karayuki-san* [Karayuki of the North]. (Tokyo: Kyoei Shobo, 1989), p. 73. This table is based on data collected by the Ministry of Foreign Affairs.

tutes in different parts of Asia suggest the ebb and flow of Japan's economic and military expansion in these regions. It should be noted, however, that these are not always the same women moving to another location. Many young women became ill and died before age thirty. Others were able to return to their homeland.

Expansion into Asian markets was linked with Japan's emergence as an imperialist power. Japanese success in the Russo-Japanese War of 1904–1905 expanded Japan's sphere of influence and gained the country new respect in the international community. In the Treaty of Portsmouth the Russians recognized Japan's military and economic interests in Korea, and ceded to Japan their leasehold on the Kwantung Peninsula as well as the South Manchurian Railway between Port Arthur and Mukden.

As industrialization in Japan increased, exports shifted from agricultural to manufactured products. In the early 1900s Japanese businessmen looked to Asia—mainland China, as well as the colony of Taiwan and the protectorate of Korea—as locations to market manufactured goods and acquire raw materials. European withdrawal from Asian markets during World War I opened new trade opportunities. Lower-middle-class workers were drawn abroad by the promises of economic success and social prestige in an overseas colony.[26] In enclaves of recent economic and military expansion the ratio of women to men was very low; hence, the demand for *karayuki-san.*

Many Japanese consuls stationed abroad viewed the presence of *karayuki-san* in their jurisdictions as a national disgrace and urged Japanese authorities to bring them home. On the other hand, some national leaders at home preferred to accept foreign capital in any form for the development of Japan's urban-industrial sector. To redeem its image in the international community, Japan promulgated a law in 1896 to prevent women from leaving the country to engage in prostitution abroad. However, because passports were not required for Japanese citizens going to Chinese and Korean ports, and because traffickers were adept at smuggling young girls onto foreign soil without proper documents, Japanese authorities had little control. This was convenient for Japanese officials who still considered that the presence of a well-organized brothel system fostered the prosperity of overseas Japanese merchants. Moreover, *karayuki-san* would continue to send much needed taxable foreign exchange to Japan, thereby bolstering their regional economies and the nation itself.[27] Consequently, official enforcement of the 1896 law languished.

Shortly after Osaki, the subject of Yamazaki's study, went abroad as a child, other events conspired to keep the flesh trade in operation. In 1915 the Japanese government presented China with the so-called "Twenty-One Demands," aimed at a major expansion of Japan's rights in Manchuria. China was also asked to recognize Japan's succession to the former German rights in the Shandong Peninsula. Outraged Chinese nationalist intellectuals fanned anti-Japanese sentiment, bringing about an explosion on May 4, 1919, when students, merchants, and workers staged demonstrations all over China. A boycott of Japanese goods spread throughout the treaty ports.[28] During this crisis Japan continued to depend on foreign currency remitted by *karayuki-san* as one means of bolstering the economy.

By 1920, however, the *karayuki-san* were finally deemed to have outlived their usefulness. Their adverse effect on the prestige of Japan now definitely outweighed their value in promoting the development of business interests abroad. The imperial government ordered consular representatives to repatriate all overseas Japanese prostitutes.[29] Pressure for their removal began in Singapore, and spread through Southeast Asia.

Some *karayuki-san* moved on to Manchuria, rich in natural resources, which became in the 1930s an economic lifeline for Japan. In 1931 Manchuria was seized by the Japanese Kwantung Army and presented to the world as the "independent state" of Manchukuo. By the end of the war there were more than two million Japanese in this region; approximately 1,270,000 eventually escaped back to Japan.[30]

As Yamazaki emphasizes in her final chapter, *karayuki-san* who returned to their country in the 1920s were simply abandoned at Japanese ports, without prospects for a new livelihood. Although *karayuki-san* had earned millions of yen for Japan, in many cases they were ostracized by family and community members, whose lifestyles had improved and ways of thinking had changed. *Sandakan Brothel No. 8* documents the fate of some of these women.

From *Karayuki-san* to Military Comfort Women

Just as *karayuki-san* formed the vanguard of colonial and commercial expansion, "military comfort women" (*jugun ianfu*) were in the vanguard of Japanese military forces in Asia. By the 1930s the established practice of providing women for sexual service to Japanese men stationed overseas no longer relied on shipments from the Japanese homeland. Now most of the women were foreign nationals. Between 1930 and 1945 approximately 139,000 women were forced to satisfy the sexual needs of Japanese military troops, in what has been described as "the legalized military rape of subject women on a scale and over a period of time previously unknown in history."[31] Of this number, approximately 80 percent were Korean, and 10 percent were from China, Taiwan, the Philippines, Indonesia, Malaya, Vietnam, and the East Indies (including Dutch women).[32] Only 10 percent were Japanese. Young Korean girls were seized in preference to Japanese women, because it was deemed that the latter should remain at home to replace men in farming and factory work, and because the troops' morale might suffer if their own sisters were pressed into prostitution.[33] Eighty percent of comfort women were between fourteen and eighteen years old, and the majority were deceived or kidnapped in the same manner as were young Japanese women who became *karayuki-san* in earlier decades.

The most frequently made promise to Korean girls was that they would be given good jobs in Japanese factories. These girls came, for the most part, from the same socioeconomic background as their Japanese *karayuki* counterparts. Their families were tenant farmers working small holdings averaging less than 2.5 acres. In economic desperation, parents allowed their daughters to be purchased by recruiters, or girls left voluntarily believing a better future awaited them. Japanese colonial authorities easily took advantage of this crisis of poverty and the low value placed on daughters.[34] Of the Japanese women recruited, some were professional prostitutes, including former *karayuki-san* who had worked off their loans and could not find other work at home. Others were conscripted believing they would clean and cook for the troops.

After the war, many Korean returnees were unable to get married because chastity for women was held in high value. Even if they did marry, many could not bear children. Many repatriates suffered from physical diseases and injuries, and all from psychological scars. Like so many of their *karayuki-san* counterparts who were repatriated to Japan in the 1920s, Korean comfort women found themselves abandoned at the bottom of the economic pile. As non-Japanese, these women had been subjected to racial as well as social and gender discrimination.[35]

Both the *karayuki-san* and comfort women systems resulted from the inferior position of women in Asian society. These systems also expressed a form of class consciousness in which the "peasantry" were considered no more than chattel to be used as tools in Japanese colonial expansion.

The Commodification of Women Following World War II

When Occupation forces were stationed in Japan after the war, a reversal occurred in the male power structure, affecting the race but not the class and economic circumstances of women recruited to serve in "comfort stations." Japanese financial institutions funded a roundup of young women in destitute circumstances, separated from their families or orphaned after the war. The organization directing this "recruitment" of women by gang members was given the English name "Recreation and Amusement Association."[36]

Today such "recreation and amusement" continues around military bases worldwide, and is further manifested in the form of sex tourism.[37] Suzuki Yoko, a specialist in women's history, suggests that the modern sex industry, whether it involves the consumption of Asian women by Japanese men at home or abroad, is a contemporary version of the Japanese Imperial Army's exploitation of Asian women as comfort women. The only difference, she points out, is that the men now wear business suits rather than military uniforms.[38]

Sex tourism succeeds when Third World women are economically desperate enough to enter prostitution. An alliance is formed between local governments in search of foreign currency and both local and foreign businessmen willing to invest in the sex-travel industry.[39] Thailand, for example, in 1986 earned more from tourism than from any other business, including the export of rice. A large part of the earnings came from sex tourism. Poor rural Thai women migrate to the cities in search of work, leaving the countryside due to a shortage of land and decently paid job opportunities. Once in the city, they can make over six times more in a massage parlor than they can in a nonentertainment-related job.[40]

As an anti-sex industry tour movement developed in Japan, Japanese women sought issue not with the seller but with the consumer. The word for prostitution, *baishun,* heretofore written with characters which mean "selling spring," was changed to "buying spring," which is pronounced in the same way. The term was then coopted by men, and used in handbooks on how to "buy spring" in Thailand and other countries.

Japanese men do not have to go abroad, however, in search of spring. Nowadays more than one hundred thousand Asian women, mainly from Thailand and the Philippines, are sent to Japan each year to work in the sex industry. These are *Japayuki-san,* or "bound for Japan," the modern-day equivalent of the *karayuki-san.* Members of organized crime syndicates (the Japanese *boryokudan,* or yakuza) approach young women with promises of well-paying jobs in factories or in the entertainment industry as singers and dancers. Upon arrival in Japan the women find their passports confiscated by gang members. Unable to speak Japanese, they are trapped as sex slaves in bars, bathhouses, or even remote houses up in the mountains.

In fall 1992 Japan's *Yomiuri* newspaper ran a series called "Victims of the Sex Industry." Their stories are all too familiar, echoing abduction tactics used with both *karayuki-san* and comfort women. One article describes a young Thai woman who needed to support herself and her child, in addition to sending money home for her family.

> One day a Thai broker approached her with an attractive offer that she believed would enable her to save up enough money to fulfill her dream

of one day opening her own beauty salon. He promised to set her up in
a factory job in Japan in exchange for eighty thousand baht (about four
hundred thousand yen). She eagerly accepted the deal, not discovering
what she would really be doing until after she arrived at Narita airport
on May 7.[41]

In another case, three Thai women killed their boss in order to seize
a bag containing their passports and some cash so they could escape
captivity. Arrested on charges of "robbery and murder," one woman
wrote a letter to the Embassy of Thailand in Tokyo, in an attempt to
dissuade other Thai women from coming to Japan.

> There are no factories where we can work, there are only bars and pubs
> and men who only think about drinking and having sex. I really suf-
> fered a lot. We had to go to bed with dirty men and strangers. If you
> don't do whatever you are told to do, you are beaten by the boss or the
> proprietress (mama-san).
>   For them we Thai women are mere animals. They have the power of
> life and death over us. Japan is not heaven but hell for us Thai women.
> It's a barefaced lie that cherry blossoms are waiting for you. What is
> waiting for you are men whose only concern is having sex. . . . [42]

With the crash of the Southeast Asian economy in early 1998, the
number of *Japayuki-san* has increased. As in the case of the *karayuki-
san,* overseas workers buttress their country's economy with money
sent home to their families. A young woman from the Philippines
interviewed by the Kyodo news service just before her departure for
Osaka in February 1998, said she expected to earn $600 per month as
an entertainer. "Life is hard in the Philippines, and I want to help my
parents and five siblings," explained Carmelita Alileo, 25.[43] With this
minimal salary Carmelita will likely face substandard living conditions, making her more vulnerable to exploitation.

The Japanese government has done nothing to ameliorate the mistreatment of women migrants, preferring to turn a blind eye on those
activities that take place at the intersection of racism, sexism, and
consumer capitalism.[44] Matsui Yayori, Southeast Asian correspondent
for the major national newspaper *Asahi,* ranks Japan as the world's
largest trafficker in human beings. This despite the fact that Japan is
party to both the United Nations Convention for the Suppression of
Traffic in Persons and the Exploitation of Prostitution of Others (1949)

and the Convention on the Elimination of All Forms of Discrimination Against Women (1979). Both the courts and police have turned a blind eye to systematic exploitation and abuse.[45]

At the International Conference on the Trafficking and Commercial Sexual Exploitation of Women and Children held in Manila during December 1997, the United Nations Children's Fund (UNICEF) released a paper in which it estimated that commercial sex workers in Asia could number more than two million, about half of them children.[46] This is a grave issue with broad social, economic, political, and public health dimensions. International organizations must exert pressure on local governments to confront the roots of loss of livelihood in the rural sector and to explore alternatives to survival in an urban setting. The clientele of sex tourism must be educated and sensitized to the devastating consequences of their activities. The indifference of certain governments or groups of clientele must be countered by international exposure and denunciation.

One of the six demands made of the Japanese government by former Korean comfort women in a widely published letter dated October 17, 1990, was "that these facts be continuously related in historical education so that such misdeeds are not repeated."[47] As the data above indicate, however, such misdeeds *are* being repeated every day, by Japanese men at home and abroad, as well as by men of other nationalities all over the globe. Asian history continues to be a product of a patriarchal system which influences historical interpretation, dictating what will be highlighted and what omitted. Historians must rewrite the past in a way that clarifies the contributions and sacrifices made by women. Documentation of socioeconomic causes of abuse as well as mechanisms of control may be the first step in assisting women from Third World societies who are still ensnared in a historical system of exploitation.

Yamazaki Tomoko

Yamazaki Tomoko notes that when she began her research, histories of women focused only on an elite minority, leaving the lives of common people unexplored. She has devoted her career to documenting the lives of the larger mass of women from the lower levels of society. Yamazaki points out that whereas elite women in Japan have enjoyed many ties to the West, lower-class women have had strong ties with the rest of Asia. Moreover, while the relationship of elite Japanese women to the West has existed for the most part on a conceptual level, dealing with thought and culture, the relationship of lower-class women to Asia has revolved around the physical realities of everyday life. This more physical, and generally bitter, relationship characterizes modern Japanese relations with Asia, toward which Japan has continued to take a stance of military or commercial aggression.

Yamazaki feels that as Japanese women assume a stronger role in society, the liberation of Japanese women must not occur at the expense of the welfare of other Asian women. She believes that through research and dialogue Asian women can document shared experiences in the past and concerns in the present, thereby assisting one another in facing a brighter future. Toward this end she established a study group called "Ajia josei koryushi kenkyukai" (Association for Research on the History of Exchanges Between Women of Asian Countries), to which women from diverse Asian backgrounds are invited to discuss issues of mutual concern. Since November 1967 the association has been publishing a journal called *Ajia josei koryushi kenkyu* [Research on the History of Exchanges Between Asian Women], which documents not only the forced movement of women from one country to another, but individually motivated exchanges in the form of study and teaching abroad, cultural and historical research, and various volunteer human rights efforts. She and her colleagues are adding a new chapter to the modern history of Asia which focuses on women and interprets events from a woman's perspective. In her book *Ajia josei koryushi* (Tokyo: Chikuma Shobo, 1995), Yamazaki discusses contacts made between Japanese and other Asian women in the Meiji and Taisho periods.

Many of Yamazaki's books and essays provide profiles of Asian women who have made significant contributions to the betterment of women's position in society. In both her current writing and lectures, she addresses such issues as means of providing redress to former comfort women; male role expectations of Asian women in service industries; Japanese women and children abandoned in China after World War II; and Asian women wed into Japanese farming communities today.

This supply of brides represents another aspect of the commodity market. Large sums of money are transferred between Japanese and foreign brokers to obtain brides from throughout Asia, but especially

the Philippines, for Japanese farmers or men working in small industries. According to Yamazaki, such arrangements are often less a "marriage" than a relationship in which a woman is fed in return for taking
care of the house and the daily needs of the husband and his live-in
parents. There are some positive scenarios in which the couples have
overcome inevitable cultural conflicts to develop a warm relationship,
but many women experience isolation and discrimination. Well-educated
contemporary Japanese women, accustomed to having a job and enjoying
personal freedom, have avoided conservative rural marriages which bind
them in traditional roles and isolate them in the countryside.

Yamazaki, who has devoted much of her life to documenting the
history of lower-class Asian women, endured many social and economic hardships herself during and after World War II. Yamazaki was
born in Sasebo City, Nagasaki Prefecture. When she was ten months
old her family moved to Kure City in Hiroshima Prefecture. In August
1940, when Yamazaki was eight, the submarine of which Yamazaki's
father was captain vanished en route to the Aleutian Islands. Several
months later the Imperial Navy issued a statement that the men on
board had died in honor of the emperor during training maneuvers. The
details of the incident were never revealed. Yamazaki has ever since
hated the imperial system to which so many lives were sacrificed and
under which so much information was covered up. Later she was to
write *Narushio no kanata ni* (1987), her own investigation of the submarine incident. After her father's death, Yamazaki moved with her
mother and sister to Hiroshima City where her mother found employment in a munitions factory. Of her life between ages eight and thirteen
Yamazaki says, "This represents a period of time when our nation
squeezed the last drop of blood out of our people."

Two months before the bomb fell, Yamazaki and her sister were
evacuated to the home of maternal relatives in the mountains of Fukui
Prefecture. On August 6, 1945, they lost almost all their classmates to
the bomb. At her relatives' house Yamazaki slept on the floor of an
uninsulated attic, often awakening to find herself covered with a light
sprinkling of snow that had filtered through cracks in the roofing. As
the oldest girl, she took care of her relatives' children. She boiled rice
and heated the bath with fires made of rice straw. Most farm families
continued to live a life of austerity for close to ten years after the war.

After graduating from high school Yamazaki commuted from this
house for two years to take evening courses at Fukui University. When

she had completed a two-year degree, Yamazaki taught at an elementary school. Later in life she would co-author with her husband two prize-winning books on Japanese preschool education.

Deciding to try out life in a large urban setting, Yamazaki moved to Tokyo, where she held clerical and waitressing positions. She married a Korean graduate student, and was for a time involved in political student movements. Although the marriage was short-lived, Yamazaki gained a new appreciation for the racial prejudice experienced by Koreans in Japan as well as an understanding of the challenges involved in balancing different cultural expectations within a single household. After the dissolution of this relationship, Yamazaki rented a room and continued to work several different jobs. One evening when she was walking home from a waitressing job, she became the victim of a violent attack, in which her face and hands were slashed with a knife. She required eighty-six stitches in her face alone. This was a period of great darkness for Yamazaki, who found herself poor, disfigured, and absolutely alone. Her doctor was extremely supportive, encouraging her to use the experience to develop her inner strength. She was young and healthy, he reminded her. She couldn't go through life relying on her external beauty. She needed to look inside.

Gradually the light began to filter back into her life, and it was at this time that Yamazaki met Kami Shoichiro, a specialist in children's culture, who became her present husband. When Yamazaki told him that she would like to devote the rest of her life to the pursuit of women's history, Kami provided his enthusiastic encouragement and support, assisting her with the early stages of her writing.

Yamazaki began her writing career with her *karayuki* trilogy, *Sandakan hachiban shokan* [Sandakan Brothel No. 8; 1972] and its sequels, *Sandakan no haka* [The Graves of Sandakan; 1974; 1977] and *Ameyuki-san no uta* [The Song of a Woman Bound for America; 1981]. The first two books have become important sources for later research on *karayuki-san*. They are quoted extensively by historian Mikiso Hane in *Peasants, Rebels, and Outcastes* (1982), and James Francis Warren, in *Ah Ku and Karayuki-san* (1993). *Ameyuki-san no uta* has been translated by Wakako Hironaka and Ann Konstant under the title *The Story of Yamada Waka, from Prostitute to Feminist Pioneer* (Kodansha International, 1985). This book relates the life of a *karayuki-san* named Yamada Waka. Lured by tales of the riches to be found in America, she accompanied a man to Seattle in 1902, after which she was forced to work in brothels along the West Coast.[48] Waka managed to escape the brothel network and return to Japan, where she became a leading social critic, playing a major role in the women's movement.

Yamazaki's personal history represents no less a remarkable rise. She discusses her life in a collection of essays, *Ikite ikete* [Living and Surviving, 1992]. When she decided to go to Amakusa in 1968 in search of the true story of a *karayuki-san,* Yamazaki was adding to the family income by taking boarders into their home. Her husband, who believes that both women and children should be free to pursue their own goals, readily agreed to take over all the cooking and housework, and the care of their third-grade daughter. At that time the total family savings amounted to no more than ninety thousand yen. Of this, Yamazaki took sixty thousand yen for traveling expenses to Amakusa. Her experiences with a former *karayuki-san,* "Osaki," not only enriched the personal lives of both researcher and subject, but launched Yamazaki's career as a writer of the history of lower-class Asian women. In 1973, one year after its publication by Chikuma Shobo, *Sandakan Brothel No. 8* was awarded the Oya Soichi Prize for Nonfiction Literature.[49] In 1974 it was made into a movie by director Kumai Kei. *Sandakan Brothel No. 8* was issued in paperback in the Bunshun Bunko series in 1975 and is now in its 24th printing.

Sandakan Brothel No. 8

Yamazaki begins her case study of *karayuki-san* by discussing the existing literature on this subject and how she hopes to augment it by providing a different perspective of the *karayuki* phenomenon. By sharing Osaki's life for three weeks, Yamazaki was able to learn the details not only of Osaki's past, but also of her present, and the text moves easily between these time frames. Within her informants' accounts of the past, Yamazaki intersperses passages from books about the South Seas—*Nan'yo,* a term referring more specifically to Southeast Asia—written between the 1910s and 1930s. These passages serve to document people, places, or events and provide further detail or another viewpoint. The translator's notes appear as endnotes to each chapter.

Yamazaki acknowledges that in her mediatory role as interviewer she will inevitably add some personal interpretation to the voices she has heard. Later in the book she also addresses the imbalance of power between researcher and her subject of study. These points, debated today by anthropologists and social historians, were not ignored by a young woman beginning her career in the late 1960s.

Had Yamazaki not heard the voices of Osaki and those close to her, we would have lost this window on the past. Osaki, like the comfort women who began to speak out only in the early 1990s, was breaking long years of silence. In this process the line between public and private becomes blurred, as Osaki's personal experiences become part of a public history. Without the testimony of such women, however, public debate on their social role is impossible. Their statements provide the evidence we need to include their experiences in a new interpretation of the past. Moreover, for *karayuki-san* and comfort women, the gradual unveiling of events so painful and socially unaccepted that they were locked up in their hearts for half a century may have served a cathartic function.

The reader may notice that dates in the *koseki,* official family registers, and dates provided by Yamazaki's informants may differ by a number of years. While Japanese are required to register the births, marriages, divorces, and deaths of family members, in Osaki's day the lower classes were more concerned with daily survival than with documenting family events. This was especially true in the case of the birth of a girl, who was considered just one more mouth to feed. Moreover, as older people recall the past, they may not be able to match an event with a specific year. The best one can do as a social historian of the lower classes is to look at a person or an event from as many different angles as possible, and in this way create an approximate chronology. It will also be noticed that children may appear on registers other than those of their birth parents, or that children born abroad out of wedlock will be officially adopted—for the record only—by a male relative or friend in Japan to facilitate their entry into Japanese society. Ages may vary by one year throughout the text depending on whether the author or her informant is determining age according to the Western system, in which a person turns one on their first birthday, or the Japanese system, in which a person is considered to be age one upon birth.

Although the historian must take into consideration the fallibility of memory over time, oral testimony provides details of personal life and local customs that are so often lost in a general recapitulation of events at a national or regional level. In the case of illiterate informants, the

Osaki, in the vicinity of her home, in Amakusa. 1968.

recording of oral history is the only way to represent their lives in written documentation of the past. Here we see the power of first-person narrative to bring life and interpretation to the past, engaging us in the reliving of history.

Black-and-white photographs of the time document and personalize *karayuki* history. Those photographs taken by traffickers or brothel owners may reveal more about the existing power structure than the personal feelings of those photographed. However, we are fortunate to have some photographs commissioned by the *karayuki-san* themselves. Because most of these women were illiterate, they would send photographs home to show their families that they were in good health. In the case of young girls like Osaki, photographs might be the only means to keep alive the memory of a daughter sold abroad and for family members to observe her growing into womanhood.

Yamazaki Tomoko has enriched this English translation with photographs documenting Osaki's *karayuki* experience, as well as with pictures taken during her stay with Osaki during 1968.

As of 1997 sales of *Sandakan Brothel No. 8* approached one million, and it has been translated into Korean, Thai, and Chinese. Although it is not possible to capture in translation the poetic idiom of the Amakusa dialect as spoken by Osaki, the spirit of her words surmounts language and cultural barriers. Japanese reader response to *Sandakan Brothel No. 8,* and a brief account of Osaki's life following the publication of her story, are included in the Translator's Afterword.

Karen Colligan-Taylor

Translator's Notes

This translation is based on the paperback edition of *Sandakan hachiban shokan: teihen joseishi josho* (Sandakan Brothel No. 8: a prologue to the history of women of the lowest classes), published by Bungei Shunju, 1975. In consultation with the author a few slight changes and clarifications have been made in the translation. *Sandakan hachiban shokan* was originally published in a hardback edition by Chikuma Shobo in 1972. Yamazaki Tomoko has provided the photographs used in the 1972 edition for this English translation.

1. *Karayuki-san,* defined in greater detail below, may refer either to the singular or plural form. *Karayuki-san,* particularly from northwestern Kyushu, reached their peak in Southeast Asia around 1916. *Karayuki-san* from various destinations continued to work in Japanese-occupied Manchuria (Manchukuo) into the 1930s.

2. All Japanese names in the text are written as in East Asia: the surname first followed by the personal name.

3. Throughout the narrative Yamakawa Saki will be referred to as Osaki, following an old custom in which the honorific prefix "o" was attached to a woman's personal name as a sign of respect or familiarity. This practice was most common with one- and two-syllable names. Today this prefix is no longer used with names, but both given and surnames, as well as professions, are followed by the honorific suffix *-san*. Hence, *karayuki-san*.

4. Edwin Reischauer and John Fairbank, *East Asia: The Great Tradition* (Boston: Houghton Mifflin, 1960), p. 582.

5. Yamazaki Tomoko, *Ajia josei koryushi* [A History of the Exchange of Asian Women] (Tokyo: Chikuma Shobo, 1995), p. 21.

6. The short stories of Higuchi Ichiyo (1872–1896), who lived just outside of the Yoshiwara, describe from a woman's perspective the sadder and seedier side of life in the "pleasure quarters." See especially "Child's Play" and "Troubled Waters" in Robert Danly, tr., *In the Shade of Spring Leaves* (New Haven: Yale University Press, 1981).

7. Cecilia Segawa Seigle, *Yoshiwara, the Glittering World of the Japanese Courtesan* (Honolulu: University of Hawaii Press, 1993), p. 34. This interpreta-

tion may say more about socially sanctioned male behavior than about the way in which this occupation was viewed. A term commonly used today for a professional prostitute, or even a woman who has simply had several relationships with men, is *kyodo benjo,* "communal toilet."

8. Mikiso Hane, *Peasants, Rebels, and Outcastes: The Underside of Modern Japan* (New York: Pantheon Books, 1982), p. 210. *Peasants, Rebels, and Outcastes* draws upon a great variety of first-person accounts, describing the miserable lives of peasants, *burakumin* ("outcastes"), textile factory workers, prostitutes, and coal miners through whose labor the modernization of Japan was accomplished. In Hane's book we see *karayuki-san* in the context of the modern history of the Japanese lower classes. To these experiences we must add those of Koreans, the Ainu, and Okinawan peoples.

9. Seigle, *Yoshiwara,* pp. 220–23; Hane, *Peasants, Rebels, and Outcastes,* p. 208.

10. Water trade (*mizu shobai*), the world of brothels, bars, and bathhouses. The term "water business" may have originated in the trade plied by unlicensed prostitutes in pleasure boats, or in the entertainment offered at teahouses along riverbanks. Clients of these businesses may be thought of as men who drift down the stream of life, awash in alcohol, wantonly partaking of carnal pleasures.

11. Yamazaki, *Ajia josei koryushi,* p. 22.

12. Kurahashi Masanao, *Kita no karayuki-san.* (Tokyo: Kyoei Shobo, 1989), p. 73.

13. Hane, *Peasants, Rebels, and Outcastes,* p. 210.

14. James F. Warren, *Ah Ku and Karayuki-san, Prostitution in Singapore, 1870–1940* (Singapore, New York, Oxford: Oxford University Press, 1993), p. 29.

15. Peter Duus, *Modern Japan* (Boston: Houghton Mifflin, 1998), p. 14.

16. To learn more about geisha, see Liza Dalby, *Geisha* (New York: Vintage Books, 1985), and Arthur Golden's *Memoirs of a Geisha* (New York: Alfred A. Knopf, 1997), a novel based on the life of a poor fisherman's daughter, sold to a geisha house at age nine in 1929. For the lives of factory operatives, see Patricia Tsurumi, *Factory Girls: Women in the Thread Mills of Meiji Japan* (Princeton: Princeton University Press, 1990).

17. E. Patricia Tsurumi, "Yet to Be Heard: The Voices of Meiji Factory Women," in *Bulletin of Concerned Asian Scholars* 26, no. 4 (1994), pp. 18–27.

18. Ibid., p. 20.

19. Yamazaki Tomoko, *Sandakan no haka* [The Graves of Sandakan] (Tokyo: Bungei Shunju, 1977), p. 195. For descriptions of the position of maid in the traditional Japanese household, see the novels of Enchi Fumiko, *Masks* (Tokyo: Charles E. Tuttlte, 1984) and *The Waiting Years* (New York: Kodansha, 1971).

20. Warren, *Ah Ku and Karayuki-san,* pp. 198–99.

21. Yamazaki, *Ajia josei koryushi,* p. 26.

22. Ibid.

23. Warren, *Ah Ku and Karayuki-san,* p. 62.

24. Ibid., 160.

25. Kaya Michiko, ed., *Japan in Modern History,* vol. 1 (Tokyo: International Society for Educational Information, 1995), pp. 116–17.

26. Duus, *Modern Japan,* pp. 201–2.

27. Warren, *Ah Ku and Karayuki-san,* p. 83.

28. Duus, *Modern Japan,* p. 205.

29. Warren, *Ah Ku and Karayuki-san,* p. 164.

30. Japanese civilians were encouraged to move to Manchukuo. The man Osaki would marry was among them. In some areas of Japan, such as Nagano Prefecture, certain villages were told to set up "branch villages" in Manchukuo and entire families were directed to move. In the chaos of escape at the end of the war, many Japanese women and children were abandoned in this foreign land. These people were ignored and forgotten by the Japanese government until diplomatic relations were resumed with China in the 1970s; since this time citizens' groups have assisted in reuniting family members. See Gavin McCormack, *The Emptiness of Japanese Affluence* (New York: M.E. Sharpe, 1996), pp. 257–59. For personal interviews with wives and children abandoned in northeast China, see Hayashi Iku, *Manshu, sono maboroshi no kuni yue ni* (Tokyo: Chikuma Shobo, 1983) and Yamazaki Tomoko, *Hikisakareta jinsei* (Tokyo: Bungei Shunju, 1982).

31. George Hicks, *The Comfort Women: Japan's Brutal Regime of Enforced Prostitution in the Second World War* (New York: W.W. Norton, 1995), p. 16. The actual number of women forced to work in comfort stations will never be known, for they were shipped from port to port as so many units of "war supplies." The number could be as high as two hundred thousand. Noriko Sekiguchi has produced an excellent documentary film on this subject, "Senso Daughters" (Icarus Films, 1989).

32. For very poignant personal accounts of the way these young women were deceived, kidnapped, and brutalized, see Keith Howard, ed., *True Stories of the Korean Comfort Women* (London: Cassell, 1995), and Jan Ruff-O'Herne, *50 Years of Silence* (Sydney: Editions Tom Thompson, 1994). Ruff-O'Herne was separated from her family in a prison camp in the Netherlands East Indies and forced to work in a Japanese brothel.

33. Warren, *Ah Ku and Karayuki-san,* p. 29.

34. Howard, ed., *True Stories of the Korean Comfort Women,* p. 5.

35. It should be acknowledged that Korean men conscripted as laborers by the Japanese government did not fare much better, either in their own country or in Japan. Not only were they stripped of their cultural identity, but they were essentially denied their humanity.

36. Hicks, *The Comfort Women,* p. 161.

37. For new approaches to the discussion of prostitution, particularly in the context of Southeast Asian tourism, see Thanh-Dam Truong, *Sex, Money and Morality: Prostitution and Tourism in Southeast Asia* (London: Zed Books, 1990).

38. Watanabe Kazuko, "Militarism, Colonialism, and the Trafficking of Women: 'Comfort Women' Forced into Sexual Labor for Japanese Soldiers," in *Bulletin of Concerned Asian Scholars* 26, no. 4 (1994), p. 13.

39. Cynthia Enloe, *Bananas, Beaches and Bases* (Berkeley: University of California Press, 1989), pp. 36–37.

40. Ibid., 36.

41. *Daily Yomiuri,* October 9, 1992, p. 3. For a more detailed account of *Japayuki,* see Nicholas Bornoff, *Pink Samurai: Love, Marriage, and Sex in Con-*

temporary Japan (New York: Pocket Books, 1991), pp. 340–53.

42. *AMPO, Japan-Asia Quarterly Review* 25, no. 4–26, no. 1 (1995), p. 65.

43. *Japan Times Weekly International Edition,* February 16–22, 1998, p. 17.

44. Although the Criminal Prosecution Codes of the Prostitution Prevention Law came into effect in 1959, the government continues to contradict itself by legalizing private baths under the Recreational Business Law. In fact, the private bath industry, a hot spot for prostitution, receives hundreds of millions of yen in loans each year from Japanese banking facilities. See Nihon kara no tegami gurupu, *Nihon kara no tegami* [A Letter from Japanese Women], April 20, 1994, pp. 8–13 and 55–56. This letter is a counterreport to "The Japanese Government's Second Periodic Report as a State Party to the Convention on the Elimination of All Forms of Discrimination Against Women (July 9, 1992)."

45. McCormack, *The Emptiness of Japanese Affluence,* p. 179.

46. *Japan Times Weekly International Edition,* December 22–28, 1997, p. 17.

47. Hicks, *The Comfort Women,* p. 185.

48. See also Yuji Ichioka, "Ame-yuki-san: Japanese Prostitutes in Nineteenth Century America," *Amerasia Journal* 4, no. 1 (1977), p. 8.

49. In 1970 this prize was awarded to a book that represents the lives of lower-class fisherfolk in Minamata, many of whom had migrated from the Amakusa Islands, just across the water, in search of jobs. This was *Kugai jodo, waga Minamata-byo* [Pure Land, Poisoned Sea, Our Minamata-Disease] by Ishimure Michiko, documenting the outbreak of organic mercury poisoning in villages along the Shiranui coast. This incident and its long coverup reflect corporate and national indifference to people of the lower class. Ishimure did not accept this literary prize, but the honor of nomination remains with her book. For selected translations and discussion of Ishimure's work in the context of Japanese environmental issues, see Karen Colligan-Taylor, *The Emergence of Environmental Literature in Japan* (New York: Garland, 1990). For a complete translation of the book, see Ishimure Michiko, *Paradise in the Sea of Sorrow* (Kyoto: Yamaguchi, 1990), translated by Livia Monnet.

Author's Foreword to the English Translation

As I once again turn the pages of *Sandakan Brothel No. 8,* preparing to write a foreword to the English translation, I realize that exactly thirty years have passed since I set out for Amakusa to gather material for this book. It was two years later that I decided how to structure my research and completed the manuscript. My book was published in 1972. Come to think of it, this nonfiction work has been in circulation now for over a quarter of a century.

About a decade after its publication, my book was translated into Thai and Korean, and last fall, a Chinese translation was published. With the appearance of this English translation, *Sandakan Brothel No. 8* will be available in five languages. As the author of this work, I could not be more pleased.

However, it cannot be said that this work underwent an easy birth. That is to say, when I wrote this book I was hardly known at all. I showed the completed manuscript to two or three publishing companies, but they declined to publish it, saying, "There isn't anyone who would be interested in reading about the life of a former overseas prostitute." Finally, a large publishing company agreed to consider the work, but the editor attached two conditions. "First, I would like you to remove the first and final chapters. Then, I would like you to rewrite the protagonist's story, emphasizing her life as a prostitute and filling it in with a lot more detail."

The first chapter explains why I began research on *karayuki-san,* overseas prostitutes, clarifying my motives and the significance of my work. The final chapter is a critical conclusion to my search for the roots of women's problems. Had I eliminated these two chapters and written only about the protagonist's life as a prostitute, I would have produced nothing more than something approximating "pornographic journalism." I withdrew my manuscript.

The manuscript returned to a shelf in my room, where it slept for several years. Then, by happenstance, a situation developed in which I loaned a rare book on women's history to renowned cultural critic Usui Yoshimi, and came to make his acquaintance. Through his support my book was at long last published by Chikuma Shobo in the summer of 1972. Not a single sentence of my manuscript was removed or altered.

Because the subject matter is sad, the publisher did not expect great sales and did not expend much effort on advertising. As it turned out, however, readers wrote back with such comments as, "Although my eyes filled with tears, I couldn't draw myself away from your book until I had finished the last page." Readers would tell their friends about the book, and soon it had undergone a number of printings. In 1973, the spring after it was published, *Sandakan Brothel No. 8* was awarded the Oya Soichi Prize for Nonfiction Literature. It received outstanding reviews and became a best-seller.

Since this time, *Sandakan Brothel No. 8* and its sequel, *The Graves of Sandakan* (Bungei Shunju, 1974), have been read widely throughout the country through the publication of inexpensive paperback editions, and these books have been made into a movie by producer Kumai Kei. Kumai's film *Sandakan Brothel No. 8* (1974) was nominated for an Academy Award in the Foreign Film category. The movie has received popular acclaim in China, throughout Southeast Asia, and in America. Reviews have appeared in many American journals, including *Ms.* magazine.

The publication of my first two books on *karayuki-san* led to another opportunity to write the biography of a *karayuki-san* who was sent to America. In the fall of 1975 I was requested by a Japanese publishing company to give a lecture for Japanese residents residing in San Francisco. While I was there, I heard about social critic and feminist pioneer Yamada Waka, whose career in Japan extended from the 1910s to the 1940s. I learned that she was one of the Japanese women sold abroad as a *karayuki-san,* although no one I met in San Francisco knew where in America Yamada had been sent.

That winter I returned to America and was able to ascertain the details of the first half of Yamada's life. This research resulted in my book *Ameyuki-san no uta—suki naru shogai,* which was translated into English under the title *The Story of Yamada Waka—From Prostitute to Feminist Pioneer,* and published by Kodansha International in 1986. I understand that this book is being used as a text in Women's Studies courses at a number of American universities.

With *Sandakan Brothel No. 8, The Graves of Sandakan,* and *The Story of Yamada Waka,* I have completed a trilogy of works on *karayuki-san.* I am especially happy at this time to see the first work in this trilogy appearing in English.

Translator Karen Colligan-Taylor, of the University of Alaska–Fairbanks, has a deep understanding of Japanese culture which is reflected in her perceptive articles published in Japan. After meeting her in Tokyo and through our subsequent exchange of letters, I have grown to appreciate her ever more as a critical thinker and strong feminist. In other words, I have been blessed with a splendid colleague, to whom I can only express my deepest gratitude.

Yamazaki Tomoko
February 1998

Sandakan Brothel No. 8

—— 1 ——

A Prologue to the History of Women at the Lowest Level of Society

As I sit before my desk preparing to write about a category of overseas prostitutes known as *karayuki-san,* I find that one particular scene continues to surface in my memory. The setting is Tenshudo, Lord of Heaven Chapel, in the town of Sakitsu, at the southern end of Amakusa-Shimo Island. At the time, I was on my second trip in search of *karayuki-san,* and I had been brooding over the possibility that my efforts would be in vain. Perhaps it was a subconscious attempt to put my mind at ease, but as soon as I got off the bus, I headed for the Tenshudo's dark gray steeple, rising conspicuously high over the flat roofs of the traditional houses around it.

In my mind's eye I can still see the early-setting sun of autumn approaching the mountain ridge line in the west. It must have been about three o'clock. Although it wasn't the time of day you would expect people to shut themselves up in their homes, in the vicinity of the Tenshudo not only were there no adults, there wasn't even a single child at play. Sakitsu was so quiet, it seemed to have been abandoned. Just behind the Tenshudo lay the ocean. Perhaps it was because the bay curved so deeply into the land, but the water was as smooth as the face of a mirror and clearly reflected the cross on the steeple.

Had I come as an ordinary tourist, I can imagine how moved I would have been by the extraordinary beauty of that scene, what peace it would have brought to my heart. But for me, who had come from afar to encounter the real form and voice of those of my same gender, women who had been sent off far away, forced to sell their bodies in distant lands, this beautiful, quiet view brought only a vague sadness.

This sadness would deepen as time passed, but it was just then that I glimpsed the figure of an old farm woman, engrossed in her prayers.

The doors of the Tenshudo stood ajar, as if it, too, were deserted. I walked in and looked around as my eyes adjusted from the outside light. When I focused on the form of a person crouched before the altar, my eyes interpreted it at first as a stone sculpture of a person in prayer. This was because, as the minutes flowed by, the old woman kneeling on the tatami, a rosary hanging from her clasped hands, neither uttered a word nor made a single movement. However, as my eyes grew accustomed to the dim interior of the Tenshudo and I could clearly discern everything from the image of the crucifixion, the statue of Mary, and each of the candlesticks on the altar in the front, to the stained-glass windows on either side, I realized that what I had mistaken for a stone image was actually the living flesh of an old peasant woman. Taken aback by the carelessness of my observation, I was at the same time profoundly moved by the presence of this elderly woman who found it necessary to immerse herself in prayer so deeply and for so long.

She looked to me as if she might have been seventy to seventy-five years old, and that was exactly the age of the *karayuki-san* that one might find still living on the Amakusa Islands or the Shimabara Peninsula. This old farm woman in silent prayer like a stone image—might she have once worked as a prostitute overseas? Of course it was quite reckless of me to reach such a conclusion, but about what could it be that she was praying so fervently to her God?

Her face, which I can see as clearly now, two years later, as if she were right before my eyes, was furrowed with a number of wide wrinkles, while her fingers were short, with knotted joints. Different patterns at the elbows and knees betrayed the patches on her work clothes. If her attire indicated the poverty in which she now lived, and the wrinkles on her face spoke of the many difficulties she had faced during the course of her life, then I would probably not be going too far in interpreting the true intent of her fervent prayer, not as an idealistic request for the deliverance of humankind from original sin, but rather as a heart-rending wish that she ultimately be saved from a life of poverty and hardship.

As is commonly known, the term *karayuki-san* is a contraction of *karahitoyuki* [a person going to Kara, i.e., China, or abroad] or *karankuniyuki* [going to China, or a country overseas]. It refers to overseas prostitutes who, from the final stages of the Tokugawa shogunate in the mid-nineteenth century through the Meiji period (1868–1911) and until the middle of the Taisho period (1912–1925) at the end of World War I, left their native country behind and traveled north to Siberia or continental China, or south to the various countries of Southeast Asia, or even to India and Africa, to sell their flesh to foreigners. These women came from all over Japan, but it is said that the great majority came from the Amakusa Islands and the Shimabara Peninsula. As I explain in the final chapter, the reason so many of these women were born in Amakusa and Shimabara can be explained in terms of the paucity of natural resources and the social poverty of these regions. If this is the case, then *karayuki-san* and the poor peasant women of Amakusa and Shimabara must represent two branches of the same tree. The soundless voice of the old peasant woman who sat kneeling like an image carved of stone before the altar at the Tenshudo in Sakitsu, silently appealing to God to recognize the unendurable hardships of her life, must be the same, fundamentally, as the inner voice of the *karayuki-san*.

Within the Tenshudo, which grew darker as the sun fell below the ridgeline, a new thought took the form of a vow within my heart. As one who conducted research on women's history, I would make it my "work" to understand the voiceless prayer of the old peasant woman from Amakusa. When at last her prayers ended, the woman put away her rosary, and, without any sign of censure for the trespasser before her, gave the slightest nod of her head and walked out of the Tenshudo. And yet, I found myself still motionless in that same spot.

I have somehow uncovered these unforgettable personal memories, and I suspect that there are readers who may ask why I am concerning myself with the *karayuki-san,* a faded memory from the distant past, when there are so many other women's issues I might confront. This is a difficult question to answer, but, frankly speaking, it is because the women of the villages of Amakusa and Shimabara who were once sold into overseas prostitution are the embodiment of the suffering experienced by all Japanese women who have long been oppressed under the dual yoke of class and gender. In other words, these women represent the "starting point" or "quintessence" of women's existence in Japan.

I am getting ahead of myself, but it should be noted that until now the majority of all Japanese history texts, from the *Nihon shoki* of the

Nara period (710–784) to contemporary collections, have been written by the dominant male sex. Since the introduction of Marxist ideology and methodology at the beginning of the Showa period (1926–1988), attempts have been made to write history from the perspective of laborers and farmers, but because these histories also adhere firmly to the male standpoint, they do not differ from earlier works. "Women's history" made its debut only after Japanese imperialism collapsed in 1945, upon Japan's defeat in World War II, and women were guaranteed political and social rights. In my opinion, however, these historical treatises were, with few exceptions, histories of an elite segment of women and nothing else.

For example, most of these women's histories follow a certain formula: they open the modern era with an account of Tsuda Umeko's study exchange to America in 1872, following this with the activities of Kishida Soen and Fukuda Eiko, proponents of the Liberal Rights Movement. Then they mention the work of Yosano Akiko, who spoke loudly through her poems of the awakening of self-consciousness at the level of the senses, and go on to discuss *Seito,* the publication of those such as Hiratsuka Raicho who were active in Japan's Bluestocking movement.[1] It is as if the authors drew a line on a graph, connecting one high point to another representing the thought and activities of a handful of elite women who emerged from the bourgeoisie, or middle class. It would be impossible to extract anything from such women's history about the daily lives and suppressed feelings of those innumerable women who lived and died as laborers or peasants.

It is not that I am trying to deny the validity of all forms of elite women's history. These modern elite women who have acquired academic learning or technical skills have some special work that only they can do to further the progress of society. However, if we draw an analogy with the icebergs that float in polar regions, elite women constitute only some 10 percent of the iceberg exposed to the sunshine above the ocean's surface, while women of the labor and peasant classes lie submerged deeply and unseen as the great mass of ice below. If a text does not follow the actual circumstances of such lower-class women and capture the essence of their joys and sorrows, then it cannot be considered a true history of women.

In order to criticize traditional women's history in a more concrete and effective manner, I would have to write a general history of women, but this is not something I am prepared to do at the present time. I wanted at least to write about the life of a lower-class woman who might be contrasted with her elite counterpart, but then the question arose, what sort of existence would provide a powerful antithesis to the elite woman's history? When I pondered this question, the image that entered my mind was none other than that of the *karayuki-san*.

It need not be reiterated here that the development of modern Japanese society was heavily dependent on light industries such as cotton spinning, silk reeling, and textile weaving, and that these industries thrived upon the sacrifice of the women they employed. In order to reduce the number of mouths, it was said, girls from farm villages throughout Japan would indenture themselves at industrial sites in Tokyo, Osaka, Nagano, and so on. The severity of their labor is documented in older works such as *Shokko jijo* [Conditions Among Textile Workers], a survey of textile sites conducted at the turn of the century, and again in *Joko aishi* [The Pitiful History of Female Factory Workers], written by Hosoi Wakizo in 1925. Recent works include *Aa Nomugi Toge* [Ah! Nomugi Pass], by Yamamoto Shigemi.[2]

Others, too, are fully qualified to denounce the prosperity of modern Japan: peasant women who were forced to crawl about in muddy paddies under the scorching sun, growing rice they were unable to afford to eat themselves, not to mention the women whose job it was to transport coal, descending deep down into the earth with only a metal hand lantern to light the way, sweltering in the heat as they confronted the coal veins. Add to these the child laborers who worked as live-in baby sitters, or girls forced to work as maids in the homes of strangers, cut off from family and friends—these girls, too, languished at the bottom rungs of society.

However, although these women were compelled to exist at the most minimal level, working long hours for low wages, they at least had the freedom to love, and even to marry if they wished. If we take it as a given that the emotion of love falls within that "free" territory that lies within us, these women could at least boast that they were in full possession of this territory. In other words, these women sold their labor, but nothing else.

When it comes to prostitutes, however, the nature of their existence dictates that they must sell for money the sexual favors that should by all rights belong to that territory of "internal freedom." Which is worse, to live by selling one's labor for the most meager of wages, or to have to survive by selling one's body?

Of course, all those women we refer to by the single term "prostitute" do not necessarily share the same type of existence or external circumstances. In postwar Japan, where the licensed prostitute no longer exists, the term "prostitute" refers to the private streetwalker who pulls at men's sleeves as they pass by. If we look at the prostitute of earlier eras, however, the definition becomes more complex. At the top we have the geisha, who entertained at banquets, selling such artistic accomplishments as the traditional dance and the singing of popular ballads. Below them are the licensed prostitutes, or courtesans, who worked in the pleasure quarters of Tokyo—Yoshiwara, Suzaki, Shinjuku, and so on—and the private prostitutes, who plied the streets outside. Yet even lower, we find the *karayuki-san,* forced to leave their homeland behind and go overseas, there to sell their bodies to customers of another nationality. There may not be much point in asking which of these categories was the more miserable, but if I were to pose the question anyway, most people would probably respond that it was the overseas prostitute.

The customers of geisha, courtesans, and streetwalkers were fellow Japanese, who spoke the same language and shared the same cultural consciousness. Of course there are some exceptions, such as the *rashamen,* who worked the treaty ports opened at the beginning of the Meiji period, and the "pan-pan girls," who catered to servicemen stationed in Japan following Japan's defeat in World War II, but most of the partners these girls encountered were men from Europe or America.[3] In the context of a nation about to walk the road laid out by the advanced countries of the West, these women did not find that taking European and American customers was such a humiliating experience. The foreign lands into which the *karayuki-san* were sold, however, were not in Europe or America, but were the nations of Southeast Asia whose civilizations lagged behind that of Japan, and which had been colonized by the Western powers. Their customers were primarily Chinese or men from one of the many indigenous ethnic groups. Since the *karayuki-san* were not liberated from the prevailing Japanese prejudice against people of other ethnic backgrounds, these women must have felt a strong sense of inferiority at having to take as customers darkskinned indigenous men whose words, to their ears, were gibberish and in whose behavior they could find no sign of refinement. And, if we accept the validity these views held for them, we can say that not only did they lead miserable lives, but that this misery extended right into the domain of their hearts and minds.

During the past century of the history of modern Japan, if we recognize that it is the common woman who has been oppressed as the subordinate of men and capital, and that among these common women it is the prostitute who has endured the most cruel circumstances, and among these prostitutes it is the *karayuki-san* whose life held the least hope for salvation, then the reader will forgive me for viewing the *karayuki-san* as the "starting point, or quintessence" of the Japanese woman. This is the reason I have chosen for my prologue to the antithesis of elite women's history neither the textile worker nor the peasant woman, neither the coal miner nor the maid, but the *karayuki-san,* the woman sent away to work as a prostitute in Southeast Asia.

My reasons for focusing on the *karayuki-san* should now be clear, but if we look closely, we will see that there has already been considerable research conducted on the topic of overseas prostitutes. For example, Mori Katsumi's *Jinshin baibai* [The White Slave Trade: Women Who Went to Work Overseas; 1959] is a valuable piece of research that adheres closely to the history and population problems of Amakusa as it attempts to depict a total picture of the *karayuki-san* as an emigrant in search of work. Miyaoka Kenji's *Shofu—kaigai roruki* [Prostitutes—A Record of Overseas Journeys; 1968], based on several thousand travel accounts, is a commendable reconstruction of when, where, and the circumstances under which Japanese prostitutes went overseas. There are also a number of works that contain verbatim accounts of and commentaries on the experiences of overseas prostitutes, including *Nihon zankoku monogatari* [Tales of Japanese Inhumanity], edited by Miyamoto Tsuneichi et al.; *Nihonjin monogatari* [Tales of Japanese], edited by the Origuchi school of ethnologists; *Dokyumento Nihonjin* [The Japanese: A Documentary], edited by Murakami Ichiro and Tsurumi Shunsuke; and *Josei zankoku monogatari* [Tales of Cruelty to Women], edited by Tanigawa Ken'ichi; all of which are testimony to the perspicacity of their editors.

I will address later the depth and limits of existing research on overseas prostitutes, but there is one more source I must not overlook at this time, which is *Muraoka Iheiji jiden* [The Autobiography of Muraoka Iheiji]. This book, published by Nanposha in 1960, is an autobiography that frankly describes the personal experiences of a man who managed brothels in Singapore and Manila between the early 1890s and the late 1930s, and who was in the business of abducting women and girls to work as prostitutes overseas. Because we have no other written works from this period concerning overseas prostitutes and because this autobiography is quite interesting, it has been considered a significant primary source in all of the books mentioned above. To put this more accurately, all of the research on overseas prostitutes mentioned above take as their foundation *Muraoka Iheiji jiden.*

However, the data I have collected to date through surveys and other means indicate that *Muraoka Iheiji jiden* is filled with errors that render it unreliable as a historical source. The logical conclusion to this is that all of the research heretofore conducted on overseas prostitutes, built as it is upon the material presented in the autobiography of this unique outlaw, must be reinvestigated from its very roots. I have questioned the credibility of *Muraoka Iheiji jiden* for two basic reasons. The first is that while materials related to the Japanese development of Southeast Asia abound, and there should still be some people alive who were active in the same area as Muraoka, there is no evidence to show that anyone knew of the Iheiji presented in the autobiography. The second reason is that there are many instances in which material presented in the autobiography does not correspond to facts in objective sources.

With regard to my first point, it should be noted that materials about the development of Southeast Asia include not only investigative reports compiled by government agencies such as the Ministry of Foreign Affairs and the Ministry of Agriculture and Commerce during the Meiji and Taisho periods, but also histories of colonization, private memoirs, travelogues, and so on published by popular presses, adding up to quite an extensive collection. Some people may censure me for doubting Iheiji's existence, saying that it is only common sense that in a small archipelago of over one hundred million people that a name might not be picked up in historical documents. However, it should be noted that from the Meiji through the Taisho periods, the Japanese population in Southeast Asia cannot be expressed in terms of a broad surface area, or even a line, but simply by a few dots here and there in such places as Singapore, Manila, and Dabo. This being the case, although Southeast Asia covers a wide territory, the Japanese community was extremely small, and for better or for worse if anyone was involved in an occupation or event that stood out in the least, his or her name would be known to all Japanese, and in all likelihood that name would be recorded in one document or another. This is why the names of brothel proprietors such as Kinoshita Kuni, whom I discuss in detail

A brothel managed by trafficker Muraoka Iheiji. Manila, c. 1900.

in chapter 9, Niki Takajiro, Shibuya Ginji, and others appear in reliable historical sources such as Irie Toraji's *Hojin kaigai hattenshi* [A History of Japanese Overseas Development].

How should we interpret the fact that Muraoka Iheiji's name does not appear once in any document? I have pursued my argument on the assumption that the reader will already be acquainted with *Muraoka Iheiji jiden,* but for the sake of those who are not familiar with it, according to his own account, Iheiji's life was divided into three distinct periods. When he lived in Singapore, from 1889 to 1895, he founded a halfway house for ex-convicts and became boss of a procuring gang that abducted young women. From 1896 to 1900 he lived on Sulawesi (Celebes) Island in Indonesia, and was appointed an "honorary consul" of Surabaya. He spent the years 1901 to 1943 in the Philippines, where he came to be known as "the boss of the South Pacific"; "wherever I went, not only among Japanese, but even among foreigners, there was not a man who did not know me." That someone who was this active in society would not be mentioned in a single document about

Southeast Asian development leads us, if not to doubt his existence altogether, at least to take his superhuman feats with a grain of salt.

In addition to this, there is the fact that hardly anyone alive today who worked at various jobs in Southeast Asia at about the same time as Muraoka Iheiji did know of him. As I explain in later chapters, when I traveled to Amakusa-Shimo Island I called upon nine or ten elderly *karayuki-san* who had worked in Singapore or Manila, but neither the name Muraoka Iheiji nor the appellation "Boss of the South Seas" triggered their memories. When I told them about Iheiji's reputed kindness to the ex-criminals and prostitutes he employed, they responded with a sneering tone, "No matter who it is, a brothel boss is a leech who thinks of nothing but sucking up our living blood, so if there had been a boss who had compassion, we certainly would have known about him. The South Seas were overrun with good-for-nothing braggarts like that." I also questioned as many people as possible who had lived in the South Seas in some capacity other than *karayuki-san,* but I met with the same lack of recognition. Among those I interviewed was Ryu Asaka, the oldest daughter of Ryu Naojiro, whose name appears in many works as the pioneer of Japanese residents in Singapore, but although she was born and raised in Singapore and her father never tired of repeating tales about prominent Japanese there, including brothel owners, this was the first time she had heard the name Muraoka Iheiji. The only exception is Hoshi Atsuhiko, a man currently living in Koriyama, Fukushima Prefecture, who had at one time been vice president of *Dabo nichinichi shinbun* [The Dabo Daily News]. According to his testimony, his deceased wife had known Muraoka Iheiji, but she always referred to him as "that big liar," he reported.

This being the case, if we can gather evidence neither from the literature nor from people, then the next thing we might attempt is to confirm the accuracy of the content of *Muraoka Iheiji jiden.* If we do this, however, we come up against the second reason I mentioned earlier for doubting the reliability of this autobiography—that the so-called facts differ from those in established, objective sources.

For example, Iheiji says that between June and November 1887 he served under Army First Lieutenant Uehara Yusaku (later to become a general), traveling to the far reaches of Siberia, and it was here that he saw large numbers of Japanese overseas prostitutes, motivating his entry into this business. However, according to *Gensui Uehara Yusaku den* [The Autobiography of General Uehara Yusaku], Uehara was then on an official trip to Tsushima, and the facts do not correlate with Iheiji's claims at all.

Again, Iheiji says that he met Itagaki Taisuke in Singapore in December 1890, and had another meeting with Ito Hirobumi in October of the following year, and he records their discussion in conversational form. However, according to newspapers of that period, it is clear that both Itagaki and Ito were extremely busy with domestic political activities, and there is no indication that they headed southward. Moreover, the voluminous work *Nanyo no gojunen* [Fifty Years in the South Seas], published jointly by Nanyosha and Nihonjinsha in 1938 includes the diary of the Japanese consul general for Singapore, covering the years 1889–1921, and though it records in detail the names of all Japanese visitors to Singapore, right down to the last businessman, the names of Itagaki Taisuke and Ito Hirobumi do not appear anywhere.

You may feel that this evidence is quite sufficient to make my point, but I would like to bring up one more matter. Iheiji announces triumphantly that in October 1890 he took the initiative to establish the Japanese Association of Singapore, where he was employed as an accountant and consultant, and that in February 1891 he established a Japanese cemetery for *karayuki-san*. However, according to the aforementioned *Nanyo gojunen,* and *Zainan sanjugonen* [Thirty-five Years in the South] by Nishimura Takejiro, who lived in Singapore for close to forty years as a practicing doctor, the person recognized for establishing both the Japanese Association and the Japanese cemetery was Niki Takajiro, who was the proprietor of a brothel and a general store. Muraoka Iheiji's name appears neither on the list of officers for the Japanese Association nor on the list of donors for the cemetery. It appears that Niki Takajiro was the ultimate boss of the prostitute trade in Singapore during the Meiji period (1868–1912), and that in addition to donating one acre of his own land for the cemetery, he worked in many ways for the benefit of overseas Japanese in Singapore. During the Sino-Japanese and Russo-Japanese wars, he collected donations from both *karayuki-san* and procurers alike and presented the money to the Japanese government. In *Muraoka Iheiji jiden* we find that Iheiji also collects donations from *karayuki-san* during the war period, but if we think about this in terms of his claims about the Japanese Association and the cemetery, one might even speculate that Iheiji wrote his autobiography claiming for himself the achievements of Niki Takajiro.

When talking to people who have no direct knowledge of our personal history, we have a psychological tendency to beautify and exaggerate past events. As we repeat this beautified and exaggerated version over and over again, we gradually come to see this modified past as the actual truth. Especially when the person who is talking about the past speaks from the standpoint of present misfortune, the further their fortunes have fallen, the more they tend to embellish the past according to a psychological substitution response. As far as we can tell from reading the Afterword to *Muraoka Iheiji jiden,* in his later years Iheiji was preceded in death by his oldest son and his work was not going as he wished. He says he wrote his autobiography at the suggestion of a traveler he happened to meet, so we can certainly expect to find a degree of beautification and exaggeration.

Perhaps I have dwelt too long on *Muraoka Iheiji jiden.* However, if the credibility of this work, which has been recognized as a major source for research on overseas prostitution, is no more than this, to what extent can we rely on the research books on overseas prostitution that I mentioned above? To the extent that they grew out of the authors' dependence on *Muraoka Iheiji jiden,* I find them no more credible than I do Iheiji's autobiography.

Of course, since the intent of the various works I mentioned before is not simply to relate historical facts, but also to expose the nature of Japanese nationalism and other ideologies through the existence of the *karayuki-san,* they will probably not be fatally affected by the discovery of falsehoods or errors. Nevertheless, I do not believe that our research on overseas prostitution is complete with these studies alone.

With the single exception of Morisaki Kazue's verbatim account, "The Life of a Certain *Karayuki-san,*" within *Dokyumento Nihonjin,* all of these studies have been written by men.[4] From the beginning I have never had the bias that only women are qualified to write women's history; in fact, I wish that more men would take part as both researchers and readers. However, in the case of prostitutes or overseas prostitution alone, I feel that there are many areas that can only be clarified by a woman.

Over 90 percent of the overseas prostitutes who poured out of Japan into destinations in Southeast Asia in the early Meiji through Taisho periods (1868–1911, 1912–1925) were illiterate, unable to write even *hiragana* [the Japanese syllabary of fifty symbols], so one cannot expect that one of them would take up the pen to bring to light her circumstances and misery. Even if they could write, they probably would have maintained their silence and not written a single line. As women they would have felt a strong resistance to writing about the inner secrets of their lives as prostitutes, but the greatest obstacle for them would have been the fear that revealing their lives would bring shame to their family and ancestors.

This being the case, I believe that if the researcher wants to grasp the true profile of the overseas prostitute, there is no other way than to elicit the details of her life and thoughts from one of the *karayuki-san* still alive today. If one proceeds in this fashion, then who will it be to open the door of her tightly closed heart and hear her unadorned tale, the male researcher who belongs to the same gender as those who purchased her sexual favors, or the female researcher who is of her own gender? Nothing reveals the answer to this more eloquently than the fact that to date all research conducted by men on overseas prostitution has concentrated solely on how the women were abducted or on the economic structure of prostitution, leaving these accounts deficient— in their failure to touch upon the actual experience of sexual intercourse, and the psychological makeup of these women.

In a chapter called "The Study of Women's History," in his *Momen izen no koto* [What Happened Before Cotton], ethnologist Yanagida Kunio (1875–1962) states that the wisdom and strength of women should be demonstrated in spheres that cannot be reached by men, even if they try, and that this is the true realm of women's learning. When we consider our previous discussion in light of this observation, is it not safe to say that only when women participate in investigations of and research on overseas prostitution do we have something that truly deserves the name of "women's history"? This is why I emphasized earlier that it is women who ought to be conducting research on prostitution and overseas prostitutes.

So, with such research as my goal, I departed Tokyo for Kyushu in search of a *karayuki-san,* with the understanding that my work would have to begin with hearing her tale. Of course there was no reason to expect that just because I was of the same gender this *karayuki-san* would reveal to a casual traveler her previous life as a prostitute, when her present life was devoted to forgetting the events of the past. I realized that I would probably have to settle down for some time in her village, or perhaps stay at her home, and, as I shared the moments of sorrow and happiness in her daily life, wait for her to reveal those thoughts so tightly locked away in her heart.

However, even though I entertained such thoughts, I did not know a single person in Shimabara or Amakusa who might provide some introduction or link to these *karayuki-san*. I did have two friends who lived in Nakama City, Fukuoka Prefecture, however—the poet Morisaki Kazue, who wrote "The Life of a Certain *Karayuki-san*," and Shima Kazuharu, born in Amakusa, who writes novels about agrarian life. If I were to ask them, they would surely introduce me to *karayuki-san* they had met in the past.

In the end I decided not to rely on these connections. First of all, it did not seem right to depend on *karayuki-san* who had already been interviewed. Such women were now living fairly easy lives thanks to the fees they had received for the interviews, and many had attained social prominence.

I wanted to meet a *karayuki-san* who had not yet been visited by researchers or journalists, an overseas prostitute who quite literally continued to crawl through the dirt. This was why I had to go to Shimabara or Amakusa, not as someone coming with formal introductions, but simply as a person with no special influence or privileges. Four summers ago I did go to Amakusa–Shimo Island on a first-trial basis, where I happened to run into just the type of old *karayuki-san* I had longed to meet.

This book, which may not be considered either as a formal research document on overseas prostitutes or as a travelogue, is an account of some three weeks I spent living with this *karayuki-san,* my chance meeting with whom provided this critical opportunity. Therefore I must begin my tale with my first trip to Amakusa, which resulted in this special encounter.

Translator's Notes

1. For a discussion of the achievements of most of these women, see Sharon L. Sievers, *Flowers in Salt: The Beginnings of Feminist Consciousness in Modern Japan* (Stanford: Stanford University Press, 1983). For the biographies and letters of Tsuda Ume (1865–1929), see Yoshiko Furuki, *The White Plum:A Biography of Ume Tsuda* (New York: Weatherhill, 1991); Yoshiko Furuki, ed., *The Attic Letters: Ume Tsuda's Correspondence to Her American Mother* (New York: Weatherhill, 1991); Oba Minako, *Tsuda Umeko* (Tokyo: Asahi Shinbunsha, 1990); and Barbara Rose, *Tsuda Umeko and Women's Education in Japan* (New Haven: Yale University Press, 1992). The reader may find it fascinating to compare the overseas journey undertaken by Tsuda Ume, a samurai daughter, with that of Osaki, a woman of the rural lower class. Tsuda studied in the United States

from age seven to eighteen. After she returned to Japan, Tsuda sent a constant flow of letters back to her American mother, filled with astute observations about a woman's place in upper-class Japanese society. She noted, for example, that women "are not often loved, often like a plaything, oftener like a servant" (Furuki, *The White Plum,* p. 57.) Ume found inadequate both public and private institutions for the education of women, limited as they were by their goal of creating "good wives and wise mothers." Following a second trip to the United States to study at Bryn Mawr, Tsuda raised money for her own academy, which would offer a liberal arts education based on a philosophy of critical, independent thinking. In 1900 Tsuda founded Joshi Eigaku Juku (Women's Institute of English Studies), known today as Tsuda College. James Stokes, one of the philanthropists who contributed to Ume's school, told her he had heard about "an awful traffic" in Japan—the selling of daughters by destitute parents. He proposed to help some of these girls, and put them in Tsuda's care (Furuki, p. 91).

2. Yamamoto Shigemi, *Aa Nomugi Toge* (Tokyo: Asahai Shimbunsha, 1968). Yamamoto interviewed old women of villages in the Hida mountains, who had once crossed treacherous Nomugi Pass between Gifu and Nagano prefectures to work in the silk mills of Suwa.

3. *Rashamen* is a derogatory term for Japanese concubines of Western men. *Rashamen* means "wool thread," originating in the Portuguese word "raxa." Popular tales of the time held that Western sailors kept sheep (wool) on board ship to engage in sodomy.

4. Yamazaki's *Sandakan Brothel No. 8,* and a later work by Morisaki Kazue, *Karayuki-san* (Tokyo: Asahi Shinbunsha, 1976), were significant sources for James Francis Warren's *Ah Ku and Karayuki-san, Prostitution in Singapore, 1870–1940* (New York: Oxford University Press, 1993).

— 2 —

A Chance Encounter—My First Trip to Amakusa

I made my first trip to Amakusa in 1968, under the blazing sun of early August. Because my father's work took him to Nagasaki, it was there I was born and lived as a young child, but those memories have since sunken into the abyss of forgetfulness, and I felt that I was setting foot on the soil of Kyushu for the first time.

Although I had made up my mind that I would gather information about *karayuki-san* without relying on the help of an intermediary, I could not help but feel a little nervous about traveling alone in unknown territory. Consequently, I first paid a visit to Morisaki Kazue, who lives in Nakama City, Fukuoka Prefecture. Perhaps she thought that easing my extreme tension would smooth the way for my research, for when she learned that this was an exploratory trip which I would combine with sight-seeing in Amakusa, she introduced me to Toyohara Reiko, who works in a library and does oil painting on the side. It would be a sketching trip, she said, and made arrangements for her friend to accompany me.

After spending one night at the Morisaki household, Ms. Toyohara and I boarded the Kagoshima-bound train at Fukuoka and headed for Minamata, at the southern end of Kumamoto Prefecture. After the so-called Five Bridges of Amakusa were built in 1966, it was most convenient to travel south along the expressway linking Kumamoto City to Uto Island, but we decided not to take that route. Instead, we followed Ms. Morisaki's advice. "If you are taking a trip to the Amakusa Islands, which have suffered years of isolation, you must by all means go there by sea, not by the smoothly paved overland route. And besides, the ocean scenery will be much nicer."

From Minamata we took a medium-size ferryboat across the Shiranui Sea, where, true to its name, you can see mysterious lights on the water which appear at about midnight in late summer or early autumn. After rocking back and forth for close to two hours we arrived at Ushibuka, the southern entrance to the Amakusa Islands. Most of the ferry passengers were clearly from Amakusa, middle-aged and elderly men and women who were on their way home after selling fish and shellfish in Minamata. Among these sat a number of young people as well, ourselves included, who you could tell at a glance from their dress and general appearance were tourists. Whether it was due to the simple, homey nature of the Amakusa residents, or the young passengers' lighthearted response to traveling under a blue sky, about an hour out of port one could begin to hear snatches of conversation between the two groups, such as "Did you come from Tokyo?" or "What should we see in Amakusa?"

Eventually we, too, entered the inevitable stream of conversation, and—perhaps it was because she remembered my purpose in traveling to Amakusa and hoped to assist me by gleaning some useful information—at some point Ms. Toyohara began asking people, an old woman over there, and a middle-aged man nearby who had the look of a fisherman, "Would you happen to know someone who used to be a *karayuki-san*?" I thought the chances were slim that this frontal-attack method of questioning would elicit the address of a *karayuki-san,* and that even if it did, it would be extremely difficult to get that person to tell me her story. This is because no sooner had Ms. Toyohara uttered the word *"karayuki-san"* than each person who until then had been talking enthusiastically about all kinds of things seemed to emit a warning signal and either fell stone silent or replied, "I've never heard of such a thing."

It was utterly impossible that these people who had been born and raised in Amakusa and lived there right now would not have known about *karayuki-san.* That, in spite of this, the mere mention of the term would be so firmly rejected seemed to reflect the love these Amakusa folk had for their native soil, and a communal sense of self-defense that kept them from revealing to strangers the shame of their native village. Next, just as an experiment, I posed the same question not only on the ferry, but also on the bus headed for Kametsu from Ushibuka, and finally on the toy-like steamboat that took us from Kametsu to Sakitsu. When these passengers also responded in the same way, I was forced to acknowledge that the people of Amakusa wore a hard armor, not easily cracked by ordinary means. Thus was I quickly apprised on the boat to Amakusa of how difficult it would be to investigate *karayuki-san.* Although the mountains and sea were glistening in the light of midsummer, by the time we arrived at the port of Sakitsu around noon I felt weighted down with gloom.

Clinging to these feelings was certainly not going to help me after coming so far, and it was not as if I hadn't anticipated such difficulties from the outset. Since I had departed that morning on one cup of coffee, I decided that this loss of energy could very well be attributed to an empty stomach, and so I asked Ms. Toyohara to join me for lunch.

Though it may be called a town, if you walk more than 100 meters through the port of Sakitsu you run out of houses, and we couldn't find anything that looked like a small restaurant. Finally we saw a little shop with the characters "shaved ice" dyed into the shop curtain in front, so we hurried in. In the tiny interior, which couldn't have been much larger than three square meters, there was one customer who had arrived before us, an elderly woman of slight build. When I jokingly said to the shopkeeper, "Auntie, do you have anything to eat? We're so hungry we could die!" the old woman turned to us, saying, "Sisters, I'd go for the fried rice. It'll keep you full until sundown."

The shopkeeper explained that besides shaved ice, all they served was fried rice and Nagasaki *chanpon,* deep-fried noodles topped with a thick vegetable sauce, so we followed the old woman's advice and ordered the fried rice. As our eyes adjusted to the light, we turned our gaze on the old woman at the table diagonal to ours.

She had already finished her rice and was using a toothpick as she drank tea. Her half-whitened hair was pulled back on her head, and the darkened skin of her face was furrowed with wrinkles. It was difficult to guess her age, but in comparing her with my mother-in-law I guessed that she must be a little over seventy. She was of slight build, and about one meter and thirty or forty centimeters tall. Her entire body was thin and frail, her arms and legs no more than chicken bones. She wore a faded blue skirt with a well-laundered shirt, and on her feet were a pair of worn rubber thongs. Judging from the old straw hat and hand towel which lay next to her on the table, she seemed not to be someone from the town of Sakitsu, but rather someone who had walked some distance to get here.

When she noticed we had ordered the fried rice, the old woman smiled in satisfaction. Withdrawing a slender pipe from a cloth bag and pulling a partly smoked cigarette out of a pack of Shinsei, she stuffed it into the pipe bowl and began smoking. As she contentedly exhaled pale purple smoke, she reached out for the three ashtrays in the small shop and, collecting the smudged-out cigarette butts one by one, she knocked off the ashes and stuffed them into the Shinsei pack.

Due to an extreme tobacco shortage during World War II and shortly afterward there were a number of people who would pick up cigarette butts dropped by others, but today, no matter where you went, you would never even hear that sort of thing mentioned. Yet here, right before our eyes, was an old woman totally engrossed in collecting cigarette butts.

Apparently the old woman could not even afford the low-priced Shinsei brand of cigarettes, and I reacted to this by seizing the opportunity to thank her for suggesting the fried rice. Pulling out a cigarette for myself from my box of Highlights, I offered one to her as well, saying, "Grandmother, won't you smoke one also?" For an instant she seemed at a loss, but when Ms. Toyohara struck a match and held it up, the old woman responded, "Such expensive cigarettes, you're too kind . . . ," and as she thanked us she pulled out a cigarette and lit up. With that as an opening, the old woman began to talk, explaining that smoking was her single pleasure, and that whenever her hands weren't busy during the day, she would light up a cigarette.

Ms. Toyohara, who had never smoked, was startled by the pipe calluses on the old woman's fingers, but her words aroused in me a different interest. That is, I felt that her accent and intonation were somehow different from the "standard" Amakusa dialect.

When people travel to a location where the native dialect is different from their own, they commonly have difficulty understanding the local speech. For me, the Amakusa dialect was no exception. Here, the younger people spoke Tokyo dialect, which is considered to be standard speech, but the elderly spoke their Amakusa dialect of old. Even when I would ask them to speak slowly, I couldn't grasp everything. And yet, though the old woman was definitely speaking in the Amakusa dialect, it was somehow closer to standard speech, and I could understand almost everything she said.

This was odd, I thought, and questioned her about it, whereupon the old woman nodded her head lightly and responded, "Well, now, sister. I certainly was born in Amakusa, but I went abroad when I was small, and no matter with whom I speak, I have no trouble." Those words took me so much by surprise that I dropped the spoon I was using to ladle up the fried rice. Although she was an elderly woman, she admitted that her speech was not imprinted with the Amakusa dialect, and that she had gone abroad "from the time I was small." Yet, though she said she'd lived abroad, from her dress and expression I felt that it could not be America or Western Europe. What did this mean? It meant that she had gone to foreign countries far behind Japan in cultural development—it would mean, for example, than she might have lived in Southeast Asia, and if one were to extend one's imagination further, that this had some connection with *karayuki-san*.

Feeling keenly the lesson we learned from our experience on the boat, not to utter the word *karayuki-san*, we conversed with the old woman, speaking on the surface in a casual way, but in our hearts heaping caution on top of caution. As the conversation progressed, I became increasingly certain that this poor, frail old woman had been a *karayuki-san*, and I determined that I must find some pretext to accompany her to her village.

Ms. Toyohara, who divined my feelings, said that she would leave before us, as she wanted to sketch the Tenshudo Chapel in Sakitsu, and, reminding me that we were to meet that evening at the inn in Miyanokawachi, she picked up her bags and left. Observing all this as if it were perfectly natural, I continued speaking with the old woman for some time on all kinds of topics. I told her that I had some business in her village, the name of which I had inquired about in passing, and we eventually left the shaved-ice shop and began walking, with the old woman in the lead.

As long as we followed a path bordering the blue inlet, a cool breeze blew in, but when we started along the narrow path through a broad expanse of rice paddies, the breeze blew our way only occasionally. Nothing could avoid the intense rays of the midsummer sun, and both the old woman and I were dripping perspiration from our faces and bodies. Now and then a motor scooter would go by, raising a cloud of fine, white dust, but no one offered to give us a ride.

Although the distance was certainly trying, I found the walk enjoyable. Perhaps I am simply lighthearted by nature, but as long as the other party doesn't rub me too hard, I immediately become friends with them. As we walked along, I felt an intimacy for this old woman, as if I had known her for years. She seemed to feel the same about me, for she volunteered all kinds of information. She told me that she had an only son who lived in Kyoto with his family; that she was now living alone with a number of cats; and that she had just returned that day from a pilgrimage to the deity who inspired her faith, Odaishisama of Ikusagaura.[1] When, now and then, she would step in a clump of vegetation that had grown up from both sides of the narrow path and a frog or a grasshopper jumped out, she would raise her voice like a child, calling out in delight, "Now, Mr. Frog, you're not to frighten an old woman." Feeling that it would be best to make myself as inconspicuous as possible, I had set off for this trip in a pair of worn slacks, a white short-sleeved blouse, and flat-heeled shoes, but as soon as I arrived in Amakusa it was obvious at a glance that I had come from the city. However, for the old woman, perhaps it was precisely because she rarely had the occasion to associate with anyone from the city that such rare companionship was an object of interest, and she grew more cheerful and animated as we went along.

At any rate, in just half an hour after we left the shaved-ice shop in Sakitsu, we had skirted the base of a hill some two hundred meters high, and entered a hamlet of thirty homes. Through the middle of the hamlet flowed a stream, about two meters wide, and the houses were scattered along both sides, hugging the banks. Sweet potatoes had sent out their tendrils everywhere, forming a mat of dark green vines.[2] "It's a dreadful house, but will you drop by?" the old woman had asked. Thankful as I was to be able to take advantage of this invitation, however, I couldn't help but feel, as I picked up each foot, that I was being overcome by a strange sensation. That is to say, because the old woman's house was at the very far reaches of the hamlet, we had to pass through the middle of the village, but below the piercing rays of the sun there was not a soul in sight. Each house seemed to be enveloped in silence, and it was very much like passing through a ghost town. This eerie feeling reached its height when we arrived at the old woman's house.

Although she had emphasized that it was "a dreadful house," I was amazed that a human being could actually live there. The house was located beneath a cliff which had been formed by an excavation into the mountainside. Although the black pillars that supported the house somehow stood up straight, the miscanthus-thatched roof, which had not been rethatched in decades, looked like a heap of compost. On the south side grew things like wild chrysanthemums and dandelions, while various kinds of ferns had colonized the north. To me, it looked just like a witch's house described in fairy tales.

The old woman trotted into the house, calling her cats as she entered, "Here, Tama, here, Mii," and beckoned me to come in. The interior was even more desolate. With only a dirt floor and a sitting room of two tatami mats, as farmhouses go it was just a toy.[3] Cobwebs three feet long hung from the low ceiling. Here and there the roughly plastered clay walls had crumbled in, and both the interior and exterior paper sliding doors, the fusuma and shoji, had, for the most part, been reduced to the skeletal structure of their wooden frames.[4] The tatami mats in the sitting room appeared to have rotted entirely, for as I stepped into the house at her invitation, my feet sank into the mats as if I had set foot in a rice paddy. Not only did the dampness of the mats cling to the soles of my bare feet, but as I braced myself to kneel down, a number of centipedes crawled up toward my knees. Overcome with revulsion, I peered down at them, only to find that the straw mats had become one giant centipede nest. Thinking it would calm my nerves, I took out two small bottles of cider I brought from the shaved-ice shop in Sakitsu, removed the lids with a bottle opener I had borrowed from the shop, and began to pour the cider into two teacups the old woman had set before me. It was just then, however, that a middle-aged and an elderly woman suddenly dropped by. Since I had not seen a soul in the entire hamlet, these women seemed to have welled up from the depths of the earth.

The first to approach us was a plump farm woman, close to fifty, carrying one basket brimming with small sardines, such as are dried and used for soup stock, and one empty basket. Without saying a word, she settled her huge bottom down on the threshold, and began snapping off fish heads and removing entrails. Since she showed no sign of leaving anytime soon, the old woman brought out another cup, and I poured some cider into it also, but before I had finished, the second woman approached, calling out, "Osaki, are you there?" Her face was white, but covered with wrinkles, and for some reason her hair was dyed blond, tinged with brown. Although her narrow eyes were open, judging from the fact that they did not seem to focus on any particular point, it appeared that she might be blind. I ended up pouring cider for this odd old woman too, but when they had drunk the meager contents of their cups, the two women began speaking volubly in the Amakusa dialect, and the old woman with blond hair began to barrage Osaki with questions, such as, just who was I, and the like. As I sat there fidgeting, trying to figure out how best to reply, Osaki quickly gave me a meaningful glance and suddenly responded in a loud voice, "This, I'll have you know, is the woman my son Yuji married."

I almost jumped in surprise at these unexpected words, and found myself utterly speechless until Osaki added, "Why, she's no better at her letters than we are; hasn't written me even once. Then she suddenly turns up like this without any warning—really surprised me, she did. Left the two children behind, she said, because it was so far. But she'll be going back this evening, without even spending the night." Inwardly marveling at Osaki's skill in satisfying the burning curiosity of her neighbors, while justifying my early departure, I found myself compelled to proffer the standard greeting, "Thank you for your many kindnesses to my mother." Then, having set myself up like this, I had to continue behaving as if I were the wife of this man Yuji, whom I not only had never met, but whose name I couldn't even spell.

The two women stayed around a little longer to exchange gossip. Then, having satisfied their curiosity about me, at least for the time being, they addressed me loudly in the Amakusa dialect, saying something I couldn't understand at all, and left. The long walk through the scorching heat and my relief at being freed from the tension I had experienced during that unexpected scene had left me utterly exhausted. Osaki noticed this at once. "When you're worn out like that, you'd best lie down. You'll be fine if you just lie still for a while." This was more than mere advice, for when she saw me hesitate, she said, "I'm tired, too, so I'll lie down with you," and she proceeded to curl up in the middle of the room, pillowing her head on her arm and beckoning me to join her.

Although I had experienced economic hardships before, this was my first encounter with tatami so old and decayed it had become a centipede nest. To be truthful, the thought of lying down on it repulsed me, but I was overcome with fatigue. How could someone pursue the history of lower-class women if they couldn't even put up with an old straw mat, I scolded myself, and I lay down next to Osaki. Osaki then picked up the only fan in the house, and waving it vigorously, sent cool drafts of air my way. Perhaps it was because I had shut my eyes, but she did not try to talk to me.

I thought I would surely fall asleep if I kept silent, and that if I did fall asleep, I wouldn't become more familiar with Osaki, but I couldn't help reflecting upon what had just happened. Osaki most certainly must have been a *karayuki-san* in the past, and in order to draw out her story, it was absolutely necessary to establish a degree of intimacy. By walking here with her under the blazing sun I had certainly opened a door, but what could she have meant by her explanation to her visitors just now? Since I had revealed nothing to her of my hopes of getting to know her well, to her I should be no more than a traveler of unknown character. Why, then, did she introduce me to her two inquisitive visitors as her son's wife? Why, when a truthful explanation like "She's someone I met at the shaved-ice shop in Sakitsu; she seems to have some business in the village" would have done nicely, did she set me up as her son's wife? Even if this didn't cause any harm to an outsider like me, wouldn't it later cause trouble for a local person like herself?

As I mentioned before, Osaki's house was so rustic as to make one wonder if it was truly a human dwelling; even within this poverty-stricken hamlet, she seemed to be the poorest of all. In a capitalist society where the possession of property is translated into human worth, it has always been the fate of the poor to find themselves the object of discrimination. Osaki must have long endured the contempt of the other villagers. Although she had an only son who worked in Kyoto, the fact that he had not returned home in years, and that his wife had not once shown her face, must have added to Osaki's humiliation.

For such a person, the planned visit of a daughter-in-law could only increase her prestige, and that may have been why Osaki had so readily introduced me as her son's wife.

However, even as I came up with that interpretation, when I recalled her childish delight whenever a frog or a grasshopper would jump up on that narrow path we took through the rice paddies, I could not help but come up with a completely different line of thought. In other words, Osaki, who had been forsaken by her one and only blood relative, her son, longed to meet, if only briefly, this daughter-in-law who had borne two children, or so she had heard, with her son. Somehow, as she found herself talking and laughing with this unexpected walking companion, could it not be that she wondered somewhere along the way if her daughter-in-law might not be a woman just like this, so that when the woman with the sardine baskets and the blind woman with the blond hair dropped by, the words just slipped out of her mouth, and before she was aware of it, she had introduced me as her daughter-in-law?

I must have fallen asleep with these thoughts running through my

mind, for the midsummer sun of this southern province had already
sunk behind the western mountains, and it was about that time when
dusk steals in to displace the day.

What should I do, I wondered. I had come to Amakusa in search of
a *karayuki-san,* without a clue as to where I would find such a woman.
Then, to run into Osaki the very same day I set foot in Amakusa—this
could only be decreed by Heaven, I felt, and not to seek her assistance
and stay there with her would be to act against fate. Osaki's introduction of me as her daughter-in-law was the best explanation she could
have offered the villagers to justify my stay. And yet, I didn't want to
push things too quickly, and when I thought about how Toyohara, who
was waiting for me at the inn in Miyanokawachi, would worry, I
decided that, for the time being, I had better leave Osaki's home.

"I'm afraid there's nothing very good to eat here," apologized Osaki
as she offered me some steamed sweet potatoes, scavenged from
farmers' discards. Not having any tea, she poured some plain hot water
into a teacup for me. After gratefully accepting this fare, I started to
thank her and take my leave, but no sooner had I begun than she sat
back down, clasped her hands together, and bowed her head, saying in
a formal way, "It's such a dirty place that even the village folk won't
come in and sit down, but you, a city person, whatever your reasons
may be, came into my house and even took a nap. When my son Yuji
comes, he never stays more than one night, and his wife hasn't sent me
a single letter. . . . "

Taken aback, I sat down on my knees and interrupted her, "Grandmother, you've got it backwards! It's I who should be thanking you!" She
continued sitting formally on her knees, however, and went on, "As you
can see, it's a dirty little house, but if you ever come to Amakusa again,
please come visit me. I'll never forget you, as long as I live."

At that instant I felt all of the doubts I had entertained about her, as I
lay there half-asleep, melting like an ice cube in hot water. Osaki had
not consciously tried to deceive her neighbors after all. When she
looked at me, nervous though I was, the first person to shake off their
fear and sit on her centipede-infested mats, she had wished that her
own daughter-in-law would come to see her with this attitude. This
feeling had given birth, of itself, to her response that I was her daughter-in-law. If this were not so, then why else would she say to someone
she had known for only a few hours and whom she had no reason to
flatter, "I'll never forget you, as long as I live."

Realizing that if I left for Sakitsu on foot I would find myself walking after dark, I stopped at the village general store to use a phone, and headed toward the inn at Miyanokawachi by taxi. There I met with Ms. Toyohara, as planned, and spent my first night in Amakusa, but after the day's excitement I could hardly sleep, and when morning came I was ready to be off. I went out and bought three dried horse mackerel as a house gift, and set out to visit Osaki again.

When I arrived at her house she was carrying on a loud conversation with her cats, but when she noticed me standing quietly in the entryway, she said only, "Oh my" and welcomed me in as she had the day before. Predicting that she would ask why I had come again, I had framed a tentative reply, but she didn't ask anything of the kind.

I spent about half the day with her, ascertaining that she had definitely been a *karayuki-san,* and that the place to which she had been sold was Borneo. I knew that to ask anything further would only serve to put her on guard, and so, with much reluctance, I left her hamlet. The following day Ms. Toyohara and I made the rounds of two or three scenic spots in Amakusa, and then headed back home.

Translator's Notes

1. This indigenous faith, in which an ordinary farm woman serves as a medium between the supplicant and her god, will be discussed further in the Translator's Afterword (More About Osaki).

2. The "humble sweet potato," notes Peter Duus, "which arrived from the New World, became a staple for poorer peasant households in Kyushu and western Japan. Requiring no irrigation, it flourished on dry upland fields where it was difficult to grow rice." *Modern Japan* (Boston: Houghton Mifflin, 1998), p. 45.

3. Tatami, a tightly packed rice-straw floor mat. Each mat is approximately three by six feet. The size of a room is measured by the number of mats required to cover the floor. In a modern Japanese home some rooms may have hardwood floors or carpet, but the guest room, at least, will have traditional tatami flooring.

4. Fusuma refers to a sliding partition of thick paper mounted in grooves on the floor and ceiling. Shoji are exterior sliding doors, or partitions, consisting of a wooden frame covered with thin, translucent white paper.

——— 3 ———

My Attempts at
a Second Trip

After I returned to Tokyo there were many times when I wouldn't get a wink of sleep at all before the short summer night had ended, as I lay awake thinking about my next trip to Amakusa. Since I had envisioned moving into the house of a *karayuki-san,* this would be the real journey. While on the one hand my heart was drawn toward Amakusa, on the other I was tormented by doubts that even if I went, it might not be possible to collect the kind of material I sought. My research methods certainly deviated from the norm, but I felt my background investigation was thorough and although I had set out initially just to test the waters, my trip resulted in a concrete objective in the form of Osaki. Yet as these thoughts went through my mind, black clouds of anxiety again made their appearance.

My primary concern was the cost of the trip and the issue of housework and child care. It was only recently that we had been able to assume a middle-class lifestyle, and since we did not employ a housekeeper, if I were to embark on a trip from which I did not know for certain when I would return, not only would I have to squeeze the travel money out of our household budget, but all the responsibility for house and child would fall on my husband's shoulders.

My husband, who conducts research in children's culture, believes that both children and women should be liberated. This viewpoint enabled him to understand my research in women's history, and he willingly assumed his fair share of the housework and child care. Therefore he agreed wholeheartedly with my plan to live for some time in Amakusa, and I didn't feel too badly about entrusting him with all our domestic affairs. But what if I failed to collect the information I needed, and my travel expenses and my husband's cooperation were all for nothing? When I considered this possibility, I was overcome with anxiety.

I was also concerned about how my only daughter, Mimi, now in the third grade, would feel about her mother's long absence. I had left her behind before on business trips, but according to my husband, while Mimi would get along fine for about five days, after a week had passed she would become extremely unsettled. And on this trip, I didn't know if I would be able to return after two weeks, or if I would be gone for more than three weeks.

One day I confronted my daughter and explained to her as clearly and directly as possible that I needed to make a trip to Amakusa that would be longer than usual. My daughter was silent for some time, then looking at me steadily with an expression stiff from excess seriousness, she replied, "It's all right if you go, Mother. I'll stay here with Father."

I don't know how the words "a poor old woman, who had once been a *karayuki-san*" affected my daughter who had just turned eight, and to what extent she understood my appeal, that "listening to this old woman's story is Mother's work." She fully accepted my explanation, however, interpreting it in her own childlike way, and was determined that she and her father could get along without me for a while.

In this way I was able to solve the problem of travel expenses and personal household affairs, but what worried me even more was whether I myself could endure Osaki's poverty-stricken lifestyle, the difficulties of which had become clear to me even in the brief two half-days I had spent there, and what I would say by way of an excuse to move into her house. The first matter hinged on my will alone, and could be dealt with simply by strengthening my resolve; but what to do about the second problem?

When I left her, Osaki had said, "As you can see, it's a dirty little house, but if you ever come to Amakusa again, please come visit me," but what possible reason could someone who was no more than a passing stranger have to pay another visit? And even if I could think of a reason, why would she allow just anybody to move in with her?

And just supposing she did let me move in, would I be accepted by most of the villagers, by the village community at whose mercy one was allowed to live or die, who determined when one was provided for and when things would be taken away?

Unlike urban areas where, for better or for worse, people are governed by a sense of individualism, Amakusa is a group of isolated islands where the vestiges of a premodern communal lifestyle are still in evidence, and where, customarily, a hamlet's sense of communal defense will be strong. Since outsiders are treated harshly, it would probably be best to anticipate that there was not much chance that the village would approve of my presence. Not only that. As we had experienced in some small degree on the ferry to Amakusa, because the issue of *karayuki-san* was for Amakusa residents a matter of local shame, if they knew that my real objective was research about *karayuki-san,* I would not necessarily be spared their sanctions. Just the thought of this conjured up unpleasant fantasies.

For some time I wavered back and forth, but finally, about two months after my first trip, well into autumn, I felt that I must be off again. It wasn't that I had come up with any definite solutions to dispel the dark clouds of doubt that filled my heart, but that I could no longer quell the urge to return to Amakusa and Osaki.

That evening my husband and daughter saw me off as far as the street in front of our house, and I said to Mimi, "Whenever I think of you, I'll take out your picture and look at it, so whenever you want to be with me, you should take out my picture too," and I patted my shoulder bag to show her where the picture was. My daughter nodded, and after she had said, "Good-bye, Mom," I walked away. My only luggage was a small vinyl shoulder bag and one Boston bag with a change of underwear and the like. My clothes consisted of a pair of worn-out slacks and an everyday shirt of synthetic material that I borrowed from my husband. My husband had teased me as I left, saying, "Don't get mistaken for a runaway wife, now," but a stranger may very well have received this impression. As it turned out, that very appearance may have served to ease my acceptance by the Amakusa villagers.

Be that as it may, the next day I arrived in Kyushu, and this time I took the bus straight over the five bridges and entered Amakusa-Shimo Island. By three in the afternoon we reached Sakitsu, the small town where I met Osaki at the shaved-ice shop. If my mind had been made up before, however, I lost all nerve once I arrived, and I couldn't bring myself to go directly to Osaki's village. To calm my nerves, I decided to visit Tenshudo Chapel, which Ms. Toyohara had seen on our last trip, but which I had missed. I have already described in chapter 1 my encounter here with the elderly farm woman who sat as still as a statue, deep in prayer.

—— 4 ——

Life with Osaki

When I saw the old farm woman praying in Tenshudo Chapel of Sakitsu, I renewed my inner vow to continue my research on *karayuki-san*. The sun of those short autumn days had already fallen behind the western hills as I walked to the one and only taxi dispatcher in Sakitsu. There I hired a car and proceeded to Osaki's village. In the field of ethnology it is an unspoken rule that when doing research on common folk, one should always enter a village on foot. It's not that I didn't know this, but the thought of being challenged by the villagers as I walked down that narrow path filled me with dread.

I had the taxi stop just past the general store, where I waited for a bit as my eyes adjusted to the now completely dark surroundings. Then I crossed the wooden bridge over the river and began to climb a gentle slope, cutting toward the north. A number of houses dotted the hillside at some distance to my right, the translucent paper sliding doors under their miscanthus-thatched roofs warmly lit by the light within. By comparison the tattered paper doors on Osaki's house glowed only dimly, giving the impression of a fox or badger home, as described in old tales. I didn't learn about this until later, but Osaki's house was lit by a single thirty-watt bulb, provided as a charity by the electric company to those who could not afford to pay an electric bill. This is why it looked much darker than the other houses.

As I stood before the tattered shoji, a human silhouette moved by, filling the frame. When I was certain there was only one person, I boldly slid open the heavy front door with all my might and jumped into the house, quickly sliding the door shut behind me as if I were being pursued. Thinking back on it now, I wonder if I wasn't in some altered psychological state. I knew I had to come up with a greeting, and without thinking I blurted out, "Mother!"—the same word I was obliged to use in front of the two villagers on my previous visit.

It seemed that Osaki had just gotten up to do something. She exclaimed something to the effect of "Oh" or "Ho" and, dropping the cat she had been holding, she stared at me as I stood frozen in the entryway. I wonder how much time passed as we each gazed at the other. "You did very well to find your way here in the dark! Well, come right in, come in." As she gestured for me to enter, I stepped up into the tatami room, saying only, "I wanted to see you, so I came again."

It is hard to believe that this was the full extent of the greetings that passed between us, but that was it. Osaki asked me if I had had dinner yet, and when I answered that I had eaten before I came, she offered me a cup of hot water, as she had on my previous visit, and gazed at me affectionately, asking if I had been well over the past two months and noting that I had put on some weight. She asked no other questions. Under normal circumstances I might have expected her to ask me why on earth I had shown up at this time of night, what my intentions were in staying, and of course she would eventually want to know exactly who I was and where I was from. But she asked none of these things, and I avoided discussion of myself or my motives.

After we had been chatting for some time, Osaki said, "You must be tired out from your long journey. You'd better go to sleep early," and she pulled a futon out of the bedding closet in the back of the house. I had thought that if she didn't have a spare futon I would go to Sakitsu or as far as Hondocho the next day to buy one, so I was thankful to know this wouldn't be necessary.

Untying a bundle wrapped in an old rain cloak, Osaki spread out a futon with a black striped cotton cover, apparently handwoven, and a cheap red comforter. There was no reason to expect that even when new they had come with accompanying sheets and coverlets.

When I tried to help her lay them out, Osaki asked me to wait a minute, and she began pounding the mattress with arms as thin as chicken legs. She was beating it too hard simply to remove the dust. She must have noticed my quizzical expression, for she explained, "This is a futon I brought home from abroad; it's made from a kind of Borneo cotton called kapok.[1] This is different from Japanese cotton, so you've got to beat it like this." Even after the dust had stopped flying up from the surface, she continued to pound the kapok. After she had pounded the futon for almost ten minutes, she laid it out for me to sleep on.

Although I was tired, I hardly got a wink of sleep that night. I was unable to relax on this mattress, filled with an unfamiliar stuffing from Borneo, besides which it was very damp from a long period of disuse, making me feel like I was soaking in a cold bath. However, what kept me awake was something else entirely. Osaki's words, spoken as she pounded the mattress, had pierced my heart, and no degree of fatigue would allow me to sleep.

Since Osaki had said that she brought the futon from abroad, this mattress must be one she had used during her years as a *karayuki-san*. Each night under the Southern Cross, which sparkled beautifully in the starry heavens of the southern hemisphere, men with different shades of skin would enter and leave, one after another, playing with her body in exchange for money, and this was the mattress upon which they lay. If this were so, then the chilling touch imparted by this futon must be due to the silent tears it absorbed as she was forced to sell her slight body to thousands of men from foreign lands. No, this dampness represented not only her tears, but the tears of untold women who were forced to go abroad, as she had done, to sell themselves in order to survive.

Some days later I learned from Osaki that it was indeed this futon which she used daily as a *karayuki-san*. When she was sold to Southeast Asia, her mother, who had remarried and entered another household, had said that the least she could do was make her child a new kimono, and she had walked through the village borrowing cotton thread. She worked through each night, weaving striped cloth, then cut and sewed the material into a lined kimono. This was the first and last time Osaki, brought up in poverty, received a new kimono from her mother, and it was this kimono she wore when she set out for Borneo. When she arrived, the brothel keeper only sneered at her, however, saying, "Do you really think you can do business wearing a plain kimono like that?" Unable to part with the kimono her mother had given her as a farewell gift, however, Osaki took it apart and made it into a futon, stuffing it with Borneo cotton. This was the striped cotton futon on which I slept.

I slept on this futon for the duration of the three weeks I spent living with Osaki, and I have to confess that I often found myself overcome with anxiety as I wondered whether bacteria bearing syphilis and gonorrhea might not still be alive within it. But I must say that being allowed to sleep on this memento of Osaki's life as a *karayuki-san* held the deepest possible significance for someone in search of the essence of the *karayuki-san* experience, and was, for me, an event to be remembered.

I was awakened by the crowing of roosters so shrill that I thought the floor cushion I had bent in half to serve as a pillow would go flying out from under my head. Osaki was already awake, and had just finished preparing breakfast. When we finished the morning meal, consisting of no more than a bowl of rice that had been cooked with an equal measure of barley paste, and some scrap potatoes boiled with miso and salt, Osaki took me off to greet the neighbors. When I told her the night before that I had brought three or four small boxes of bean-jam buns, Osaki had responded, "Well, then, let's at least make the rounds of my relatives," and we did just that.

First of all we went to a tiny house part way down the narrow path leading toward the river. According to Osaki, only one person lived there. "You met her when you came last summer. The one who had lost her sight, and had her hair dyed blond, remember? That was my brother's widow." Next we visited the two farmhouses to the west, and I learned that these houses belonged to the old blind woman's sons, in other words, to Osaki's nephews.

I had been introduced to Osaki's sister-in-law before, and at the homes of Osaki's nephews, whom I was meeting for the first time, I expected to be introduced in a similar fashion, as the wife of her son, Yuji. However, Osaki took one look back at me and said only, "She's going to be staying with me for a while." Since I had planned on passing as her daughter-in-law, I was baffled by this sudden switch in tactics and responded with a simple "Pleased to meet you" and offered them each a box of sweets. As I watched them bite into the buns with an enthusiasm one would never see in Tokyo, we took our leave.

You might say that making the rounds of these three houses was a rite of entrance into this hamlet. On my part, it was a declaration that I would be staying for a while at Osaki's house, while on the hamlet's part it was a gesture of solemn approbation. Having somehow passed this rite of entrance, I officially began my life with Osaki.

Osaki's way of life, which I was to experience firsthand, represented the most extreme degree of destitution I had ever encountered. I came to learn that Osaki's income consisted of only four thousand yen, sent to her each month by her son Yuji in Kyoto.[2] Other than the money he sent, which tended to fall behind schedule, she had not a bit of income. Even the Livelihood Protection Law, widely criticized as a policy for abandoning people, makes welfare payments of 9,587 yen per month to the elderly in farm villages. But Osaki had to make do with less than half of this sum to cover all expenditures for clothing, food, and shelter. And besides herself, she cared for nine cats left to die by previous owners. "These, too, are living creatures," she explained. "I feel sorry for them."

If we follow the word order in the standard phrase "clothing, food, and shelter" and begin with a discussion of clothing, I observed that Osaki had only a few items of clothing. The clothes Osaki was wearing when I first met her at the shaved-ice shop—a plain faded navy skirt and a shirt of "ripple" cloth, worn from many washings—were her go-to-town clothes. She had dressed up purposefully that day to make her monthly pilgrimage to pray to Odaishisama in Ikusagaura. On days when she stayed at home, she wore an old thin, gray cotton skirt and an even flimsier short-sleeved shirt of staple-fiber. Staple-fiber, colloquially known as *sufu,* is a kind of cloth that arrived on the market during World War II, and "ripple" is a kind of cloth which became popular just after the war. Other than these items which she either made or received around the time this cloth was popular, Osaki owned no clothes. Once, when there was a death in the village, she did pull out a silk kimono from an old chest and wear it to the funeral service, but this, I learned, was a gift she had received upon the distribution of keepsakes of a deceased friend or relative, and was something she saved for only the most special of special occasions.

As for footwear, other than the rubber thongs she wore everyday, whose soles had worn down to a polished surface, she had only a pair of old *geta,* or wooden clogs, with frayed thongs attached to the course-grained platforms. These she stored neatly under the threshold to the tatami room, bottoms clamped together. Considering that Osaki wore these only once on the aforementioned condolence visit, they must have been her dress shoes. As for her bedding, which might be considered part of her nightwear, she had the futon of Borneo cotton, which I described earlier, but no pillow, and she did not use any sort of sleepwear. Every night I slept in the same clothes I wore all day, a pair of slacks and my husband's shirt. Other than the matter of sleepwear, in the short period that I stayed with her, Osaki's wardrobe had little direct affect on me. When it comes to food, however, we are talking about the daily diet that sustains our lives, and here, I must admit, I encountered serious problems.

Beginning with the cooking facilities, Osaki's house was entirely lacking in anything like the kitchen you would find in the average home. No matter where I looked in the house, there was no evidence of a well, piped water, or a sink. All she had was a primitive, makeshift sort of oven which she had fashioned out of clay with her own two hands and placed on the dirt-floored room. Above it hung a kettle, black with soot, and next to the oven was placed a *mikan* box, bearing her single iron pot. Next to that was a leaky metal washbasin, containing five or six rice bowls, and that was the extent of her kitchen utensils. She had no soup bowls or plates, and so both rice and side dishes had to be eaten from the same bowl.

One couldn't cook without water. I wondered how she was going to handle this, until I learned that there was a water barrel about three feet high placed under the eaves just outside the door, and that Osaki would haul water here in a dented bucket from a well under a small pine, twenty to thirty meters from her house.

Having written this, I may be accused of lying, since I said earlier that there was not a well or any plumbing, but I'm not sure her source of water deserved the name of well. The place she referred to as a well, and from which she hauled water every day, actually may have been a well some decades ago, but now it could only be described as a hole yawning open right in the middle of the road, no more than eighty centimeters in diameter. Not only did it not have a lid, but it was not even enclosed by a stone fence. Looking down into it, you could see that the water was cloudy at the bottom. When water was pulled up in a dented bucket, attached to a rough straw rope, there were always leaves and small insects floating on the top. This water was used after it had settled in the water barrel, but Osaki told me that she had received the barrel just two years ago when her younger sister-in-law's family had moved to Nagoya. In the long months and years before that, she must have had to go all the way to this well each time she needed water.

Well, then, what sort of cooking did Osaki do in this kitchen which could not be called a kitchen? I mentioned already that the breakfast I had the morning after I arrived consisted of rice mixed half and half with barley paste, but during the entire time I stayed with Osaki, she never once prepared the meal with any more rice than this. Based on what she told me later, Osaki was preparing the highest-quality meal she could afford. Usually she used a greater proportion of barley. Not only was the rice cut fifty-fifty with barley paste, but it was red rice, one of the lowest-quality rice grains. It was bad enough to eat it warm, but once it was cold, it was so dry that it just wouldn't go down my throat. Of course she didn't have a rice cooker, and she had to use the dried leaves and firewood she collected sparingly, so she would cook as much rice as she could at one time in a large pot. For that reason she ate dry, cold rice almost all the time. I tried to disguise this rice with the side dish, but that wasn't much more appetizing, consisting routinely of scrap sweet potatoes boiled down with salt or miso. Osaki never ate miso soup or pickles. Once a week she would buy small leftover horse mackerel, at three for ten yen, from an itinerant fish peddler. Stewed potatoes with horse mackerel were her only special meal, but according to Osaki, "I just buy the fish for the cats." When the neighbors wanted to prepare a special dish, they would make things like *udon,* soup with large wheat noodles, or deep-fried vegetables, but at Osaki's house this was unimaginable. For her, it was a steady diet of dry rice and scrap potatoes boiled in salt, day in and day out.

These meals, which almost defied linguistic description for someone from the Tokyo middle class, were ultimately due to Osaki's meager budget of four thousand yen per month. But another reason was that Osaki was a woman almost totally unfamiliar with the art of cooking.

Even to my untrained eye there were all kinds of edible plants in the village, and had she known how to use even one of them she could have enriched her menu, but because Osaki had spent that time of her youth, when she would have learned to cook and sew, as a *karayuki-san,* she knew almost nothing of the art of cooking.

This was true not only for Osaki, but, based on my later observations, was a common trait among almost all women who had once been *karayuki-san.* In today's society knowledge of cooking is an important quality in a wife; *karayuki-san,* for this reason as well, had been deprived of their qualifications to become wives.

With regard to the "shelter" in Osaki's life, I need not mention the dilapidated condition of her house, which has already been discussed. What I must record at this point, however, is the fact that she had neither bath nor toilet. A bathtub is a relatively expensive item, so she probably could not have afforded one. Besides, it was her habit to go and borrow the use of the bath at her nephew's house, who lived not too far away. I joined her any number of times, but what passed for a bathtub at her nephew's house was nothing more than an oil drum, raised off the ground by several bricks, under which a wood fire was lit to heat water. The room itself was lit by neither electric lamp nor candle. Rather, one had to grope one's way around by shafts of moonlight piercing through the rough roofing and siding. The first night I tried out the bath, the warmth of a living thing touched my shoulder. Automatically freezing in place, I strained my eyes, only to find that right before my nose was the large, black eye of a cow. Osaki's nephew's bathhouse consisted of one corner of his cow shed.

Since I could get along without a daily bath, the occasional trip to the nephew's bathhouse was sufficient, but I found it a major problem that there was no toilet. As I learned several days later, this was not the house in which Osaki grew up, but a place she had been able to purchase for an extremely low price, sometime after she was repatriated from China. Certainly the previous occupant would have had a toilet. Indeed, there was evidence of a former toilet in the small storage shed that was barely hanging together in the northeast corner of the house, and it was to this spot that I first ventured. Osaki stopped me, however, saying, "You'd better not use that toilet. The floorboards are rotten, and with just enough pressure you might find yourself falling into the cistern underneath." Then, responding to my questioning eyes, she pointed to the vacant field at the foot of the cliff behind her house and said, "Do it there. That's what I do. No one will look."

It certainly wouldn't do to cling to the old toilet and take the chance of falling through rotten boards into a stagnant pool, so I decided to follow Osaki's advice. When I just had to pee I went empty-handed, but at other times I would go out below the cliff, hoe in hand, and find a soft-looking spot in the ground where I could dig a hole. When I was done, I would fill it in. I was always afraid that some villager working in the mountain fields would look down and see me, but what was even more trying was having my exposed flesh attacked by swarms of horseflies which seemed to appear from nowhere.

Osaki's life was certainly the poorest of which I had ever seen or heard. For me, accustomed to a middle-class urban lifestyle, life with Osaki was almost unbearable. To pretend otherwise would be a lie. Time after time I sought to relieve my own suffering by thinking I might just put out some money to bring home white rice, meat, and fish, or order some lumber and hire someone to build a simple toilet. I could have done this easily, simply by parting with a small portion of the money I had brought with me, and perhaps it was my duty to do so as someone sharing the same living quarters.

But every time I reached for my wallet, I would begin scolding myself. Didn't you make this second trip to Amakusa so that you could experience life with Osaki just as she lives it? If you can't eat Osaki's barley rice day in and day out, sit on rotten tatami crawling with centipedes, and sleep on her futon of Borneo cotton on which she had to lie with thousands of foreign men, and finally, if you can't dig a hole and do your business below the cliff out back, how can you expect her to look at you as an equal? If you can't do that, surely she won't tell you about her life as a *karayuki-san*. Shouldn't you be depending on Osaki's goodwill in all things, and sharing her life of poverty?

So, for three weeks I did not once supplement Osaki's household budget, but rather received the favor of being allowed to make her everyday lifestyle my own. Having to eat barley rice, to which just a few grains of red rice had been added, and a side dish of scrap potatoes boiled in salt, morning and evening, day in and day out, was a hellish torture. Thinking that if I didn't eat this food, I wouldn't be able to hear her story, that the act of consuming this food was my passport to her heart, I resigned myself to eating every last bit of barley stuck in my bowl.

After living this way for a week to ten days, casually I began to extract from Osaki the tale of her years as a *karayuki-san*. When we would spread out the mattress of Borneo cotton at night, I would shift the conversation away from kapok and try asking her such questions as how old she was when she went to Borneo, about how many Japanese were there at the time, and what kind of work they did there.

Osaki did not respond to such questions readily. "I went to Borneo when I was small," she would say. As for such questions as how she came to be sold to Borneo, what route she took to get there, how she felt at that time, and so on, she kept her lips sealed and wouldn't reveal a thing.

It was precisely because I had no illusions that I could draw out her tale by ordinary means that I devised the plan of living with a former *karayuki-san* in the Amakusa Islands. But when I still had no significant results after one week, and then ten days, I couldn't help but feel anxious.

It was not long afterwards, however, that Osaki began to tell me everything that I wanted to hear, not concealing anything. This change in her attitude seemed to have been brought about by the open distrust with which the villagers had come to view me.

This open suspicion displayed by the villagers was rooted, of course, in their doubt that I really was Osaki's daughter-in-law. The wife of her only son, Yuji, had never come to this village to visit her mother-in-law, and Osaki herself knew her only through a photograph, so no one had actually seen her face; but it seems that the daughter-in-law of the old blind woman with the blond hair, whom we encountered earlier, began saying things like, "Once when I went to Kyoto I had dinner with Yu-chan, and Yu-chan's wife looks nothing like this woman. His wife is a shorter, more heavy-set woman." Perhaps out of consideration for me, whom she had become accustomed to seeing when I came for a bath, it seems that the daughter-in-law made this observation only once or twice. Not so the old blind woman with blond hair, who had nothing to do but kill time. She made the rounds of the hamlet trumpeting the news to everyone.

Soon there was no one in the village who hadn't heard the rumor that I might not be Osaki's daughter-in-law. Only I, the very person involved, was unaware of it. Therefore, when the fishmonger came by one day, bringing horse mackerel for the cats, and began questioning me about things, I inadvertently mentioned that I lived in Tokyo and knew the town. This made the rounds of the village, falling on every one's ears, and served to stir up their suspicions even further.

Everyone in the village, including Osaki's sister-in-law, the old blind woman with blond hair, could talk of nothing else but the mystery of my identity. Finally, after much speculation, the villagers quieted down, satisfied with the opinion that "that woman is either Osaki's illegitimate child from her *karayuki-san* days, or else she's the child of one of Osaki's *karayuki* friends. She must have been tracking down Osaki's whereabouts and finally found her. Either that, or she's part of the water trade and came to hide here because she got into some kind of trouble."

Actually, as we will see in the case of Ofumi, Osaki's co-worker, it was not unusual for *karayuki-san* to give birth to children who were then hidden away. It would not be unusual, then, for Osaki herself to have one or two such children, and it seemed plausible that one of these children might yearn for her real mother and seek her out. Then again, even if she were not Osaki's child, if she were the daughter of a friend from her *karayuki-san* days, there might be any number of reasons for her coming to visit. Compared to these speculations, the hypothesis that I was a prostitute who had come to hide seemed rather far-fetched, but from the viewpoint of the villagers, any woman who stayed for very long at the home of Osaki, a one-time *karayuki-san,* could not possibly be very reputable. Add to this the fact that I still bore a number of scars on my face from an accident I had over ten years earlier. These scars formed part of the basis for the villagers' water trade theory.

Once the villagers had decided that one of the three previous descriptions must reveal my true colors, they began to treat me with unusual kindness. Some expressed kindness out of a sense of pity—she's a poor, unhappy girl, so we should do all we can for her. And some out of a sense of superiority, for being upright people who stood above my inferior type—if she's not the child of a *karayuki-san,* she must work in the water trade.

This was all reflected as a subtle light and darkness in Osaki's heart, and she began to reveal more to me than ever before. As always, she refrained from asking my identity, but on nights when we lay down and the chorusing of insects outside defied sleep, she would suddenly offer me advice. "You know, men are really evil creatures. No matter how nice you may think a man is, you mustn't seriously fall in love with him. If you really fall in love, you'll end up bringing ruin upon yourself."

Her voice bore the tone of one who considered me to be the same type of person as she, and who was offering advice as one older and more experienced. These words, which represented the sum total of her life wisdom, distilled from decades of experience as a *karayuki-san,* wrenched my heart as I took them in.

After this, whenever I asked Osaki about her life in Borneo, she spoke openly about everything. Which country were most of her customers from? How many men did she serve each night? What did they pay? What were the feelings she experienced with regard to selling her own flesh? What were the circumstances that compelled her to embark upon the life of a *karayuki-san*?

I didn't confront her with a consistent series of questions. I approached her, rather, as someone sharing her life who would like to know as much about her as possible, asking her about things as the occasion permitted. It was unavoidable, therefore, that I heard her story in disconnected pieces. Just when I thought she was telling me about her life in Sandakan, Borneo, she would begin reminiscing about her childhood in Amakusa, and then suddenly she would jump back into an account of her life as a prostitute.

For my part, I needed to record Osaki's tale as accurately as possible, preserving not only her words, but the spirit in which they were uttered; however, this was not the sort of situation where one could use a tape recorder or pull out one's notebook. As I lay in bed at night listening to her speak, I would reflect upon every word, chiseling her tale into my memory down to the very last detail. The next morning, after making certain that I was alone, I would furiously record everything on stationery, which I would then run and post at the village mailbox. This became a daily pattern which served two purposes. Osaki aside, who couldn't read, this routine ensured that even if the villagers should find some pretext to go through my belongings, they wouldn't find anything that would cause any trouble. Secondly, it meant that this material, so valuable to me, would be kept safely in my husband's hands in Tokyo.

After leading this sort of life for three weeks, I was able to grasp the gist of her childhood and years as a *karayuki-san*. What you will read in the next chapter is what I learned from Osaki about the course of her life. Because I heard her story in fragments and because the act of hearing itself is subject to personal interpretation, I cannot say that the life story I here record is a precise reconstruction of Osaki's own words. However, I feel that I used the only methods available to me at that time, and while I must endure the knowledge that this is something like scratching the sole of one's foot through one's shoe, I have presumed to use the first person as I weave the pieces into a coherent story of Osaki's life.

Further, as I have noted any number of times earlier, because Osaki was completely illiterate, unable to read either *katakana* or numbers, I recorded the names of people and places she mentioned phonetically, not knowing which characters to assign them.[3] After returning to Tokyo I made use of family registers to assign the correct characters to people's names, but there were limits to the information I could obtain, and so some names will remain in *katakana*.

Translator's Notes

1. What Osaki calls "Borneo cotton" is kapok, grayish white fibers, dry and air-filled, found within the fruit of the kapok tree, *Ceiba pentandra,* occurring natu-

rally in tropical America and growing as a plantation tree in Southeast Asia. The fibers are too short and smooth to be spun for textile thread, but, being only one-eighth as heavy as cotton, are used as stuffing in cushions, mattresses, life jackets, and the like.

2. The exchange rate at this time was 360 yen to the U.S. dollar, so Osaki's monthly allowance was equivalent to $11.11.

3. *Katakana* is the simplest of the two Japanese syllabaries, consisting of forty-six symbols. Generally children learn *katakana* in kindergarten.

—— 5 ——

Osaki's Story—The Life of an Overseas Prostitute

The date of my birth, well, I'm not exactly sure. I'm certain of the month and the day, January 29, but I don't know what year it was, although I think I'm about seventy-two this year. When my son, Yuji, got married, he went to get our family register from the town hall, and according to it, he said, I was born around 1907 or 1908. But that's wrong. My mother and father were in no rush to go to a place like the village hall, so they didn't report my birth; then, when I was close to ten and was about to go abroad, my brother registered my birth for the first time. But my own honest calculation and the calculation made by the village hall differ by ten years, and so my neighbor, who is the same age as I, is able now to get money for the elderly from the government, while I don't get a speck of dust.

My father—his name was Yamakawa Manzo—comes from a family who have been farming in this village for generations, but I don't know how much land he had. He fell sick and died when I was four, and I don't remember his face or what he was like. If my older brother were still alive—Yasukichi is four years older than I am, so he would have been eight when Father died—he would have known something about him, but he passed away a long time ago. I've heard, though, that Father just couldn't resist gambling whenever he had a chance, so eventually he lost all of his farmland and my parents ended up working together as day laborers in the fields of a wealthy man.

My mother's name was Sato, and she came as a bride from the Kawashima family in the same village, but she wasn't a very kind woman. It's not very nice to speak of one's own mother in this way, but since I'm not lying, I hope you won't mind my saying so.

Even if you had land, you could barely eke out a living here, so I'm sure my parents' life as day laborers must have been really difficult. Because, you see, they also had three children—my older brother, Yasukichi, my older sister, Yoshi, and me. Even so, we somehow made ends meet while my father was still living, but when he became ill and died, we just couldn't make it. Eventually we had to sell the large house we'd lived in until then. When we sold the house we had nowhere to go, but my mother's older brother was very fond of his younger sister, and so he built a small house close to the one we had sold and moved us all in there. It was so small I wonder if you could have laid out even four full tatami mats. I was about four or five at the time, and I just couldn't understand why we moved to such a tiny place. I was told that I caused all kinds of trouble, crying to my mother, "Let's go back to Osaki's house."

After that my mother put even more energy into her work as a day laborer. My older brother, who had just turned nine or ten, said he would go to work as a baby-sitter for a nearby farming family, so Mother wouldn't have so many mouths to feed. Even so, our life didn't become any easier. There were days when I would have nothing to swallow but water from morning 'til night. Even when noon came around, or when the sun had set, I still hadn't had even the neck of a sweet potato to eat. It's bad enough for an adult, but let me tell you, when you're a young, growing child and need food the most, it's really miserable not to have one bite to eat all day.

> According to the official copy of her family register, Yamakawa Saki was born on January 29, 1909, the second daughter of Yamakawa Manzo and Yamakawa Sato at No. 1,629 of XX Section, XX Village in Amakusa County, Kumamoto Prefecture. Her brother, Yasukichi, was born on March 27, 1896, and died on September 19, 1947. Her older sister, Yoshi, was born on July 11, 1898.

After we had lived this sort of life for a number of years, there was talk that my mother would get married. The wife of my uncle Tokumatsu, my father's older brother closest to his age, had died, and my mother was told that as the widow of his younger brother, it would be convenient for her to become his next wife.[1] I don't know how old Uncle Tokumatsu was then, but he had six children by his first wife, and his oldest daughter was only three years younger than my mother.

So, when my mother went as a bride to my uncle's house, this oldest daughter no longer lived there. She had gone to Java to work as a prostitute. I don't know why, but she came home deaf, and ten years after my mother went to her home as a bride, this girl died. Poor soul.

I wonder how old my mother was when she went to Uncle Tokumatsu's place. With all those small children at his place, my uncle would have had a hard time with no one to cook, and since at our place we were so poor there were times we couldn't even eat sweet potatoes, the two households might as well join—this was his reasoning for marrying my mother. Actually, he had promised that in return for her hand in marriage, he would take care of the three of us children.

When I heard this from my mother, I was embarrassed, and I didn't say either that I agreed or didn't agree, but my brother, Yasukichi, was really against the idea. I've forgotten now why he opposed it so strongly. After all, this happened sixty years ago. My brother was someone who held the spirits of the deceased in deep respect, and he must have said something like, "I can't make any excuses for this to our dead father." Nevertheless, my mother did go as a bride to my Uncle Tokumatsu's place, but it was decided that we three children would stay in our tiny house and take care of ourselves. I remember how my eyes filled with tears as I thought in my childish heart that a mother who would just abandon her children and go to another man's place could no longer be my mother.

> According to the official family register, Yamakawa Saki's mother, Yamakawa Sato, was born on March 6, 1873, and was remarried to Yamakawa Tokumatsu on December 15, 1913, at No. 1,657 of XX Section, XX Village, Amakusa County.

Around that time my older brother had stopped working as a baby-sitter, and had taken a job as a pit worker at Mitsubishi Coal Mine nearby, but when my mother left, he quit and tried to stay at home every day. He rented some fields not far from our house and began growing barley and sweet potatoes, and my older sister and I threw ourselves wholeheartedly into helping him. Since this wasn't enough to keep us going, when I was seven I got a baby-sitting job for two years at the home of Shoda Joi. I took care of a little boy named Yoshinori, but because I was small for my age, when I would tie Yoshinori on my back with my obi, his feet hung down right next to

mine. They fed me lunch and dinner, and I earned a salary of four yen
per year. Because I had to work like this, I didn't spend even one day
of my life in school. Neither my older brother or sister, nor I, went to
school. It wasn't just my family that didn't go to school, though. At
that time, unlike today, there were many children in my village who
didn't go to school, and it wasn't a bit strange. But because I didn't go
to school, I can't read at all, not a single syllable. You young people
are really fortunate. You can read books and newspapers to your
heart's content. You can write letters to anyone you want. I'm like a
blind person with open eyes. Even when I went abroad I couldn't write
home a single letter saying something so simple as that I was in good
health and hadn't been sick. When I sent money home, I had to ask
someone to write the letter for me each time, and when letters came I
had to have someone read each one. You probably wouldn't understand, but it was really humiliating.

I'm probably talking about too many different things. No matter
how hard the three of us worked, a child's income was no match for
that of an adult. By the time winter arrived, the barley box and potato
tub were empty, and days would go by when not only was there no
barley gruel, but we couldn't even sip potato broth. Unlike the big
house we lived in before, this little house didn't have anything like
tatami. We were able to keep a fire going from dried twigs we gathered
in the hills, but when the three of us would sit with empty stomachs on
the wooden floor, we could think of nothing but food. On those nights
as I sat thinking, my mother's face would appear in my mind—but she
was no longer our mother, and I hated her. If I spoke of her in this way,
it would anger my brother, so I just bit my lip and remained silent.

Once she went to Uncle Tokumatsu's place, my mother hardly ever
came to visit us. Although she lived in a different neighborhood, it was
within the same village, and she could have dropped by now and then.
I'd like to think that the reason she didn't come wasn't because she
didn't feel sorry for us, but because she didn't want to cause any
trouble for Uncle Tokumatsu and her stepchildren.

In this situation, it was my mother's older brother, who built our
house, and her older sister, my aunt, who had no children, who often
visited us, saying, "How are you doing, have you been eating?" We've
made some rice cakes, my aunt would say, bringing some over on a
tray, or she would drop by with new potatoes, saying they'd just been
digging some. Their kind words gave us strength. "The three of you

should try and get along well together. If you have any trouble, feel free to come talk to us."

In the meantime, my older sister, Yoshi, turned ten or eleven, and it was arranged that she would work as a maid in the home of Shoda Toichi whose house was in our neighborhood. Shoda Toichi was not that well-to-do, so he had other reasons for taking my sister on as a maid.

Toichi had an older sister named Otoku. The villagers would call her "Otonjo," but anyway this Otonjo opened a brothel in Rangoon, Burma. Toichi wanted prostitutes to take to Otonjo's brothel, and so there was no doubt this is why he set eyes on my sister, Yoshi. It wasn't long before my sister was forced to accompany Toichi to Otonjo's brothel and start working as a prostitute. Shoda Onami, who lives just a little bit up the road from me now, became Toichi's wife in Rangoon.

Shoda Toichi, now there was a bad man. He took every cent Otonjo saved at her brothel. After they returned to the village together, she went crazy, running around town saying whatever came into her head. Toichi shut her up in a single room at the back of his house, which never saw the light of day, not providing her with sufficient food and drink, so that finally he allowed her to die before his very eyes. But Toichi, too, is long gone. Onami is still strong, and owns a store in town. Remember when you said you wanted some soap the other day, and you went out and bought some? That was her store. But she keeps everything about her return from abroad strictly to herself.

What happened to my sister Yoshi? First she was sent to Rangoon, and from there she moved to Singapore and then to Java, and in the year that the current emperor was enthroned, she returned to Amakusa.[2]

She said she set up house in the South Seas with a seaman born in Kyoto, but he got sick and died, and she came home with his ashes. After that she never returned to the South Seas, but joined up with Shoda Kaikichi, elder brother of Shoda Onami. Yoshi died just last spring. She was one or two years short of seventy-five.

> According to the official family register, on May 1, 1914, Yamakawa Yoshi was married to Daizaburo, the second son of Tanaka Mitsuyoshi, of No. 694 of XX Section, XX Village, Amakusa County. On February 26, 1922, she was divorced by mutual agreement. On March 7, 1936, she married Shoda Kaikichi of No. 1,125 of XX Section, XX Village, Amakusa County.

Osaki's older sister, Yoshi. The photograph was taken in Rangoon around the middle of the Taisho period (1912–1925). Most *karayuki-san,* including Yoshi, were illiterate, so they would send photographs home to show their families that they were in good health.

Since the last war no girls from anywhere have gone to the South Seas, but when I was small, girls from this house and that house would all go. They didn't come just from families without two parents. Even from this one village there were more than twenty young girls who went abroad at the same time I did.

Those who went to foreign countries to work as prostitutes had all kinds of difficult experiences, and in many cases we don't know where they finally went, so we don't have information on all of them. Among those I know, Shoda Osana across the river below lives in a big house, and she even has foreign chairs and a refrigerator. Osana went as a bride to the home of one of my distant relatives, and she gave birth to one girl, but for some reason she left that house, and she was taken by a different boss than ours to Phnom Penh. She got together with a Frenchman there named Gagnon who was quite wealthy, and it seems that she lived in luxury. This Frenchman died a long time ago. His younger brother from France took all of his property, so Osana went to court and did quite well for herself. Even now she receives funds from abroad every year, and so she's able to lead an easy life. You could say that Osana is the most successful of all of us who went abroad.

Okazu, who lived below here, also became the mistress of a Frenchman when she was abroad, and continued to live quite well after her return. She died a year or two ago. If I'm not mistaken, Shigemura Natsuno was sold to a place in Tientsin. I heard a rumor that Yamashita Tatsuno's older sister—I've forgotten her name—became the wife of a Chinese, and after that she never returned to Amakusa. I haven't heard of any letters from her either; I wonder if she's still living. There are many more than these, but other than Osana and Okazu, not one of them has any good thoughts of the past or the present.

Even within my own family, many of us went abroad. First there's me and my sister, Yoshi. Then there was Haru, my father's oldest brother's daughter—that's right, she would be my cousin, wouldn't she? She was in Rangoon for twenty years, and the man named Ryoji, from Shimabara, who became her husband had spent a long time in the South Seas also. My sister Yoshi's first husband, the sailor, also worked in the South Seas, and her second husband, Shoda Kaikichi, was a clerk for a brothel in Rangoon, and his younger sisters, Onami and Oyae, worked as prostitutes at the same brothel. Kitagawa Shintaro, the man who became my husband, also worked abroad, and Uncle Tokumatsu's oldest daughter went to work in a brothel, as I mentioned earlier.

I wonder how many of us that makes. Six women and four men, you say? This many people went to the South Seas from one family alone, so if you look at other households I imagine it would be about the same. [See the chart on the next page.]

It was the year I turned ten that it was arranged for me to go abroad. We children couldn't get anywhere by ourselves, farming rented land. My brother Yasukichi was becoming a young man, but someone who

Genealogy of Kitagawa Saki.

*Refers to familiy members who spent time Southeast Asia or China between the late Meiji and early Showa periods (approximately 1900-1930). Over half of the family in Osaki's generation went abroad in search of jobs.

```
                                       Ryoji* (from Shimabara; Rangoon)
                                         ‖
                                       ____Haru*  (Rangoon)
          wife                         ǀ
 ǀ___‖  --------------------------     ǀ _____    younger  brother
 ǀ    Manzo's eldest brother           ǀ_____younger  daughter
 ǀ
 ǀ    Previous wife                                         Eldest daughter*
 ǀ    ‖                                                     ǀ         (Java)
 ǀ__Yamakawa Tokumatsu (younger brother of Manzo; remarried to Sato)   ǀ---
 ǀ    ‖                                                     ǀ---
 ǀ       -----Saki's stepsister                             ǀ---
 ǀ    ‖
 ǀ    ‖             ǀ---Yasukichi
 ǀ    ‖             ǀ    Previous husband* (from Kyoto; Rangoon)
 ǀ    ‖             ǀ    ‖
 ǀ    ‖             ǀ ---Yoshi* (Rangoon; Singapore; Java)
 ǀ___Sato (mother)  ǀ    ‖
 ǀ    ‖   _____ǀ    Second husband
 ǀ    ‖             ǀ    ‖
 ǀ ___ Yamakawa Manzo    Third husband, Shoda Kaikichi* (Rangoon)
          (father)  ǀ             ǀ__Nami* (Kaikichi's younger sister; Rangoon)
                    ǀ             ǀ__Yae* (Kaikichi's younger sister; Rangoon)
                    ǀ
                    ǀ    Yamashita Giezo (previous husband)
                    ǀ      ‖
                    ǀ___SAKI* (North Borneo; northeast China)
                         ‖
                         ‖_____Yuji* (eldest son; born in northeast China)
                         ‖
                         Kitagawa Shintaro* (last husband; from Kyoto; northeast China)
```

didn't own a single paddy or field wasn't treated as a respectable man, so no one offered to come as a bride. I felt really sorry for my brother and I wanted somehow to help him become a real man. I saw that the girls in my community were getting a lot of money for going to work abroad, and in my child's heart I thought that if I just went abroad my brother would be able to buy some farmland, build a large house, receive a bride, and become a splendid man. That's how I decided to work abroad.

If you head for Oe from Sakitsu, and then veer farther west, you reach a place called Takahama. There was a boss named Yoshinaka Tarozo who had gone from Takahama to the South Seas and done very well. One evening this boss dropped by our house. My brother and the boss sat at the hearth and talked deep into the night. As the conversation drew to an end, it was concluded that for the sum of three hundred yen I would be taken by the boss to Sandakan in Borneo.

Kneeling and bowing his head to the floor, my brother Yasukichi begged, "Please consider going to work abroad." Thinking that it was to make my brother a man, I replied "OK, I'll go," but when the boss told me to keep my word, I somehow felt uneasy, and sulkily responded, "If Ohana goes also, I'll agree to work abroad; if you don't take Ohana, I won't go."

> According to the official family register, Yoshinaka Tarozo was born on July 28, 1876, the eldest son of Yoshinaka Torajiro and Komu, at No. 1,013 of XX Section, Takahama Village, Amakusa County.

Ohana was my closest friend from early childhood. She was a year younger than me. She lived just a glance away from my place, and her father cultivated a few fields, but Ohana wasn't really a child from that family. It seems that she was born in another village, that her parents had died for some reason, and that she was taken in by the Shoda family when she was two. I've mentioned the name Shoda over and over, but that's because it's a very common family name in these parts. Still, even though she had someone to call "Father, Mother," they weren't her real parents, and because they had children of their own, she always felt second-class. You can see how she would be a good companion for someone from a house with no parents at all.

When I met Ohana the next day, I told her what I had heard about going abroad, and just as Boss Tarozo had said, I told her, "If you go to work abroad, every day is like a festival, you can wear nice kimono, and every day you can eat as much white rice as you want. Won't you come with me?" Ohana answered without a moment's thought, "I'll go."

> According to the official family register, Shoda Hana was born on January 10, 1901, the fourth daughter of Yamashita Tokitaro, head of the family at No. 1,669 of XX Section, XX Village, Amakusa County. On April 28, 1917, she was registered as the adopted daughter of Shoda Yoshimatsu and Shoda Kimi.

No, it wasn't only Ohana. Another friend, Takeshita Tsugiyo, was also there when we were talking. Tsugiyo said, "I want to go abroad to work too. Let me go with you." Tsugiyo's home was located in a rocky area near the mountains where you can't grow decent radishes or potatoes no matter how much fertilizer you apply. This happened after we left for the South Seas, but Tsugiyo's older brother had to go to Brazil to work. Because that's the sort of family she came from, you can see why Tsugiyo would say, "I want to go abroad too."

According to the official family register, Takeshita Tsugiyo was born on July 26, 1902, the eldest daughter of Takeshita Saburo and Takeshita Tayo, at No. 2,992 of XX Section, XX Village, Amakusa County. She died on February 9, 1962, at No. 410 of XX Section, XX Village, Amakusa County.

When they came home from playing that day, both Ohana and Tsugiyo faced their parents and said, "Please, let me go abroad to work." I don't remember clearly, but it's likely that Boss Yoshinaka visited their parents as well, stacking up bills before them as he promised, "If you give me your children, I'll give you three hundred yen for each one."

In this way it was decided that the three of us would go abroad, but when the decision had been made we had mixed feelings, sometimes very happy and sometimes sad. I don't know whether my brother told my mother, or whether she heard it from someone else, but she knew that I was going abroad, and she came to visit for the first time in ages. She brought me a new kimono that she had made. I was so happy— after all, it was the first time in my life I had received new clothes since I was born. It was a black cotton kimono with white stripes.

When I returned from the South Seas for a visit, my mother told me that in order to make this kimono, she had to conceal the whole process from my Uncle Tokumatsu. It had been no easy task, she said. She had no secret savings to buy thread, so she had to walk through the village borrowing cotton thread, promising, "I'll return it in no time." She used the thread to set up her loom and weave cloth, and she would sew late at night without sleeping. As she wove and sewed, she worried and cried for me, her daughter who was to be sold and sent away, and her eyes became red and swollen.

It was with such thoughts my mother had made this kimono, but when I arrived at Sandakan, Tarozo became angry and said, "How do you think you're going to be able to work as a prostitute with a shabby kimono like that?" So, I took out the stitching, filled the material with kapok, and made it into a mattress. It's the very same mattress you are using now. I used it all the time at Sandakan, but when I returned to Amakusa for a visit, I brought it home with me.

Don't you think I've talked enough about the kimono? So, this was the way my mother made me the kimono, but she wasn't able to go so far as to make a new sash. Even so, she somehow managed to get her hands on someone's used sash—it was a red Hakata obi—and she tied it around my waist. For the first time since I was born she put a decorative comb in my hair, and when I had bundled up a few under-skirts in my *furoshiki,* my packing was complete.

Then Yoshinaka Tarozo came to get me, and finally we were ready to set off. Ohana and Tsugiyo's fathers took off from work to accompany them, and my mother came with me. You know that path through the rice paddies we walked in on together, well, we all walked single-file down that path to Sakitsu, and below Tenshudo in Sakitsu we boarded a small boat and went to Takahama. My mother couldn't tolerate being in vehicles, of which boats were the worst, maybe because when she was young she got sick on a steamship and even threw up blood. This time, too, her face turned ashen as she accompanied me to Takahama.

My mother snuggled close to me in the boat, the tears rolling down her cheeks. "You're going off to work in a distant country, so this will be our final parting in this lifetime. I wonder if we shall ever be able to meet again?"

I fell into a deep silence and tried to comfort my mother, wiping away her tears with a hand towel. "Mother, please don't worry so much. Three or four of us are going, but I'll somehow endure any hardships and be the first to return."

In Takahama, at the harbor where we were to board a boat bound for Nagasaki, we parted from the mothers and fathers who had come to see us off. As soon as our boat started moving, Tsugiyo and Ohana's fathers cupped their hands to their mouths and called out over and over "Tsugiyoo—Come home in good health as soon as you can!" "Ohanaa—You're not to get sick, now!" but my mother could only stand there crying and was never able to say a word. Even though I had felt for some time that my mother had no compassion, when I saw my mom like that I felt sorry for her, and I remember that my heart went out to her as I thought, "It's a long way from Takahama back to our village; how on earth will she make it?"

The trip from Nagasaki to Borneo was dreadfully long. No sooner had we had arrived at Nagasaki than we had to board a steam train and ride to Moji. From there we were put on a huge steamer, which took seven days to reach Keelung in Taiwan. We stayed in Keelung for about forty days, waiting for another boat. At last the boat left, and seven days later we arrived in Hong Kong. We stayed there another forty days waiting for a boat; from there it took ten days to reach Sandakan in Borneo.

We thought we had come to terms with the fact that in order to work abroad we would have to part with our parents, our brothers, and our sisters, but from the moment we parted from our parents in Takahama we grew deeply homesick. All of us—Ohana, Tsugiyo, and I—fell totally silent, unable to speak about anything. But it was painful, being silent so long, and finally I said, "What are you thinking about? I don't think we'll ever be able to return to our parents. What should we do?" At this, both Ohana and Tsugiyo started crying loudly. I was so upset that I soon joined them.

Then Boss Tarozo, the same man who had been so gentle until then and had treated our parents so kindly, flew into a rage, and shouted, "If you want to go home, you can leave any time. Stop that bawling!" If until now the boss had been a Buddha, he was suddenly transformed into Emma, King of Hades. We were terrified, and fell silent again, keeping our lips sealed all the way from Nagasaki to Moji by train, and then from Moji to Hong Kong by ship.

The trip had its frightening moments, but we were just children, and there were many things that we found really interesting. We had never set one foot out of the village, so even a look at Tenshudo Chapel in Sakitsu was a first, and you can imagine how strange everything else must have been—boats, trains, inns, tile roofs. At the inn we were served polished white rice for breakfast, lunch, and dinner. I remember that the three of us feared that if we ate such a luxury three times a day, every day, we might face some kind of divine punishment, and for a while we were afraid to pick up our chopsticks.

Our eyes really popped out when we arrived in Hong Kong! We heard that Hong Kong was called "the London of the East," and that it was even more lively than Tokyo. I don't know what Tarozo was thinking, but when it grew dark he took us sightseeing through the town. Of course, he didn't buy us a scrap of cloth or a single thing to eat. We simply walked through the streets. But, when we saw neon lights of red and blue and yellow flickering on and off, we were thrilled. After all, we were raised in a village that didn't even use oil lamps, let alone electric lights. At times like this my longing for my brother and mother, and my fear of traveling to a strange land, vanished like a puff of smoke, and I would say, "I didn't know there were such beautiful things in this world. It's like heaven. I don't need to go home." Ohana, Tsugiyo, and I would hug each other and laugh for joy.

I left Amakusa at the height of the summer heat, but when we arrived at Sandakan it was already the end of the year. Of course, even if we talk about the end of the year, since it was the South Pacific, it was even hotter than Amakusa in the summer. Not only were the trees full and green, but flowers were blooming. It really didn't feel like December, and I thought that the South Pacific was a very strange place.

> Sandakan is the largest port town in the English colony of Borneo, and there is nothing which may be ranked with it save Jesselton [Kota Kinabalu] in the northwest. It is located in the eastern corner of the English colony of North Borneo. It is 1,000 miles from Singapore; 1,200 miles from Hong Kong; and 660 miles from Manila. The town is four miles from the port, and the port itself is five miles wide and fifteen miles long. Because the water is very deep, it is impossible to construct a landing pier, but many large ships can anchor in the bay at the same time. The population of Sandakan is about twenty thousand, and it is said that the greater part is Chinese. Sandakan is a small city facing south onto Sandakan Harbor, and flanked by low hills to the north. As I gaze out on the city from my warship, the city roofs, all painted a bright red, present an unusual scene.[3]

> — Tazawa Shingo, *Nangoku mita mama no ki* [A Record of Observations of Countries of the South Seas] (Tokyo: Shinkodo Shoten, 1922).

In Sandakan the majority of the brothels were managed by Japanese, nine all together. Brothels managed by Chinese took second place. Korean or local girls were not employed by the brothels, so they took in men secretly. This was called undercover prostitution. But even if they conducted their business in this way, the Korean girls had the prettiest faces and the best figures. I heard that in the Philippines there were brothels with white women, but in Sandakan there wasn't a single one. [See Table 1.]

Table 1

Occupations Held by Japanese Residents of the Region

Because Sandakan is the capital of the country, the population of resident Japanese is relatively large. The following is a description of the occupations held by the Japanese residents of this region:

Occupation	No. of House-holds	Male	Female	Comments
Photographer	1	2	1	Husband/wife with one assistant
General store	1	2	1	Husband/wife with one clerk
Employed at government printing office		1		
Laundry	1	2		
Inn for travelers	2	7	2	Two couples; four employees; one child
Carpenter		2		
Prostitute	7	7	21	19 prostitutes
Concubines to Westerners			6	Five live in Patopote
Confectioner	1	2		
Concubines to Chinese			1	
Concubines to Malays			4	
Concubines to Filipinos			1	
Concubines to East Indians			1	
Rubber plantation laborers		1	1	Man and wife
Confectioner		1	1	Couple in Patopote
Palm plantation owner	1	6	5	Man/wife owners; his parents; employees
Palm plantation owner	1	1	1	Couple
Palm plantation owner	1	1		

Total households/ establishments = 16
Total men = 35
Total women = 46

Source: Miho Goro, *Hojin shinhattenchi toshite no Kita Boruneo* [North Borneo as a New Region for Japanese Development] (Tokyo: Tokyodo Shoten, 1916), p. 85.

After dinner I strolled through the streets enjoying the evening spectacle, making a special point of looking in on the "flower and willow" quarters. This was a flourishing area, with seven or eight Japanese brothels and fourteen or fifteen Chinese brothels facing each other on opposite sides of the same street. After that I passed by the front of a gambling house run by the Chinese with government permission—quite a grand place.

> —Miho Goro, *Hojin shinhattenchi toshite no Kita Boruneo* [North Borneo as a New Region for Japanese Development] (Tokyodo Shoten, 1916).

The nine Japanese brothels did not have names, as would an inn, but were simply referred to by numbers, as Brothel No. 1, No. 2, No. 3, No. 4, and so on. The brothel owned by Tarozo was No. 3, and it was here that we were forced to live. This is something I didn't learn until later, but in most cases a brothel owner will buy his girls from a procurer. But Tarozo was a trafficker himself before he owned a brothel, so rather than pay a large sum to some procurer for his girls, he would simply return to Japan and buy the girls directly.

This is how we came to be sold to Tarozo's brothel, but we weren't forced to work as prostitutes right away. At that time Brothel No. 3 kept two prostitutes, Ofumi and Oyae. At first Ohana, Tsugiyo, and I ran errands and worked as maids for Tarozo and his wife, as well as for Ofumi and Oyae. Ofumi and Oyae were only three or four years older than we, probably 13 or 14; I'm sure they weren't even 15 yet. Later Ofumi became my closest friend. She was from Oe. Oe is the village just over the mountain from Sakitsu, the place we got on the boat. In Oe there is a Catholic chapel, Tenshudo, just as in Sakitsu. Oyae was not from the Amakusa Islands; she said she was born in Shimabara.

According to the official family register, Yoshimoto Fumi was born on January 18, 1900, the fifth daughter of Yoshimoto Naojiro and Yoshimoto Tayo, at No. 7,400, Oe Village, Amakusa County.

When Ohana and I arrived at Brothel No. 3, Ofumi and Oyae were already working as prostitutes. Although customers sometimes came during the day, generally the girls were free at this time, and they would take naps or amuse themselves. At night, however, they would paint their faces with white powder and lipstick. Sitting in front of the house, they would wait for an opportunity to catch a man passing by. At Brothel No. 3 we had only Ofumi and Oyae, but next to us was

Brothel No. 2, and next to that, Brothel No. 5. Girls would come out of those brothels, too, to sit in front and wait. The entire street seemed to be lined with prostitutes. When a man came by, they would call to him in Japanese, English, Chinese, or a native dialect, depending on where he was from. When ships came into the harbor we might also see Americans or French. This clamorous crowd of prostitutes would suddenly dwindle as now one, then two, and then another would disappear, customer in hand. But in a short time they would be through with that customer and would descend again from the second floor to line up outside and attract another man. This would go on all night long.

Those of us who had not yet debuted as prostitutes would refer to Ofumi and Oyae as *oneesan,* older sister. Watching them every evening, I would ask Ohana and Tsugiyo, "Do you think we'll have to do that when we get older?" Although I had some idea of what a prostitute was, no one explained to us exactly what went on and we didn't ask. We really didn't know anything.

Our boss, Tarozo, kind enough until we left our village, turned into a demon once he boarded the ship. After we arrived in Sandakan, he became even worse, with never a kind word. Wheezing through his chronic asthma, he would abuse us with his filthy language as he drove us to work harder, constantly reminding us that, "I've got good money invested in you." As old as I am, I can still hear that voice right next to my ears. Even Tarozo's wife hated him, but she never once treated us kindly.

> According to the official family register, Yoshinaka Tarozo's wife, Moto, was born on October 9, 1898, the eldest daughter of Kawakami Tsunejiro and Mishi, at No. 5874 of XX Section, XX Village, in Amakusa County.

But the two older girls, our *oneesan,* treated the three of us as if we were really their younger sisters. Ofumi, especially, would stick up for us whenever the boss or his wife said horrible things. "After all, the three of you are from Amakusa, just like me." We're good friends, even now. Ofumi also returned safely from abroad, and is now living in Oe, the village where she was born. I haven't seen her in four years, but she should be doing fine, living with her son, Matsuo.

So this was the kind of life we led until we were initiated as prostitutes, and we weren't unhappy about coming to the South Pacific. This was partly because we didn't fully understand our sisters' work, but the main thing was that we were able to eat white rice morning, noon, and night. In Amakusa the only time we saw white rice was at New Year's, O-bon, and at local Shinto festivals, and even then a parentless child like myself couldn't count on so much as a taste.[4] Here, we had plenty to eat every day. The rice was different from Japanese rice, though. It was Siamese rice. Japanese living in Sandakan called it "purple rice." It wasn't sticky, it was loose, and when cooked it wasn't white, but a pale pink. When we arrived as children we took one look at this rice and clapped our hands for joy, exclaiming, "Red rice! Red rice!"[5]

We even had fish to go with our rice. Although Amakusa is surrounded by the sea, and our village is just a short distance from the harbor of Sakitsu, we had never before eaten fish. Deserted by my father through death and abandoned by my mother in life, I was lucky at least not to have stepparents. Ohana, on the other hand, was taken into the Shoda family, so all year long she had to swallow their complaints; that was her food. Which was better: that, or life with rice and fish on your tray?

By the time our sisters went to work in the evening, our chores were done, so we would often wander down to the sea. In Sandakan the water was so clear you could see right down to the ocean floor. It was beautiful. Black porgy and large fish with red and green stripes—I'm not sure what they're called—would swim by. We would roll up the hems of our kimono and wade out into the shallow water. The fish weren't afraid of people, so they would come right up close. We would entertain ourselves by chasing after them, or collecting the most beautiful shells you can imagine.

My village is not on the coast, but you can follow your nose to the sea, sniffing the salt air. Because Sakitsu is on a bay, you can swim and collect shells there too, but I had never once been in the ocean. Even though I was just a child, I was somehow always busy working. When I went to the South Seas I was able to play in the ocean for the first time. After wading in the water we would stroll along under coconut trees or through flowers as red as blood. Ohana, Tsugiyo and I would say to each other, "I'm so glad we came to the South Seas. Maybe I'll never go back to Japan."

It was two or three years after our arrival that we were forced to take customers. I had just turned thirteen. I will never forget that day when, right after lunch, Tarozo faced the three of us and said, "Starting

From left to right: Osaki, Ohana, and Tsugiyo, in a commemorative photograph taken the day before the girls took their first customers. They are dressed in their best kimono.

tonight you're to take in customers, just like Ofumi and the rest." Ohana, Tsugiyo, and I immediately retorted, "We aren't taking customers; no matter what you say, we refuse!" Then Tarozo flew into a demonic rage, yelling, "Not going to take customers? What do you think you're here for?" Clinging to each other, we responded, "You brought us here when we were little without ever mentioning that kind of work, and now you tell us to take customers. You liar!"

He didn't flinch. Then, like a cat drooling over a captured mouse, he said, "I've invested two thousand yen in your bodies. Pay back the two thousand yen and you can forget the customers! Well, let's have it! Hand it over. If you can't pay me back you'd better just settle down and start taking in men tonight." How could we even think of repaying two thousand yen when we didn't have a single sen?[6] So in the end we lost, and no matter how much we hated it, we had to start taking customers that night.

It was just about that time that Ohana and Tsugiyo first had their periods. I must have been late in maturing, but I still hadn't started. It wasn't until years later that I finally started menstruating; I must have been more than twenty. The bleeding, which should have lasted only three or four days, would last for half a month or a full month, and sometimes I thought I was going to die. You would think that at least when we had our period, we wouldn't have to take customers, but the boss wasn't one to let that get in the way. "Just stuff some paper up inside you; it's no big deal," he would say, and sent the girls to work as usual. My period was irregular until I was thirty-four or thirty-five; then it stopped completely. When I asked others, they said that women usually have their period into their forties and that they can even bear children at that age.

Well, I've gotten stuck here talking about my period, but the first customers Tarozo had us take in were native men. As I said before, the brothels of Sandakan were visited by men of all colors, from sailors of British, American, and French ships, to Japanese and Chinese, but Japanese prostitutes didn't like to take in Malaysians or natives of Borneo. Whether the man was English or native, the price was the same, but the natives were black, and to make matters worse, they were not civilized in the least and were made fun of by everyone. When we slept with these men we would feel that we, too, had somehow been transformed into natives. Among the native men there was an ethnic group called Mangage, whose bodies were larger than those of white men, and who had darker skin than other native men. Just looking at them would make our hair stand on end, and no one wanted them as customers. But Borneo was, after all, their native land, so there were far more native men than whites or Chinese. It wouldn't be good for the brothel business if prostitutes were to refuse native clients. The boss assigned us to native men from the first night, so that we wouldn't reject them later. And for two years straight we were forced to take native customers.

This was how the boss got us to sleep with native men, but after our first night, we were terrified. We hadn't realized that was what men and women did. It was so horrible, we could hardly believe it. That was how the three of us felt.

The population of northern Borneo, which the British had claimed as colonial territory, is quite sparse. In an area of 76,000 square kilometers, there is a population of about 270,000. The most prominent ethnic group is the Dusun, numbering about 100,000. These are primarily an agricultural people, who follow a primitive religion and who know nothing of modern civilization. Next we have the Bajau, who number 30,000, most of whom are fishermen and are Muslim. The Muruts number about 20,000. These are a savage people who are extremely skillful hunters. They move their dwellings through the mountains and plains, and adhere to a primitive religious faith. In addition to these, native ethnic groups such as the Idahan, Brunei, Sungei (river people), Kendayan, Bisaya, Sulu, and Tidong, all of whom are Muslim, are scattered here and there, but the population of each group is small. Nowadays one almost never hears anything about the Dayak, famed as head-hunters, who are now just barely holding out in the depths of the mountains, but when the author was living in Tawau City around 1918, one would get news of them from time to time. It seems that one had to be especially cautious around the twenty-fifth or twenty-sixth of February when they held a festival.

> —Ouchi Hisashi, M.D., Professor of Medicine, Taihoku [Taipei] Imperial University, *Nettai no seikatsu jiten* [Encyclopedia of Daily Life in the Tropics] (Tokyo: Nanpo Press, 1942).

In the morning, East Indians serving as soldiers and guards would perform military drills. This was a most unusual sight. Two ethnic groups were employed as police in this region. One was a people called Bengali who were of large build and dark skin, with unkempt beards; the other, men from Luzon, were of short stature, with dark skin. Both groups wore khaki-colored uniforms with short pants, and held guns over their left shoulders. In place of a shoulder strap the Bengali squadron leader wore a three-inch strip of red cloth on his shoulder. Under his command were giants of over six feet, and small men, under five feet, all mixed together. As they advanced in line, or formed columns, they presented an extremely amusing spectacle, and I could hardly refrain from laughing when I watched them.

> —Tazawa Shingo, *Nangoku mita mama no ki* [A Record of Observations of Countries of the South Seas] (Tokyo: Shinkodo Shoten, 1922).

I talked it over with Ohana and Tsugiyo, and we went over to the boss and said, "We'd rather die than do what we did last night! We won't work as prostitutes!" Tarozo glared at us and replied, "Well, if you're not going to do that, just what kind of work *are* you going to do?" We braced ourselves and said firmly, "We'll do the same kind of work we used to do. But no matter what anyone says, we're not selling ourselves like we did last night!" Tarozo looked over at his wife and grumbled, "Osaki, you're the troublemaker here." But when night fell, the boss came over and started in again about the money. "Ready to hand over the two thousand yen, now?" And with that, he sent us off to work. When it came to a sum like two thousand yen, we didn't know what was what, but we did know it was an awesome amount and we couldn't say anything else to his face. There was no way out of it, so we went back to taking customers.

Still, he had really cheated us. The payment my brother Yasukichi received for my body before I left Amakusa was three hundred yen. In three years it had suddenly become two thousand yen. It was the same for Ohana and Tsugiyo, and was probably no different for Oyae or Ofumi, our older sisters at the brothel. When we asked Tarozo about this, he spat out that the amount beyond three hundred yen was spent for transportation by boat to Sandakan and for taking care of us for three years. Unlike money today in the postwar era, back in the Taisho period (1912–1925) two thousand yen was not an insignificant sum. Our thirteen-year-old bodies were firmly bound by that debt of two thousand yen, and we were to pay it back by selling our flesh. If a customer went home right away, without staying the night, we earned two yen. A single night's stay was ten yen. We were to split the earnings evenly with the boss. It was arranged that our room and board would be taken out of his share; we were to pay for our own kimono and cosmetics out of our share.

You asked if our loan payment was included in the boss's half of the earnings. No, that's not how it worked. The two-thousand-yen loan was considered separately from his take of our nightly income. It came out of what remained of our share. Even if we took ten customers a night and earned twenty yen, the boss would take half of that, ten yen, and if he applied an additional five yen toward the loan, then we would have five yen left. If you subtract the cost of clothes, cosmetics, and other things, there was nothing left. If a girl had to borrow spending money or clothes money from the boss, or if she lost work time by being sick, she might owe well beyond two thousand yen. The loan would snowball, and she could never break away.

Of course, clothing expenses differed according to the item, but a *yukata* [light cotton kimono] would cost about one yen, while a kimono made of various types of crepe or brocade would cost about ten yen. A Hakata obi was about two yen.[7] We could buy these things at a dry-goods store opened by a Japanese. We didn't buy cloth and sew our own clothes; instead, we asked the store clerk to cut and sew the material for us. There wasn't one among us brothel girls who had taken sewing lessons. The cosmetics we had to have were a paste of white face powder and lipstick. The white facial paste was ten sen per bottle and lasted for about one month. In addition to these, we also had to buy underwear and tissue papers, so all together we spent about ten yen per month on cosmetics and related items. The brothel bosses would cut a deal with the owners of the dry goods and sundries stores, encouraging them to sell us kimono and cosmetics we didn't even need.

At the end of every month the boss would pull out his abacus and calculate our earnings. Calling out our names one by one, he would announce, "Osaki, your earnings are such and such, and your debts are such and such." He only revealed the results of his calculations. Oyae could read a little, but because Ofumi, Ohana, and the rest of us were totally illiterate, we didn't know how he came up with these figures. The boss could manipulate the accounts as he saw fit. Even so, if we received the same salary on months when we had an unusually high number of customers as on months when we hadn't done very well, even we couldn't help but feel that things were amiss. If we got angry and tried to approach him for an explanation, he would refuse to hear us out, rewarding our effort with nothing but his scolding.

Still, if you were determined to pay off your loan and worked very hard, it was possible to pay back one hundred yen per month. Be it ever so little, I looked forward to nothing more each month than hearing how much my debt had shrunk. No matter how revolting the work, when the boss made it clear that we either worked or coughed up two thousand yen, we understood that we had no choice. "Ohana, Tsugiyo, every extra customer is going to count. We've got to try to pay back that money as soon as possible and go home." After we had talked it over, we worked as hard as we could. Besides, in my heart I truly believed that my reason for going to the South Pacific was not to play, but to help my brother, so I threw myself into the work, hardly stopping to rest.

If I wanted to work hard to save money and reduce my loan, without ever slacking off, I couldn't be choosy about the customers, taking only Japanese or whites. By welcoming native men who were rejected by other prostitutes, I was able to return one hundred yen per month. I truly hated this work at first, but after I had determined to save money to help my brother Yasukichi and return home as soon as possible, I went out of my way to allure every indigenous man on the streets.

Of course, the local native men paid the same as any other customer. It's just that I treated them all the same whether they were native men, or whites, or Chinese or Japanese. In order to attract native men, I needed to learn the native language. They taught me their language, word by word, until I could speak about almost anything. Of course there were other girls who picked up some of the local tongue, but none as fast as I did.

You want me to teach you some native words? Well, when I was in Sandakan I could speak the local dialect as well as Japanese, but now I've forgotten it completely. After all, I haven't used it in forty years. . . . I can remember about as many words as you can count on the fingers of one hand. The word for "water" is *airu.* Rice is called *nashi. Maakan'nage* means "let's have some fun together." "Good night" is *tedo,* and *tedoru* means "to spend the night." "Go home" is *puran,* and when we said this, the native men would leave right away.

There was not a single native who became angry, even if we said *"puran"* as soon as they had finished their business. The native men treated us well. Never did they do anything rough. When it got out that I could speak their language, there were even natives who would regularly come from some distance just to visit me at Brothel No. 3. They all had very gentle dispositions. Having sex with them was easier for us than with other men, as they went about it simply and quickly. After the native men, the next best customers were the Americans and the English. Chinese men were kind enough, but they were persistent and clinging. Because we were so homesick we were all happy to receive Japanese men, but among them were our most disgusting customers. They treated us roughly, without the least consideration.

Besides the words I just told you, I can also remember how to count money. One yen was *sadodenge,* and two yen was *doadenge.* I can't remember how to say three yen. I think four yen was *anpadenge.* Five yen, six yen, seven yen, I've forgotten them all. Eight yen was *rappadenge* and ten yen was *supporodenge.* Of course there were many different ethnic groups among the natives, but no matter who it was, they produced two yen when you said *"doadenge"* and four when you said *"anpadenge,"* and they never tried to haggle down the price or jeer at us like the Chinese and Japanese. Since the job was the same whoever came, I tried to attract as many native men as possible so I could save up enough money to go home. Eventually I had the top earnings at Brothel No. 3. Whereas he had once said, "Osaki, you're the troublemaker here," now Tarozo would look at the others and say, "There isn't one of you who draws in customers and works as hard as Osaki. You ought to follow her example!"

But even though I worked hard without discriminating among customers and paid back one hundred yen a month, the interest on my loan kept adding up. Things just didn't work out the way I had hoped.

How many men did I see in one night? Well, it's difficult to talk about. I don't know how much I can say.

Ohana, Tsugiyo, and I had shared the same room since we arrived at Brothel No. 3, but when we began to take customers we were assigned separate rooms. It was the same at other brothels as well, but because Brothel No. 3 was built by a Chinese man, it was built in the manner of a Chinese house. It was a two-story wooden house, surrounded by a brick wall. The roof was made of galvanized iron sheets, painted red, and the floors were laid with hardwood. It was only when we served liquor to the customers that we laid two or three mats down on the floor. The boss and his wife had the four-and-a-half-mat tatami room downstairs. Only that and one other room had tatami. This was a small sitting room of just three mats, where we took turns eating our meals.

Each of us prostitutes had one of the ten rooms on the second floor. They had wooden floors, but were about the size of a four-and-a-half-mat tatami room. The rooms were furnished only with a sleeping platform, a camphor wood trunk, and a basin of disinfectant. There were no curtains on the windows and not a thing you could enjoy looking at it. I love flowers. Since they were always in bloom, I would pick some any time I had a chance to get out and stick them in a bottle of water. You don't find those bright red flowers in Amakusa like they have in the South Seas.

When customers came we would lead them up to our second-floor room and have sex with them. If they left when they were done and did not stay the night, it was two yen. How long did it take for each man to come? Well, I'd say it was about three to five minutes. If the customer just couldn't seem to get on with it and took a long time, we would demand a bonus. If they stayed half the night, not from early evening, but from sometime after 11 P.M., the price was five yen. To stay the entire night was ten yen, but this meant we had to be with the same man from evening to morning, and so the entire night's earnings were only ten yen. If the customer didn't stay over, but left right away, we could take in any number of customers in one night, and so this was much better for us economically. The men who stayed overnight wouldn't let us get a wink of sleep. I really disliked these customers, but somehow I enticed them into doing things like taking me for a stroll along the beach and so on, and so there were some good times too.

We never forgot to disinfect ourselves when the man was done. Near the bed, in the corner of the room. was a basin filled with a red disinfectant solution.* Each time we finished we would carefully wash both the man's and the woman's private parts and wipe them with tissue paper. Because this solution chilled us inside, we prostitutes hardly ever got pregnant. They said it was to see if we had contracted a disease, but every seven days, without fail, we had to go the hospital for an examination. Syphilis—if you got that, you know, your body would rot. Your whole body would be covered with pustules and you would die a terrible death, or else you would go mad. We never missed an examination, because we didn't want that to happen to us.

*This refers to a disinfectant rinse. Usually the rinse consists of one thousand parts of cresol liquid soap (Lysol), one thousand parts lysoform, one thousand parts potassium permanganate, and so on. Corrosive sublimate solutions are seldom used. It is feared that especially in women a corrosive sublimate solution could be absorbed through the mucous membranes causing poisoning, and there is also the inconvenience that metal wash basins cannot be used. Moreover, because this type of solution causes proteins to solidify, it is not suitable as a disinfectant.

—Ouchi Hisashi, M.D., Professor of Medicine, Taihoku [Taipei] Imperial University, *Nettai no seikatsu jiten* [Encyclopedia of Daily Life in the Tropics]. (Tokyo: Nanpo Press, 1942).

The following is extracted from a conversation with former vice-president of *Dabao nichinichi shinbun* [The Davao Daily News] Hoshi Atsuhiko. (Mr. Hoshi spent two years, from 1919 to 1921 in Davao, working for the Department of Sanitation of the Philippine government as a syphilis inspector of Japanese prostitutes.) "In order to inspect for gonococcus, we would extract uterine secretions with a loop, transfer it to a glass and heat it over a burner. We would then add a liquid dye, rinse it with water, and look at it under a microscope. Inspection for syphilis was done by the Wassermann reaction. Inspection for gonococcus took place once a week, and for syphilis, once a month or once every two months. In either case, a schedule was observed regularly. If someone did not pass inspection, they had to stop work until the following week, and they were hospitalized in the Oriental Hospital run by the Philippine government. Gonococcus inspections were three yen per visit, and syphilis inspections were ten yen per visit. The prostitutes paid the fees. Inspections were compulsory, and a fine of thirty yen per inspection was assessed on prostitutes who did not show up."

Most of the time we weren't deluged by customers, but when a ship anchored out in the harbor, every brothel in town was filled. While we were busy taking care of one customer, others would be lined up waiting outside the door. My very worst experience was having to take thirty customers in one night. A customer is a customer, so it didn't really matter to me how many of them bought the use of my "box," but this was far more than the usual gang, so I was totally exhausted. No matter how accustomed I had become to this work, once or twice a month I hated taking customers so much I thought I would rather die. There were times when I would break down and cry, wondering what sort of karma I had brought upon myself that forced me into this role. On days when I was feeling sorry for myself like that, I would have given anything to have a day off, but we were not given a single holiday. Couldn't we take a day off for New Year's and festivals, you ask? Sandakan was under English rule, so on British holidays the English stores and plantations would take the day off. When others had holidays, our establishments would be even busier than ever. Because Sandakan was a port town, steamers on the sea route from the Philippines would often enter the harbor, and whenever they did we didn't get a wink of sleep. The boss wouldn't let us off even when we had our period. We simply stuffed paper way up inside and kept working. Not even when we were sick, whether it be colds, or upset stomachs, or headaches, could we take time off. Because we stretched our endurance to the limits, it was only rarely that one of us got pregnant. If a girl did get pregnant, she still had to work until the month the baby was due. I never conceived while I was doing this work, but Ofumi met someone she liked and got pregnant twice, giving birth to a boy and a girl. Both times Tarozo made her take customers right up to the final month.

I don't know about the other girls in this business, but I did not once enjoy this thing that happens between men and women. I heard that there were some men and women who had good experiences, and the women even let out cries of ecstasy, but I never felt this way. Of course, I also uttered these cries. What did they call it? Service, that's it, extra service. But in my heart I just wished that the man would hurry and be done with it and leave. If I could have worked on my own to support myself I would have had no use for a man. The only reason I got together with Yuji's father after I stopped working as a prostitute was so that I could eat. It was certainly not because I wanted a man.

Well, this is what the prostitution business was like. After he had us trained in the business, our boss, Tarozo, became more foulmouthed than ever. As long as we brought in a lot of money, things were fine, but just let the customers dwindle for a while and the money grow short. There was no end to his complaints. Tarozo had chronic asthma. Whenever he became angry or received some unexpected news, he would go into a coughing fit. When earnings dropped, his complaints would inevitably bring on a bout of wheezing. Since it gave him so much pain, it seemed that he could have let up on the complaining, but he went right on.

Not a single one of us, not I, or Ohana, or Tsugiyo, or Ofumi, or Oyae liked the boss. And we weren't the only ones. There was also a girl named Toshiko who came three years later than we. She was Tarozo's niece, whom he brought from Oniike in Amakusa to work as a prostitute. Toshiko absolutely loathed him. Not only that. Even Tarozo's own wife hated him, and she became involved with a photographer named Kinoshita. This wife of his who was also from Oniike had been sent to work at a brothel in Oura in Nagasaki. Tarozo either bought her out, or stole her away, and brought her to Sandakan to be his wife, but until shortly before we arrived, he had her taking customers as well. This didn't happen only to Tarozo's wife. There were lots of other wives of brothel owners who were forced to take customers. Since Tarozo's wife was from Oniike, it's possible that even though Toshiko was referred to as Tarozo's niece, she may actually have been one of his wife's relatives.

As I said, we all hated the boss, but then came the big event. It must have been about two years after we started working as prostitutes. Tarozo's asthma worsened, and even though he shifted from one doctor to another, none could help him, and finally he died. Under normal circumstances, the wife would have taken over as proprietor of the brothel, but as I just explained, she was having a relationship with the photographer Kinoshita. So, when the boss died, she married the photographer as if she had been waiting for this day, and they both took off for Singapore.

> According to the official register, Yoshinaka Tarozo died in the English colony of Sandakan in North Borneo on October 29, 1918, time of death unknown. Yoshinaka Komu, of the same residence, reported his death to the authorities on December 3, 1918.

Since both the boss and his wife were gone, you might think that we were then free to go where we pleased, but that's not how it was. I don't know what sort of arrangements had been made between them, but when the boss's wife went to Singapore, his younger sister, Toyo, came to take his place and assumed the management of Brothel No. 3. Toyo had come to Borneo at the same time as, or just a little after, Tarozo, and at first she had worked as a prostitute. I heard that she worked in Jesselton. A Kilin native bought her freedom, and she had a daughter named Michiyo. This Kilin man had dark skin, and was tall and thin, and so Michiyo was also a dark-skinned child. I heard that Michiyo returned to Japan after the last war. Tarozo was born in Takahama, so Michiyo may have gone to live there. She would have been a small child of three or four when I met her, so she must be getting on in years by now.

> According to the family register, Yoshinaka Toyo was born on May 6, 1880, at No. 1,013 of XX Section, Takahama Village, Amakusa County, the third daughter of Yoshinaka Torajiro and Komu. [Translator's note: The original text is in error as to Toyo's birth date and father's name. The author corrected this information for the translation.]

> According to the family register, Yoshinaka Michiyo was born on March 10, 1906, at No. 2,301 of XX Section, Tosaka Village, Aki County, Hiroshima Prefecture, as an illegitimate child of Riyo, the younger sister of Yamagata Yakichi. Yoshinaka Tarozo acknowledged the child and reported this to the authorities on May 8, 1913. Michiyo was then registered in Yoshinaka's family register.

Well, as soon as Toyo arrived from Jesselton, she sold Brothel No. 3 in a snap, thinking she would just take off with the money. Ofumi and Oyae had made arrangements to move next door to Brothel No. 4. Since they were old-timers they had probably paid off their debts, and it was unlikely that Toyo could stop them. However, she said that because the four of us—Ohana, Tsugiyo, Toshiko, and I—still owed her money, she could not let us make our own plans for the future. Then she sold all of us except Toshiko—I'm not sure of the price—to a procurer named Matsuo Yashiro who had come from Singapore. Toyo must have realized that if she told us that she had sold us to Matsuo we would set up a clamor, so she silenced us by saying, "Circumstances are forcing me to have you move to a new place, but Matsuo will take you there and see to your needs. So please go quietly." Then Matsuo took the three of us to Jesselton. We thought we were to live in Jesselton now, and although it was painful to part with Ofumi and Oyae, there was nothing we could do about it, so off we went. But this wasn't just a change of residence. Toyo had sold us to Matsuo Yashiro, but then that loathsome man sold us to someone else. In the end we were taken from Jesselton to Tawau Island. If Jesselton was new to us, Tawau was equally strange. And it seems that when Matsuo sold us to another procurer he pocketed quite a sum of money, so that when we arrived at the brothel we were told that the loan we must pay off was even higher than before. After I had worked so hard at this disgusting business to pay off my debt and send even one more sen home each time to my brother, things turned out like this.

The three of us got together and made plans to escape Tawau and return to Sandakan. We decided on the day, and when our boss and his buddies weren't observing us, we bought tickets in advance for the boat to Sandakan. On the day we were to leave, we went out in the middle of the day as usual as if we were just going to stroll about, and then we went right to the harbor and got on the boat. Everything seemed to be going well until we were on the boat and Ohana suddenly said, "When they discover we've run away, the boss at the brothel will figure that the only place we could have gone is Sandakan, and he's sure to come after us. I've heard that there are a lot more Japanese in Singapore than in Borneo, and the brothel business is flourishing, so why don't we just pass by Sandakan and go on to Singapore?" I thought this made sense, but Ofumi was just like an older sister to me, and I really wanted to stay in Sandakan to be close to her. Besides, I thought that we might have a chance with one of the brothel madams, Kinoshita Okuni. "I'm sure that if we all went to Okuni's place and begged her, she would think of something clever to say when the Tawau boss comes to search for us," I said, looking convincingly at Tsugiyo and Ohana.

Kinoshita Okuni was known as "Okuni of Sandakan," and there was no one in the South Seas who hadn't heard her name. She was born in Futae, in Amakusa. When she was young she was a live-in mistress for an Englishman in Yokohama, and she was waited upon as "the lady of the house." When this man returned to England Okuni was past thirty. She went to Sandakan and opened a general store and a brothel. When I met her she must have been close to sixty, and she was considered in a sense to be the manager of the Sandakan brothels. Usually the bosses of these brothels were all men, who could think of nothing else but squeezing the lifeblood out of us prostitutes, but being a woman, Okuni looked out for the needs of her girls. The prostitutes of Sandakan were constantly calling upon "Okuni-san" for one thing or another.

> According to the official family register, Kinoshita Kuni was born on July 7, 1854, the second daughter of Kinoshita Tokuji, at No. 2,755, Futae Village, Amakusa County.

> In this place there is a single female boss. Her surname is Kinoshita, and her given name is Okuni. This year finds her an elderly woman of sixty-three, and she single-handedly manages a general store and one brothel. When I questioned her, she said that her assets are worth more than ten thousand yen. She came to this place over thirty years ago, and when I asked, "When did you most recently return to Japan?" she replied, "I returned seventeen years ago. My granddaughter is now attending a girls' high school in Nagasaki." This Kinoshita Okuni is truly the commander of the Japanese women's brigade in North Borneo, and whenever a newcomer arrives, she seeks Okuni's guidance. This elderly woman goes out of her way to help her fellow countrymen, and not only do the young flowers of Japan, our *Yamato nadeshiko*, receive her nurturing care, but even many Japanese men heed her counsel.[8]

> —Tsubotani Zenshiro, *Saikin no nangoku* [Countries of the South Seas in Recent Times] (Tokyo: Hakubunkan, 1917).

I decided to pay a visit to one of the famous products of Sandakan, Grandmother Okuni. She is extremely gentle in demeanor, with a slightly elongated face. Her distinguishing feature is a birthmark, the size of a bean, on the right side of her chin, from which grow three long white hairs. In addition to her lifelong role as commander of the women's troops, she is very patriotic.[9] She told me the tale of the boycott of Japanese goods which took place last year over the entire South China–South Seas region. Even though this is just a small part of her story, the episode describes her vividly. "Those were really terrible times. Once the Chinese found out that a shipment consisted of Japanese goods, they burned them, one after another. So I said to them, if you don't want that stuff, give it to me. If you give those things to me, I'll pray to God for your happiness. They had no personal reason to deny my request, but they said if they gave the goods to me, they would be in trouble with the others, so it couldn't be helped. Watching them burn everything was so trying for me. If I had been a young man I would have killed the ten of them at once." Tears rolled down her cheeks as she recalled those days.

> — Tazawa Shingo, *Nangoku mita mama no ki*
> [A Record of Observations of Countries of the South Seas] (Tokyo: Shinkodo Shoten, 1922).

At the mention of Okuni's name, the other two took strength, and as soon as the boat arrived in Sandakan and we set foot on land, we rushed to Brothel No. 8 and told Okuni our story. "Please help us," we begged, prostrating ourselves before her. Then Okuni answered, "I understand your whole story from beginning to end, and somehow I'd like to help all three of you. But if three of you run away from Tawau and refuse to return, things get complicated. I know how bitter this must be for you, but one of you has to return to Tawau. I'll talk to the boss there about the remaining two of you and pay off your debt." She was as straightforward as a man, and we knew that if she promised to do something she would stick to her word to the very end. We were so relieved that tears came to our eyes.

But, no matter how hard Okuni tried to smooth things out for us, one of the three of us would have to return to that place we had been so successful in escaping. Of course none of us could bear the thought of returning, so finally we decided to pull straws. We cut long, thin strips of paper and twisted them up tightly. The one who drew the shortest strip would be the loser. It was Ohana. Ohana protested, saying "I won't go. I want to stay with Osaki and Tsugiyo." But there was no way out, and finally she returned to Tawau. That was the last time I saw Ohana as a young girl. The next time I met her, I wonder how many decades had passed. It was after the war, when I returned to Amakusa. Still, I was happy just to see her again in this lifetime. After we were deceived and sold off to Tawau, I never again saw Yoshinaka Tarozo's niece, Toshiko. I have no idea where she went. I haven't seen her since then, and I haven't even heard anything about her. It would be nice if she hadn't died and were still alive somewhere.

> According to the official family register, Shoda Hana was married to Shimooka Toyohiko on October 7, 1943, at No. 1211 of XX Section, XX Village, in Amakusa County. The next year, 1944, she was divorced by mutual consent. She died on December 5, 1948, at No. 1211 of XX Section, XX Village, Amakusa County.

Because Ohana returned to Tawau, Okuni was able to save face, and Tsugiyo and I were able to move into Brothel No. 8. When Okuni negotiated with our former boss, she ended up paying two hundred yen for each of us.

For us, Okuni's establishment was just like heaven. Although it was the same old business, and we had to take customers, we were well seasoned by then, and we were simply grateful that Okuni treated all of us so kindly. At Brothel No. 3, Tarozo and his wife ate well, while we were served much cheaper food. In all things they treated us as if we were many times their inferior, but at Brothel No. 8 it was completely different. Not only did Okuni treat us as normal human beings, but we always ate the same food. Okuni was fond of pork and chicken, so we found such dishes on our tray almost every day. I wasn't used to meals like this, and I had never been fond of meat. Okuni noticed this. "It's because you don't like meat," she said, and kindly bought snapper for me and served it as *sashimi*.

Okuni told us that she had learned to play the shamisen when she was in Yokohama. "This is how you pluck the strings," she would show me, and when we all had a little free time she would sing with us. Although she sang and played the shamisen, Okuni would not touch a drop of liquor. She had such a fine character, and she spoke English fluently. She loved to take care of people, and she would often help someone out even if it meant borrowing money herself. It was strange that someone who liked people so much wouldn't drink at all.

But the rest of us drank. We didn't have any *sake*, so we drank beer or whiskey. When it came to beer, I could drink a dozen bottles of Kirin beer with no effect. I was seventeen or eighteen when I went to Okuni's place, and by the time I was twenty I drank like a fish. There was no reason that I had to drink, but if I drank and encouraged the customers to drink, our liquor sold well, and if the beer sold well, I made that much more money off the customer. Even now, though, I can't get along without *shochu*.[10] After I moved into Brothel No. 8 I remained friends with Ofumi and Oyae, just as before. Brothel No. 4 and No. 8 were so close, it was like the distance from your nose to your eyes. There were a number of other girls at No. 4 as well. Ofumi had hit it off with a girl named Oshimo, and she and I became good friends also. Oshimo was born in Shimoda in Amakusa. If you go beyond Oe, there's a hot spring called Shimoda Onsen. I've never been there, but that's where my friend was from. After the last war was over she did return to Shimoda, but shortly after that she hung herself from a willow tree, and so she's no longer living. I feel so sorry for her.

> According to the official family register, Mita Shimo was born on January 18, 1887, the third daughter of Mita Yutaro and Mita Sayo, in Shimoda Village, Amakusa County. She died on September 9, 1946, at No. 2,961 of XX Section, Shimoda Village, Amakusa County.

Oshimo was not at Brothel No. 4 for very long. A Malay native who lived in a place called Kozatoko took a liking to her, bought her freedom, and made her his wife, and so she moved to Kozatoko. "I'm lonely, so please come visit me," Oshimo had told us, so we went to see her many times. It was just a small boat, but her husband, the native man, was the boat captain, and he also owned some forest and flatland, so Oshimo was able to clothe herself in silk kimono. It was this Oshimo who, shortly afterwards, was to raise Ofumi's child.

I brought this subject up suddenly, so you don't know what I'm talking about, but because Ofumi was a beautiful woman, any number of Japanese and foreigners came to see her regularly. She was selective about her customers and never took native men. Among the Japanese men who came to visit her, one who was especially taken by her was a man named Yasutani Kiyoji. Yasutani had a huge coconut plantation in

Osaki, after she moved to Brothel No. 8. Osaki had the photograph made to send to her family in Amakusa.

Sandakan, and already had a wife and children. He couldn't have a permanent relationship with Ofumi, but he came to visit her often. Ofumi became pregnant by him, and ten months later gave birth to a boy. Of course she couldn't very well raise him in the brothel. So, she approached Oshimo, who had married a native man but couldn't have children, and asked, "Would you take care of my child?" Oshimo was delighted, and agreed right away. This child is Matsuo. Now he is living with his real mother, Ofumi. She gave him up to Oshimo's care when Matsuo was an infant of one month.

Oshimo, in her best dress, on New Year's Day, following her marriage to a Malaysian. In the background, on walls thatched with nipa, hangs a picture of her husband. In the foreground are the tiered boxes of special foods prepared as part of Japanese New Year festivities.

According to the official family register, Matsuo was born on August 14, 1925, in Sandakan of the English colony of North Borneo, to Yoshimoto Fumi as an illegitimate child. He was registered by his mother Fumi on February 3, 1926. On December 6, 1929, Nakamura Ichiro of No. 94 Yachimata-cho, Imba County, Chiba Prefecture, legally recognized Matsuo as his own child.

Ofumi, with her infant son, Matsuo. c. 1926, Sandakan.

After that, Ofumi gave birth to one more child, a girl. This child was given over to the care of Oyae, from Shimabara, who had become the concubine of an Englishman. I wonder what happened to this girl. If she is still living, she would be about your age. I don't know if this was Yasutani's child also, or someone else's. Women who had to go to the South Seas to work as prostitutes could not fall in love, even if they met a man they liked, so usually things ended up like this.

I went by sailboat to Tanjonaru on the shore opposite Sandakan to take a look at the Yasutani coconut plantation. As we had favorable winds, we reached our destination in an hour. Yasutani Kiyoji is from

Amakusa. A number of years ago he purchased a seventeen-acre coconut plantation from an Englishman for six thousand dollars. Almost half had already been planted in seventeen hundred coconut trees from which were harvested six thousand to eight thousand coconuts per month. After this he was able to get a 999-year lease from the government on 140 more acres, to be paid off over a number of installments, and he is now planting it with seedlings. On this portion he must pay 50 cents per year for five years on each quarter acre, and after that it will go up to $2.50, but the first seventy acres are designated "Garanmate" and they are exempt from tax. Yasutani plans to live here and has brought over his wife and children, as well as his elderly parents. He built a pretty house on his plantation, which he makes his permanent residence. Besides four or five Japanese, he also employs five or six Chinese. He devotes himself wholeheartedly to cultivation and seems to live a comfortable life. One could say he has taken the first step to success.

> —Miho Goro, *Hojin shinhattenchi toshite no Kita Boruneo* [North Borneo as a New Region for Japanese Development] (Tokyo: Tokyodo Shoten, 1916).

In order to pay a visit to Yasutani Kiyoji's coconut plantation in Tanjonaru, on the opposite shore from Sandakan, we got together ten midshipmen under the commander of the warship, along with ten Japanese who reside in this area, and dividing up between our ship's launch and a sampan, we left the ship at 10 A.M. . . . First we were guided to Yasutani's home for a brief rest. As is typical of homes in the South Seas, Yasutani's house had an extremely elevated floor. It was a new house of two stories. The roof was thatched with *nippa*, unique to the South Seas. There were a large number of rooms, and it was a very pleasant home indeed. Mr. Yasutani kept two monkeys, a number of dogs, and one orangutan.

> —Tazawa Shingo, *Nangoku mita mama no ki* [A Record of Observations of Countries of the South Seas] (Tokyo: Shinkodo Shoten, 1922).

Didn't I ever meet a man I really liked? I feel embarrassed to tell you personal things about myself. Doesn't everyone feel like that?

Basically, I felt that I didn't need a man, so I neither liked nor disliked them, but there was just once when I was young that I thought, if it could be with this man, I'd like to set up house. Of course I have never revealed this to anyone but Ofumi, but it won't hurt for me to tell you about it.

He was a young man hired by Mitsubishi to patrol their rubber and coconut plantations. He said his family name was Takeuchi. He told me he was born in Nagano Prefecture. Are you familiar with Nagano Prefecture? This happened when I was around twenty. Takeuchi was a year younger, about nineteen. He saved up his money and came to see me once every three days. He wasn't what you would call handsome, but he had an honest character, and I was attracted to his personality. Takeuchi was attracted to me, as well, and he even thought about getting married. Although we were in love, I still had a debt to pay off, and Takeuchi didn't have enough money to buy my freedom, so two or three years later Takeuchi married a girl who was staying at the same lodging house as he. "Please forgive me," he said, "but I don't have enough savings to pay off your debt." Then he gave me all the cash he had, and made it possible for me to take a month off without receiving customers. Instead of buying my freedom for life, he freed me for only one month.

As I think back on it now, Takeuchi couldn't have said or done anything else. He was a plantation guard, he was still young, and he didn't get much in the way of salary. No matter how hard he tried, there was no way he could have bought my freedom. But at that time he was the first man I had loved, and I wished he would save up his money for ten or even twenty years and then come take me away. I felt that I had been betrayed and I vowed right then, "I will never again give my heart to a man." A while ago I told you that although Okuni never drank, I could handle almost any amount, but it must have been after the affair with Takeuchi that I came to be able to drown myself in beer without getting drunk.

As life went on like this at Brothel No. 8, perhaps it was due to karma from a previous life, but Okuni and I became very close to each other. I would call her "Mother," and she would call me "Osaki," treating me with special kindness. She was the first person who had ever treated me as an equal, and was the most considerate person I had ever met. Although the mother who gave birth to me still lived in Amakusa, to me Okuni was much more like a real mother. After three years had passed Osaku said that she wanted to see her daughter, Mineo. As she prepared to return to Amakusa, she said, "Mother, you're getting older now, so why don't you leave Sandakan and return to Amakusa with me?" But I didn't want to let her go.

I haven't mentioned Osaku yet, but she was Okuni's adopted daughter, and she had a single daughter herself, Mineo, who I heard was being taken care of in Nagasaki or some place like that. She would have been about six or seven then. Osaku had come to Brothel No. 8 sometime after we did in order to help her aging mother and in order to be able to send home money for her daughter's education. So, when she decided to go back to see Mineo, she encouraged Okuni to return to Amakusa with her. I'm not sure why, but Okuni didn't seem to want to return to Amakusa. Even though she was still alive, Okuni had her grave built on top of a hill. The grave was quite an eye-opener, with its large, white stones.

> According to the official family register, Kinoshita Saku was born to Kinoshita Kuni as an illegitimate child on July 15, 1882. On June 13, 1899, Kinoshita Saku gave birth to a boy, Takayoshi, as an illegitimate child, and on March 1, 1903, she gave birth to a girl, Mineo, as an illegitimate child.
>
> It was Kinoshita Kuni's idea to give the baby girl a boy's name, Mineo.
>
> [Translator's note: In Chapter 9, Osaku indicates that she was the daughter of a samurai, adopted by Okuni at age four, but Yamazaki believes that the official register is probably correct. Osaku may have provided this interpretation to maintain her respectability, especially in deference to her son-in-law's position as a teacher. Moreover, this may have been what Okuni told her.]

There are probably very few people alive today who know this, but Okuni had a Japanese graveyard built to pray for the souls of those Japanese who died in Sandakan. I believe even now that this was a great accomplishment which could only have been carried off by Okuni. She cleared part of a hill that looks out toward the sea, and made room for several hundred graves. Next to the gravesite she built a small hut, just six tatami mats in size, in which she kept a wooden bucket and a water scoop. She had a conduit pipe built of cement to collect water running off the mountain, and in these ways she ensured that even if someone came to visit the graves empty-handed, they would have everything they needed to pay their respects. Since there was not such a splendid Japanese cemetery to be found in either Jesselton or Tawau, Japanese who landed at Sandakan would inevitably have heard about it and would pay their respects at the cemetery just to say they had been there. It must have been when Okuni was several years past sixty, but she had gravestones ordered from Japan and built her own grave at the very top of the hill, in a place that had the best view. It was an impressive grave, so big and white. She planted bamboo grass, and there was even a gate that led to the site. If she hadn't planned all along to turn to dirt in Sandakan, never to return to Amakusa, she wouldn't have built such a fine grave.

> On the slopes of the mountains behind this town there is a place with two huge tombstones, which can be seen even at some distance from the sea. I heard that this is a community cemetery for the Japanese. In order to take a look at these tombstones in such an incongruous place, I scaled the steep mountain slopes with several others. Next to the Chinese cemetery was the Japanese cemetery, about seven thousand square feet in area. Almost all of the hundred graves belong to women. The older ones were simply grave mounds, and most of the wooden markers were so weathered by wind and rain that the writing could no longer be deciphered. Among these the newest was a marker about two feet high which read, "Tadamune Toyo, age 19, of 71 Kozuka, Yoshino Village, Kounu County, Hiroshima Prefecture, Japan." When I thought about the fact that all of these grave mounds, piled up here one next to the other, represented flowers, fallen and scattered in their prime, having succumbed to one tropical disease or another, although we may blame it on their own emotional state or carelessness, I felt a deep sense of sympathy for these fellow countrymen, the *Yamato nadeshiko*, young girls of Japan. As we gazed at each level of these graves, gradually ascending the slope, at the very top we came upon a rectangular granite tombstone, about two feet wide and four feet high, which stood on two kinds of foundation stones. On the front of the tombstone, chiseled vertically, were the words "muen hokai no haka" and on the other side, "erected by Kinoshita Kuni."[11] One level above that, on the same kind of tombstone, were inscribed the words "Homyo Shakusaisho Shinnyo."[12] Here, the inset characters had been filled with red paint. On the side was chiseled "Kinoshita Kuni, Futae Village, Amakusa County, Kumamoto Prefecture." All of the stones had been ordered from Japan. This year she is sixty-three, and already she has amassed a fortune of over ten thousand yen. But whereas most women would have pocketed

this money and returned to Japan to live a comfortable life of retirement, she is determined to remain here for the duration of her life, and
the fact that she erected her own grave before she dies indicates that she
plans to join this soil in death. Her spirit can only be described as
worthy of great admiration. Not only this, but if you climb up to the
highest level spot, you will come to a small hall of worship, at the very
back of which are a Buddhist altar and a Buddhist image made in Japan.
A native man with the shaven head of a priest stays nearby to care for
the grounds. If you look at the list of names of those who donated to the
building of the cemetery, you will see that the majority of the money
was contributed by Kinoshita Kuni. In a sense Grandmother Kinoshita
is one of the founding mothers of Sandakan, and the most influential of
its senior women. It has been more than thirty years now since she
ventured into this distant and unknown territory, and I believe that her
distinguished service in taking the lead in the development of our empire is deserving of the greatest praise.

> — Tsubotani Zenshiro, *Saikin no nangoku*
> [Countries of the South Seas in Recent
> Times] (Tokyo: Hakubunkan, 1917).

Then there was also the fact that Okuni's personality tended to clash
with Osaku's. Okuni loved to help people out and was very outgoing,
but Osaku was just the opposite. Osaku was pretty tight about money
and she couldn't bear to look at something that was slightly out of
place without adjusting it immediately, so there was no reason to expect that they'd get along. I got along with Okuni much better than her
adopted daughter, Osaku, and Okuni was always saying things to me
like, "Osaki, now *you* are someone I can live with."

Since this is the way it was, when Osaku approached Okuni saying,
"Mother, won't you return to Amakusa with me?" I replied, "I'll take
care of your mother, Osaku, so you should return to Amakusa without
worrying about her," and I sent her on her way. Since Okuni didn't
return to Amakusa, business went on as usual at Brothel No. 8. I helped
Mother out, and the days went by. When Osaku arrived back home in
Amakusa she found that there was nothing good there waiting for her,
and after several years had passed she sent a message saying, "I'd like
to go back to Sandakan," but Mother never invited her to return.

After Osaku left I helped Mother manage Brothel No. 8. She was
called "Okuni of Sandakan," and she was a stouthearted woman who

could compete with the male bosses without ever coming out on the losing side. But just let someone come ask her for help, and she would lend her strength to anyone, paying for their needs out of her own pocket. That's why no matter how much money we seemed to take in at Brothel No. 8, on the inside we were barely keeping our heads above the water. Among those folks that Mother helped, there were those who said, "The fact that she's willing to help out everyone indicates she has a great fortune," but in reality we were just scraping by. No one understood this better than I, since I lived right at her side. And it wasn't just Japanese that she rescued either—she even held out her hand to Dutch, Chinese, and Kilin. Just think, that even in the South Seas where there were nothing but demons wearing the skins of man, there should be a splendid person like her.

That being the case, I continued to work, thinking of Brothel No. 8 as heaven, but presently, through the good offices of a friend, I became the concubine of an Englishman. Whether it be at Tarozo's brothel or Brothel No. 8, I had to pay back my debt, and even if business was very good, I still couldn't send as much money as I would have liked to my brother Yasukichi in Amakusa. If I became a live-in mistress for a foreigner, I wouldn't have to serve the needs of man after man, I would receive a lot of money, and it was quite an advancement for me. "It would be good for you to go to this Englishman's place," Mother encouraged. So I gave Mother all of the money I had saved up so far at No. 8, which made it possible for her get two new girls to take my place, and then I left.

The Englishman I went to serve was called Mister Home, and he worked at a customhouse operated by the North Borneo Company of Sandakan. I have no idea how old he was. He could have been ten or twenty years older than me; probably he was around forty. In Sandakan the English, the Dutch, the French—at any rate, all of the white men—had splendid homes on top of the hills overlooking the sea. Mister Home had a wife and children back home in England, but he had come to Borneo alone, where he lived in a fabulous house, with his Chinese cook and houseboy.

> North Borneo has a national polity unique in the world. The government is a stock holding company, and its directors are in effect the Cabinet. Moreover, this Cabinet is located in London, and beneath the governor-general elected by the Cabinet is someone equivalent to our

prefectural governors who is placed in Sandakan and in three other locations. Below this person are regional officers in each section who have the dual role of county official and chief of police. This is rather the same principle we see in Southern Manchuria, in which the South Manchurian Railway Company of Japan controls Southern Manchuria by itself. Here, too, the board of directors selects the governor, directs the garrison, and controls the custom house.

The North Borneo Company was established in November 1881. Long before that, India was controlled by the British East India Company, and Dutch Java by the Dutch Colonial East India Company. It would appear that each colony's affairs were managed for the most part by the colonizing nation, but now these powers have largely been transferred to the home government, and the only place in the world where a company still operates as a political system is here through the North Borneo Company. The government, in other words the company's structure, is tightly controlled. With a capital outlay of 5,000,000 pounds, it has the objective of developing northern Borneo. But, in spite of this level of development, Borneo is still known to the world as the home of orangutans and long-tailed monkeys. Nominally it is an independent country, but the governor-general, who should be the President, is appointed by the Board of Directors residing in London, so everything must be done with the permission of the British government, including negotiating treaties with foreign countries, declaring war, making peace, and selling its land, and so, in reality, it is part of the British Empire.

> —Tsubotani Zenshiro, *Saikin no nangoku* [Countries of the South Seas in Recent Times] (Tokyo: Hakubunkan, 1917).

What was my life like after I went to live with Mister Home? Because the cook and the houseboy prepared the morning and evening meals, and also took care of the cleaning and the laundry, I didn't have to do anything. Even if I had been told to do these things, because I had learned nothing but the prostitution business since I was a young girl, I wouldn't have been able to do a thing. So, when Mister Home left every morning, I had so much free time I didn't know what to do with myself. I would start drinking brandy and whiskey and gin during the day. Oh yes, I also did a lot of gambling with *hanafuda*.[13] After I went into Mister Home's service I was told, "You mustn't go visiting the brothels." So I couldn't visit the brothels where my friends were—

not even Brothel No. 4, where Ofumi and Oyae, and Oshimo from Shimoda worked. Since there was nothing else to do, I would go to the store that sold women's cosmetics and accessories and gamble every day in the guest room. But Mother Okuni was trusted by Westerners, so I was permitted to go to Brothel No. 8. I was probably better off than most concubines of white men.

Whether it was the women's goods store or Brothel No. 8, my greatest pleasure was gambling. When we played *hanafuda* we would make fifty-sen bets per game, but I didn't win even once. Aside from the money I sent my older brother, I pretty much wasted the rest of it gambling. Okuni liked to gamble also, but she wasn't very good, so she was always getting taken.

> I went to see a Japanese woman who had become the wife of a Malay, but the door was closed. I thought it was unfortunate that I should come all this way and not meet a Japanese, so I went to see some Japanese involved in shameful callings. There they were, one man and four women sitting in a circle totally absorbed in a game of *hachi hachi*. When I looked more closely I saw that the wife of the Malay was one of them. When the man saw me enter, he stopped the game and greeted me, but the women wouldn't stop playing. When I said, "You've been playing *hachi hachi* since morning; do you intend to go on all night?" the woman with the darkest skin and a pointed nose gave me tit for tat, resounding, "No, no, we have another kind of job in the evenings." In this place, Kuudatsu, there were no Chinese brothels, but there were two Japanese brothels, this one, and the one next door. Women though they were, they were really quite a shocking lot, sitting cross-legged from early morning playing *hachi hachi* in nothing but their underwear.
>
> — Miho Goro, *Hojin shinhattenchi toshite no Kita Boruneo* [North Borneo as a New Region for Japanese Development] (Tokyo: Tokyodo Shoten, 1916).

Since I mentioned money, I'll tell you about my wages. I received one thousand yen per month. All this money was for me alone, and I guess if we knew how high the salaries were of the Westerners living in the South Seas, our eyeballs would have popped out in amazement. Out of this thousand yen I sent four or five hundred yen four or five times to my brother Yasukichi. Since I couldn't write, I would ask

Osaki (right), when she was a concubine to an Englishman. Standing next to her is a friend, Fumiko, who was also the mistress of an English resident of Sandakan. In the background is the home of Fumiko's partner.

Mother Okuni or one of the young men at the women's store to send the money to Japan for me. My sister Yoshi was also sending money home from a brothel in Rangoon, and combined with what I sent, eventually Yasukichi was able to build a house. You know, it's the house you've been going to for your baths. Now my brother's son is living there.

Among the friends I made after going to Mister Home's place were Tamako and Fumiko. Neither was from Amakusa. They said they came from Shimabara. Fumiko was a real looker. She was about two years older than me and was the concubine of an Englishman who supervised road construction. She could even speak a little English. Tamako had a large build and poor eyesight. She suffered many hardships. I don't remember the nationality, but she was also some Westerner's mistress. Mr. Home made no complaints if I visited with these friends.

Okuni probably would have known how many people in Sandakan

On the left is Fumiko, from Shimabara, who became a concubine to an Englishman. Osaki is standing on the right. Tamako, who sits in the middle, is holding a doll, because of the Japanese superstition that if three people are photographed together, the one in the middle will die early.

were employed by Westerners, but I couldn't tell you. Among them were concubines to Englishmen and women who had been made legal wives, but these were just a few jewels among the rocks. Dalby Company, was it called? An English company with that sort of name came to Sandakan, and the wife of the second most important man in the company—I've forgotten her name now—was also a friend of mine.

Dalby Company opened a branch office in Jesselton, and besides conducting a general import export trade, they also served as representatives for Hong Kong Shanghai Bank, China Borneo Lumber Mill Company, Sebatik Coal Company, various rubber companies, India China Shipping Company, Sabah Steamship Company, and Osaka Merchant Company (for shipments to the United States). Recently they also became the representative for Kaikyo Steamship Company, and with their widespread influence they monopolize nearly all of the trade in English colonial North Borneo. . . . Dalby Company also owns a shipyard in Sandakan, where they can accommodate three-hundred-ton ships. In addition, they are the suppliers for all government purchases, and so their collusion with the government is firmly estabished. As a result this company often wields a tyrannical attitude, which creates opposition among the foreign residents, especially the Chinese. I've already mentioned that the Sabah Steamship Company is actually owned by Dalby Company, and that their ships of some three hundred tons ply the coastal waters.

> —Miho Goro, *Hojin shinhattenchi toshite no Kita Boruneo* [North Borneo as a New Region for Japanese Development] (Tokyo: Tokyodo Shoten, 1916).

These flower girls of Japan, who shun the dew, find their sleeves wet with tears after being used by the American men who rain down upon them. In the morning they see off white men, and in the evening they welcome in black customers. Although there are some who criticize these women, saying they expose the most dishonorable face of our nation, in Sandakan these Japanese women are an especially vital force, and there are not a few who have become the wives of powerful white men. . . .

The wife of one of the managers of the huge Dalby Company is also a Japanese, and one evening I received a dinner invitation from her husband. . . . There are many bachelors sent from distant England to work in Sandakan, who, out of loneliness, became involved with a woman, but after a period of time developed a true love for her and now support a warm family. The object of this love is the Japanese woman. If we are to gradually transplant Japanese vitality in these faraway soils, we must not overlook those who have rendered distinguished service to their country through this particular approach.

> —Tsubotani Zenshiiro, *Saikin no nangoku* [Countries of the South Seas in Recent Times] (Tokyo: Hakubunkan, 1917).

There is now a woman in Sandakan [other than Kinoshita Kuni] who has a rather high status. Her husband is an American, and because the formalities of registering the marriage in the official family register have not been completed, she cannot be called a legal wife, but she is not your typical concubine. She already has a child by this man, and for all purposes is considered his wife. Her husband is the assistant manager of Borneo's largest company, Dalby, and I have heard that he commands the highest of social positions. It seems that in the future he plans to spend the rest of his life in Japan with his wife, and that he has already purchased a home there in Sasebo. Many Japanese living in Borneo are indebted to this woman for her assistance.

> —Miho Goro, *Hojin shinhattenchi toshite no Kita Boruneo* [North Borneo as a New Region for Japanese Development] (Tokyo: Tokyodo Shoten, 1916).

I guess when you become a proper wife, the word used is legal spouse. If you are a legal wife, when Western guests come to visit you are allowed to join them in the parlor, but we servants were not supposed to show our faces in front of guests. This rule applied not just to male guests, but was especially strict in the case of female visitors. Of course there wasn't anyone who didn't know about me, but because I was thought of as a secret lover, I wasn't supposed to show myself.

After we went into service as concubines we had only one lover, so everyone commented on how happy our lives must be. But the way we were treated at the Westerner's house wasn't any different than the way we had been treated at the brothel. Since they looked upon Japanese women as former prostitutes, as soon as we had sex with the Westerner we had to wash him carefully with disinfectant just as we did at the brothels. No matter how long we lived with these men, they still made us do this even though they knew we didn't have any diseases. They probably didn't consider us as equal human beings.

Let's see, I stayed with Mister Home, one, two, three, four, yes, altogether exactly six years. At first I worked four years straight, and then I took time off to visit Amakusa; after I returned I stayed with him for two more years. During my first four years with him Mister Home approached me only two or three times. You asked if this was because something was wrong with him. No, that's not it. Mister Home had an English lover who was already married, and he was always going over to see her, or bringing her over to his house. There's no doubt that he paid me one thousand yen a month just so this woman's husband wouldn't become suspicious. Since he only slept with me two or three times in four years, you say, didn't I become lonely and have another man? Because I had this Westerner, I had no problem making a living, so I had no need for another man. Never once while I was at Brothel No. 8, or when I was with Mister Home or after that, did I ever feel any need for a man. Of course, there were women who felt differently than I did. In addition to a Westerner, Tamako of Shimabara also had a secret lover who was Chinese, and when the Westerner returned to England, she went to Singapore together with the Chinese. After that I never saw Tamako again. I wonder how she's doing now. I wonder if she managed to return safely to Japan, or did she die in the South Seas?

The reason I was able to return to Amakusa for a while was because Mister Home received a vacation to return to England. Westerners who worked in Sandakan were generally given leave once every few years to rest up in their home country. Then they would return to the South Seas. It was Mister Home's turn to take leave, so he called me aside and gave me five thousand yen, saying, "Please wait for me until I return." When I replied, "I'd like to go back to Japan," he said, "Do as you like," and gave me permission to go.

I tucked away the five thousand yen, filled a trunk full of presents, and returned to Amakusa. Tomoko, that futon that you've been sleeping on every night—it was then that I brought it home with me.

I asked someone to write a letter to my older brother Yasukichi, telling him that I would be home for half a year, and that I would arrive in Nagasaki on a certain ship. But when I finally arrived in Nagasaki by steamship, and even when I got in a small boat and took it from Nagasaki to Sakitsu, no one at all was there to welcome me home. My brother had already gotten married, and he probably thought it would be scandalous to go meet someone like me who had returned from abroad. So, I carried that heavy trunk and returned to the village alone.

I was close to ten when I left home, and now I was seeing my hometown again after being away for more than ten years. There were changes everywhere I looked. The river that had seemed huge to me as a child was just a narrow creek you could almost jump over, and the mountains I had thought were so high now looked like mere hills. That wide field that we couldn't finish cultivating in one day, no matter how

Osaki and her mother, in Sakitsu Village, Amakusa. This is a commemorative photograph taken on the occasion of Osaki's visit home some years after she began working in Sandakan.

hard we worked, now looked like a cat's playground. At first I couldn't believe that this was really the place where I was born. Still, relying on the familiar houses that remained on both the east and the west side, I finally arrived at the spot where the tiny house of my childhood had stood. But now, in its place, stood a new house of wood. Just as I was wondering if this could be Yasukichi's new house, a tall woman came out. It was Yasukichi's wife. At that time she was not blind, as she is now.

My mother had gone to Uncle Tokumatsu's, and my sister Yoshi was in Singapore, so I decided to stay at my brother's place. Although

I thought of it as the house that had been built with the money that Yoshi and I sent, my brother was no longer a bachelor. I couldn't very well boast that the house had been built with my money, and somehow the atmosphere was very uncomfortable. After I divided some of the money I had brought home between my brother, my mother, and my close relatives, I took the rest with me to a traditional restaurant at Sakitsu, called in some geisha, and enjoyed everyone's company.

There were a few villagers who said, "Osaki, how about staying in Amakusa now? Forget about going to faraway places!" But there was actually nowhere I could live comfortably. If I returned to Sandakan, Okuni would be there, as well as my friends Ofumi and Oshimo, so I decided that I really belonged in Sandakan, and before half a year was up I boarded a ship for the South Seas.

When I arrived at Brothel No. 8, in just the half year that I had been gone, the shop had really gone under. For some reason the two prostitutes who were there didn't do a good job at all, but nonetheless they continued to eat fine food and gamble from morning to night. Okuni was deep over her head in debt. I went to Brothel No. 4 to borrow some wisdom from Ofumi, and we decided that since Mother was getting old, she ought to quit the brothel business and lead an easygoing lifestyle. After she sold Brothel No. 8 and paid off her debts, I encouraged her to rent a two-story house and live quietly. She was, after all, Okuni who had been respected by Westerners, so in her time of need they helped her out in many ways.

I went back into service with Mister Home as before, but when the Westerner left for the day I would go over to Okuni's place to visit. We would exchange gossip, and I would look after her needs. Two years passed in this way, but Okuni grew weaker as she aged, and finally she passed away. Until seven days before her death she was still cooking her own meals. "I'll steam the rice for you," I would offer, but she wouldn't hear of it.

Even as Okuni grew weaker she insisted, "There is no reason to go back to Japan." The only doctor available was a Westerner, and she would say to him, "The only time I'll take your medicine is the day I die." And she refused to take anything. I was the only one at her side when she died. Gazing at me peacefully, she said, "Osaki, thank you for taking such good care of me. My grave is already built, so please have me buried there." Those were her last words. She must have been seventy. Well, then, what to do about the memorial services—there wasn't a Buddhist priest in Sandakan. The only thing we could think of was to have the owner of the Japanese hotel come over and read the sutras. After she was cremated we had her bones placed in the grave on the hill. Mother must still be looking out at the blue, blue sea of Sandakan from her grave of white stones at the top of the hill.

After Okuni died and left me, I just fell apart. After all, she was the one I had called "Mother," and I truly thought of her as my mother from the bottom of my heart. After the funeral I fell into a deep depression. It was some kind of mental illness, but I don't remember what it was called. My body felt light, while my head felt like it had been stuffed with rocks. I couldn't make myself think about even the most important things, and even if I felt like saying something, the words just wouldn't come out. When I was seen by a Western doctor, he said, "If things go on like this, she'll die." Mister Home decided to send me back to Japan. Once again he gave me several thousand yen, and put me on board a ship. And this wasn't all. Even after I had returned to Amakusa he sent me money to use while I was convalescing, but my brother and his wife, Kane, took advantage of my illness to take all the money for themselves.

On the boat back to Amakusa I felt that if I had one thing to be grateful for, it was Okuni's enduring devotion. Although Okuni had died, and I had placed her remains in her grave at Sandakan, I felt her ghost or her spirit next to me. When I lay down to sleep, she was next to my pillow; when I sat, she was at my side. I'm sure she was there with me. She took care of me. When the steamship arrived at Moji, I was told by the captain, "Your brother came to meet you. Hurry and get your things together." It was at that instant that Okuni's form vanished, and no matter where I looked I couldn't find her.

[Author's note: According to my consultation with Dr. Nozue Etsuko of the Obstetrics and Gynecology Department at Aiiku Hospital affiliated with Boshi Aiiku Kai (Mother Child Loving Care Association), Osaki's symptoms were not related to a gynecological disease, but to a nervous breakdown.]

When I returned to Amakusa I had nowhere else to go, so I had to depend on my brother Yasukichi again, as I had when I came back to visit two years before. I went to see a doctor in Sakitsu, but no matter how much time passed, my head didn't get better. But this interminable mental illness finally left as if it had never happened, thanks to the god Odaishisama in Ikusagaura.

I may have mentioned her name in passing, but my father's oldest brother had a daughter named Haru. She would be my cousin, wouldn't she? Well, she was a little older than I. She spent ten or fifteen years in Rangoon. This cousin told me, "There is a Buddhist deity, Odaishisama, who can cure any kind of illness." One day she pulled me out of the house, and took me past Sakitsu toward Oe. This was the Odaishisama enshrined at Ikusagaura. When Haru made an offering and entreated the medium to help me, my illness vanished immediately. People like you from Tokyo probably don't believe in this sort of thing, but it really happened. I haven't told you a lie even as small as the tip of my little fingernail, either about my work in the South Seas or about Odaishisama.

Ever since then, I've worshipped Odaishisama at Ikusagaura. As long as I've been in Amakusa I've visited this deity on the eleventh of every month, without fail. How far is it from here to Ikusagaura? Probably less than seven miles. If I ride the bus I start feeling sick, and besides there is the bus fare, so whether it's raining or windy, I always go on foot. When I visit Odaishisama I pray with all my might. No matter what you do, you should throw your whole self into it. Tomoko, I first ran into you on the way home from visiting Odaishisama, and I believe that it was probably due to Odaishisama's will that we met.

Well, then, when my head cleared up and I came to understand what was going on in the house and the village, I realized that someone like me had a lot of nerve showing up at my brother's house. Since Yasukichi had received a lot of money from me, he didn't say anything, but his wife, Kane—at that time she had not yet started dyeing her hair, and her eyes were still good—would manage to throw me piercing looks. And besides that, whenever I saw other women from the village who were about our age, they all had homes and husbands, and those that didn't were only women like me, who had come home from abroad. Each new day brought nothing interesting, so I would approach the young men in the village and say, "Let's go have fun somewhere. Let's go!" And I would take a gang of them along to one of the restaurants in Sakitsu, and call for every single geisha to amuse us. We would get very rowdy, and waste money as if we were millionaires. I didn't like sewing or book learning, but I did enjoy playing the shamisen, singing, and having a lively time, so I drank like a fish, and bought drinks for the others as well, until their eyes were spinning.

Even so, Yasukichi never said anything to me, but his wife, Kane, gossiped all over the village. "She drinks so much you wouldn't believe she's a woman, and then she goes around amusing herself with geisha." But I just replied, "What's the problem with my spending the money I earned however I like?" and went ahead drinking with the young folk. I felt that it was only when I was drinking, buying entertainment from geisha, and carrying on loudly that I could forget everything else and live. Once when I asked about it, I learned that one of the geisha that I hired when I was partying all the time is still alive in Sakitsu.

While all this was going on, one of the young men approached me once and asked, "Will you marry me?" Since he was from my village, he knew all about my work abroad, and he said his parents didn't object to my becoming their daughter-in-law. I neither liked nor disliked this man, but I had nothing going for me then at all, and I had no idea how I was going to support myself in the future, so I agreed and became his wife. This man's family were farmers, so I became a farmer's wife. Since both my father-in-law and mother-in-law lived with us, I tried to please them by working as hard as I could in the fields. It was really exhausting, but when I thought that eventually this house and field would be ours, I persevered the best I could. I worked outside until I was black from the sun.

But it seemed that for someone like me, no matter where I went, things didn't go well. While he was drinking and being entertained by geisha in Sakitsu, the man who became my husband seemed like a generous man, but he was completely different on the inside than he seemed on the surface, and he turned out to be quite a miser. Although he drank every night, he wouldn't give me a drop, and he would complain about my using too much miso or pouring too much soy sauce on my green vegetables. If I made him mad, he would raise his hand and slap me, or kick me. Before half a year was up I had had enough of being a wife.[14]

One day when I was working in the fields, I heard a voice calling out behind me. "Why, if it isn't Osaki!" When I looked up, it was Yasuyo, who had been to a brothel in Manchuria and was back for a visit. Yasuyo is still doing well now, and works as a massager in the village downriver. Since Yasuyo was a childhood friend, we stood there talking for some time, and when I told her that married life wasn't worth it, because I was always being abused, Yasuyo replied, "You're crazy to stay in a place like this and turn black doing a farmer's work. Why don't you come to Manchuria with me?" she invited quite seriously. Manchuria was cold, totally different from the South Seas, but people from Japan were going over in droves, forcing the Manchurians and Chinese to work, and developing the country more each year. She said life there was easy, and it was possible to make a living without being a prostitute.

As she told me more and more about Manchuria, I felt my spirits picking up. I had no regrets about leaving that man, so I decided to go to Manchuria. "Just wait here, Yasuyo," I said. "I'll just go tell them I'm leaving," and I ran to the house and told my husband. My husband had been listening with a blank face like a pigeon hit with a pea-shooter, but when he understood the gist of what I was saying, he screamed at me, "I'll never allow it, never!" and he dragged me around the house by the hair. Until that moment, even though I say I had decided to go to Manchuria, I really wasn't sure about it one way or the other. But as he pulled me around by my hair, I knew that I had to go. That night, when everyone was sleeping, I groped in the dark for the chest of drawers, got some clothes together, and left the house with everything tied up in one bundle. That was how I came to cross the sea to Manchuria with Yasuyo.

When we reached Manchuria, we went to Mukden, and got a job at a tavern in a town called Kobai.[15] The name of the shop was "Kaiku." There were a number of brothels in Mukden as well. Let's see, there were ten Chinese brothels and there were Japanese brothels too, but this time I didn't go into that business. I had built Yasukichi's house, and I didn't need to pay off any debts to a boss. At Kaiku all I had to do was serve drinks and snacks, and talk to the customers. There were some Manchurian and Chinese customers, but the shop was run by a Japanese, so most of the customers were Japanese.

I don't think I worked there for quite a full year. During that time I became good friends with a co-worker named Midori, who had a husband. "Why don't you have a family?" she would encourage, and she introduced me to a trunk-maker named Kitagawa. As I've said from the beginning, I didn't want a man, and I regretted that I had a husband, so at first I had no inclination to marry him, but when I added up the years, I realized that I was getting older. I was past thirty, and I couldn't go on forever applying makeup and entertaining men while they drank. I didn't want to grow old and die by the wayside for want of being able to feed myself, so I decided to join up with the trunk maker. He was Kitagawa Shintaro—the father of my Yuji in Kyoto.

> According to the official family register, Kitagawa Shintaro was born on May 18, 1896, at No. 31 of XX Section, Fukakusa-machi, Kii County, Kyoto, the third son of Kitagawa Yasaburo and Sue. His marriage to Yamakawa Saki was registered on January 28, 1932.

He was a kind man, who treated me well. Because I had lived abroad from the time I was a young child, I couldn't sew a stitch with a needle, and I could barely steam the rice, let alone make any tasty side dishes. The first man I had married would heap abuse on me with his parents, saying, "A woman who can't even steam rice is totally worthless," but this man never complained once. When he learned that I was no good either in the kitchen or with sewing, he readily did all those things himself.

However, he did like to drink and play around with women. Still, he was a good person, and since I felt that working as a prostitute had made me an undesirable woman, I didn't say anything. Was I jealous? No, that sort thing is a waste of time, and I had no special reason to feel that way. I did tell him, though, that if he messed around with amateurs he'd be sorry later. "If you're going to play with women, make sure they are professional prostitutes," I told him. "I'll come up with the money for you." So I got together the money I had earned working at the bar and handed it over to him. I have no idea which brothels he visited.

After we got married, we first lived in a rented room in the house of a Manchurian, and it was pretty cramped, but although my husband played a lot, he also worked hard, and soon he had a good business going. In the meantime Yuji was born, and now that he had a son, that man must have thought he needed to start saving his money, because he worked really hard and eventually was able to build a large, two-story house. Because Manchuria is very cold, unlike the houses in Japan, you build an *ondoru*, a Korean floor heater, out of clay. I was so happy when the house was finished and we could finally move in. I kept thinking, this is my home, this is really my own home, and I loved every bit of it, from the walls to the heater to the furniture.

What? What year was it when I went to Manchuria and built the house? Well, I'm not sure. Yuji was born in 1934—October 5, 1934. At any rate, it was a little bit after that.

According to the official family register, Kitagawa Yuji was born on October 5, 1934, the first son of Kitagawa Shintaro and Saki, at No. 14, Miyajima-machi, Mukden City, Manchukuo.

But even that house which we had been able to build only after working so hard, and for which we felt so much affection, vanished the instant Japan lost the war. It was when Yuji was eight. Russia broke its promise to Japan, got involved in the war, and all of Mukden was in an uproar. Then, when Japan lost the war, women and children were told to flee Manchukuo immediately. While we were trying to figure out what to do, I don't know if it was the Chinese Communist Eighth Route Army or Chiang Kai-shek's troops, but Chinese soldiers came into town, and destroyed the homes of all Japanese. They stole everything in the stores, took off with money and ammunitions, and raped any woman in sight. It was so horrible, there aren't words to describe it.

Chinese soldiers broke into our place, too, and took all the trunks we had for sale. What they didn't want they had fun destroying, slashing at things with their swords. I carried Yuji on my back; his body had stiffened from shock. We didn't think we could survive this holocaust. When I was in the South Seas, I had been pitted against unruly sailors and drifting scoundrels, so there wasn't much that shocked me anymore, but there was no way I could deal with those Chinese soldiers. They were stark raving mad. Still, I was one of the luckier ones. Because my husband had always treated the Manchurians and Chinese kindly, everyone around us offered us food. Whether a person be Japanese or from any other country, they should always treat others well.

It was hot when Japan lost the war, but soon the autumn winds were blowing, and it came about that every last Japanese had to return to Japan. We were no exception, but we had to leave behind our house and all our fortune. Even if we wanted to sell our house and turn it into cash, there wasn't a single person who would buy it, so we just let it go for a song, and the three of us returned to Japan with just the clothes on our backs. We went from Mukden to Tsuka [Tonghua] by steam train, and then on to a place called Koro Island.

Somehow we were able to get a ride on a boat called the something or other Maru, and crossed the sea, but our rations for all three meals consisted of nothing more than barley gruel or millet gruel, and only one bowl apiece at that. As we sipped it up, there would soon be nothing left. If this was difficult for the adults, it was a source of constant distress for the children, and I felt really sorry for the little ones. "We're hungry, give us something to eat," the children would cry, but their fathers and mothers could do nothing about it. Yuji was hungry too, so after I had taken just one sip of my gruel, I would let Yuji finish my bowl. By the time the boat arrived in Sasebo and it was time to get off, my whole body was so drained of energy I could hardly walk. An American soldier grasped my hands and pulled me along, helping me up onto dry land.

On the boat I heard people say that tens of thousands of Japanese had been killed in Manchuria. In villages at some distance from the towns, Japanese must have been hated for seizing farmland from Manchurians in order to develop it for themselves. There were even cases where Manchurians destroyed entire Japanese villages, killing men, women, and even all the small children. I should be grateful simply that the three of us were able to return safely to Japan.

But, you know, when we returned to this village, it was really difficult to live here. We had nowhere else to go, so we asked my brother Yasukichi to put us up for a while. While I had been alone when I returned from the South Seas, however, now I had a husband and child with me, and my brother also had several older boys and girls. We borrowed just one room, which was enough to get us out of the weather, but food was a problem. Just take a good look at the fields in this village! I don't know if you grew up in Tokyo or someplace else, but I bet you've never seen such poor, rocky soil anywhere. No matter where you go in Amakusa, the soil is like this. Rice doesn't grow well, and even sweet potatoes won't get very big for us. Aside from a few wealthy landowners, most households had trouble putting food on the table, so no matter how we begged for someone to sell us sweet potatoes, they would hardly relinquish a one. There were some households that said, "We won't sell food for cash, but we're willing to trade." We had just returned with nothing but our own bodies, however, and had nothing to trade.

There was no way we could survive here, so my husband and I discussed the situation, and together we decided to go to Kyoto. Kyoto was where my husband was born. It was a big city, where we might somehow be able to make a living. With this hope, we set off for Kyoto. In the end we stayed in Amakusa for less than half a year. My husband could read, so he got a job with the post office, delivering mail. Yuji was about to start school, and both rice and fish were so expensive, we couldn't get along with my husband's earnings alone. I decided to go to work also, and begin helping out a local farmer in the fields. I didn't make much, but it covered my share of the food, at least, and that in itself helped us a lot. My husband never changed jobs after that, but because I was just a temporary helper, I moved from this spot to that, doing cleaning, laundry, baby-sitting, anything at all. As we worked like this, ten years went by, and suddenly my husband took sick and died. I wouldn't know unless I counted back on my fingers, but I think it was eight years ago. That's right, if it was eight years ago, that would be 1961.

> According to the official family register, Kitagawa Shintaro died at 3:08 P.M., July 23, 1957, at Fushimi-cho Fukakusa Mukohata in Kyoto. [Translator's note: Osaki does not remember the year correctly.]

Yuji was past twenty, so he was ready to be on his own. He was working as a laborer for a construction company in Kyoto, and I felt comfortable about his future. Yuji was a hardworking boy, and after his father died he worked even harder. But after two or three years he suddenly came up to me and said, "Mom, why don't you go back to Amakusa? After all, that's where you were born, and there's no doubt that everyone will help you out."

"Even if I were to return to Amakusa, my brother Yasukichi is dead, and there isn't any work there for old folk, so I'd rather stay in Kyoto where I can work," I responded. The autumn of the year after we moved to Kyoto, Yasukichi had become ill and died. But no matter how much I pleaded with him, Yuji would not be dissuaded, so there was nothing else I could do but return here alone. Just at that time, the person in the house next to my brother's had to move to Osaka, and the house was for sale, so I bought it with the fifteen thousand yen Yuji had given me. That house is the one I'm living in right now. It's the shabbiest house in town, but I'm not renting from anyone. It's all my own!

Shortly after I returned to Amakusa, I received a letter from Yuji, informing me that he had gotten married. Since I'm illiterate, I usually have the mailman or Kusuo who lives just above me, my brother's oldest son, read the mail for me. Yes, I remember that in that letter there was a photograph of a woman.

I realized afterwards that Yuji had sent me back to this village because he wanted to take a bride. Because, you see, I'm a woman who has a history of going abroad and working as a prostitute. Yuji was probably worried that if the girl he liked found out about me, she wouldn't agree to marry him. And he was probably right. He was probably also embarrassed that his mother couldn't read a single letter. That's why he sent me back here without saying a word about this woman, and he didn't tell me a thing until he'd heard her say, "I do."

I don't feel any hatred for Yuji. But even though he's been married six or seven years now, his wife hasn't shown her face here once, or even written a letter, so I can't say I'm fond of her. We old folk will be the first to cross the River Styx, though, so I'm satisfied if the young folk live their lives the way they want. The old folks have to take what they get, and just endure it. It's much easier for her without having a mother. Every time she looked at me, she would be reminded that her mother-in-law had worked as a prostitute, so it's much better for me not to be with her. I'm glad I returned to Amakusa. I have two grandchildren by Yuji and this woman, and although not a day goes by that I don't long to see their faces, I don't know if that wish will ever come true. It's pretty lonely living by myself, without being able to look at my grandchildren, but it's best that way for Yuji and his wife, so I just endure it without saying anything. And every morning I pray to Odaishisama, and to the sun, and to the Buddha that Yuji and his family will avoid colds and live in good health, and will be safe from car accidents or mishaps at work.

Yes, that's right. Did you notice that I pray every morning? I'm an old lady, so I wake up early, but you're a city person, so you take it easy in the morning. It seems a pity to awaken you when you're sound asleep, so I slip outside to pray without making a sound. But you say you wake up anyway?

Ever since he cured the mental illness that overcame me after Okuni died, I've had faith in Odaishisama of Ikusagaura, and I ask him to help me out with all kinds of matters. From this village, Ikusagaura is in that direction, so every morning after I've washed my face, I fold my hands in prayer to Odaishisama. I always pray out loud, "Please, Odaishisama, take care of everyone in my Yuji's family in Kyoto. Yuji's been healthy since he was a little boy, but city life must be so much more difficult than life in Amakusa, so please do protect him. And please take care of his wife and my grandchildren that they may live through the day without getting sick or having an accident." Then

I pray to the sun, and to the spirits of my husband, father, and mother. Only after I've prayed to everyone do I feel relieved.

Praying like this is my job. I haven't missed a morning since I returned to this village. Whether it's raining or blowing, or even in the autumn and winter when my asthma gets bad and I'm coughing so hard I can't bear it, I still haven't missed a single day.

I've become old now and can't move around very well. I live on the money Yuji sends every month, but I'm not able to do anything in return. All that's left for such a superfluous woman to do for her son and grandson who carry on her genes is to pray with my whole heart to the sun and to Odaishisama, in whom I place my faith. Tomoko, when you return to Tokyo this time, you can bet that I'll be praying for you too, so you're to take care of yourself now.

You say it's an awkward question, but would I mind if you asked anyway? Haven't I told you everything you wanted to hear, about the South Seas and about working as a prostitute? You can ask me about anything. What, you want to know how much Yuji sends me every month?

Every month he sends me four thousand yen. He always sends it in a cash delivery envelope, so I receive it after affixing my seal. Until four years ago he sent three thousand yen a month, but now it's four thousand yen. Things must be difficult for Yuji, too, but if I didn't have this money I don't know what I'd do. Once Osana from across the river told me about social welfare. "There's something called the Livelihood Protection Law which lets the municipal office give money to poor people like you. Why don't you go there and ask about it?" It's not that I hadn't heard about it before, but Yuji said, "If you accept that money, everyone will think I'm not a filial son," and he begged me not to take it. I haven't received that kind of money even once. Some people say I should just accept money from the town office without telling Yuji, but lying isn't part of my character.

It's almost impossible to survive for one month on four thousand yen. If I bought rice to eat, I'd run out of money in no time, so I just eat the sort of thing I'm serving you, barley with rice. When my allowance from Yuji is late and I run out of barley, then I eat sweet potatoes. These days I'm about the only one left in the village who mixes so much barley with rice.

Some of the villagers say that I have no business supporting cats when I'm having such a hard time myself. Just counting the ones that live with me there are one, two, three, four, five of them. Mii here, and Tama, as well as Pochi stretched out over there, were all abandoned by someone, and were meowing in hunger. No one knows better than I do how painful it is to be starving, so I couldn't just overlook them. I brought them home, and fed them. Pochi is a dog's name, you say, not a cat's name? Dogs and cats are like relatives, so he doesn't care, do you, Pochi?

The cats I asked you to bring some rice to yesterday in the house down below—there are four of them all together, so combined with my five, I have nine. That house belonged to my younger sister, the child born to my mother and Uncle Tokumatsu after she went to live with him. That would make her my stepsister, but anyway the whole family, she and her husband and kids all moved to Nagoya to work. They couldn't take the cats, so they left these two behind. It's not that they especially asked me, "Would you take care of the cats?" but they are, after all, living things too. As I was taking food down to them, another two showed up from somewhere, and then there were four. Just as you say, I wouldn't mind bringing them up here and having all nine of them live here with me, but cats prefer to stay in the place they've become accustomed to living. So if I bring their food to them, they don't have to move.

Those cats know exactly what time I come, and when it's dinner time they're all lined up waiting at their feeding spot, all four of them.

If I'm eating barley, the cats get barley; if it's sweet potato, they eat sweet potato. I don't know how many years I have left to live, but until I'm taken away by the Buddha I plan to keep living exactly as I am. But when I think back on those days when my father died, my mother left us, and I lived with Yasukichi and Yoshi, the three of us shaking from hunger, with nothing to swallow but water, I feel like I'm living like a queen just to be able to eat barley or sweet potatoes three times a day.

Translator's Notes

1. It was common practice at the time for the widow of a younger brother to marry an older brother-in-law if his wife died. Osaki and Yoshi did not move to their uncle's house due to the opposition of their elder brother, Yasukichi. After the death of his father, Yasukichi became the head of his household.

2. Emperor Hirohito, the Showa Emperor; reigned 1926–1989.

3. Yamazaki Tomoko has interspersed throughout "Osaki's Story" excerpts from books written about the Nanyo (literally "South Pacific," but referring more

specifically to Southeast Asia) in the 1910s through the 1930s. These passages provide another perspective on the people and places Osaki mentions.

  4. O-bon, the Festival of the Dead, is in mid-August.

  5. *Aka no manma* = *sekihan*, rice boiled with red beans, served especially on festive occasions. The children associated the color of the rice in Borneo with this special treat from their own country.

  6. One hundredth of a yen.

  7. A sash of glossed silk, produced in Hakata, Kyushu.

  8. "Flowers of Japan"/*Yamato nadeshiko* is a euphemism for Japanese prostitutes. (*Nadeshiko* = a pink.)

  9. "Women's troops" is a euphemism for prostitutes. The latter half of this passage refers to the Chinese boycott of Japanese goods which followed Japan's "Twenty-One Demands."

  10. *Shochu*, a low-grade alcoholic drink.

  11. *Muen no haka* refers to the grave of one who has no surviving relatives to perform Buddhist memorial services. *Muen hokai* refers to a Buddhist realm of equality in which discrimination does not exist. This term may also refer to all of those people in this world who have no relatives upon whom to rely.

  12. *Homyo* refers to a posthumous Buddhist name. *Shinnyo* is a title that follows the posthumous Buddhist names of women. *Shakusaisho*, Okuni's posthumous name, might be interpreted as "the ultimate victory of Buddha."

  13. *Hanafuda*, "flower cards"—Japanese card game that developed after the Portuguese introduced Western playing cards about 350 years ago. *Hachi hachi* is one of many ways of playing *hanafuda*.

  14. Osaki's "marriage" was not recorded in her partner's family register, so there was no need to get a formal divorce. This type of arrangement, called *naien*, was common among the lower classes, and often took place in upper-class relationships as well. A marriage might not be registered until the woman proved her worth in the husband's family through her domestic skills, deference to her husband and his parents, and bearing a male child.

  15. The Japanese set up a puppet government in Manchuria, and announced the new state of "Manchukuo" at Mukden on March 1, 1932.

——— 6 ———

Many More Voiceless Voices

Considered by the villagers to be either Osaki's illegitimate child or the child of one of Osaki's *karayuki* friends, and considered by Osaki to be someone from the water trade who for some complex reason had taken shelter in her home, I was at last able to learn Osaki's life story. As we lived together, day after day, she began to respond little by little to my nonchalant questions, until at last I had a clear picture of her life as a *karayuki-san.* Although I should have known quite well what the life of a prostitute who wandered abroad might be like, I could not help but be touched by her heartrending account.

Of course, among my readers there may be those who say that from what they have read so far, Osaki's life as a *karayuki-san* wasn't really all that terrible. Documented in the various types of literature related to *karayuki-san* are many accounts of women who were victims of a far crueler fate.

For example, in his *Shakai kakuseiron* [Treatise on the Purification of Society], published in 1914, Yamamuro Gumpei—who, as leader of the Salvation Army, had already been working toward the abolition of prostitution since the late 1880s—enumerates in a section of chapter 6, called "Overseas Prostitutes," the life histories of *karayuki-san,* whose appeals he heard for the first time when he was traveling to a world conference of the Salvation Army. One woman with whom he spoke was twenty-year-old Himeno Katsu, born in Toyogo. When Katsu was traveling to Moji, a man approached her, saying, "Why don't you come with me to Kokura?" She followed him there, only to be forced onto a ship transporting coal. For one week she was given hardly any food, and when the ship finally reached port, she was no longer in Japan as she expected, but in Hong Kong. Without having any say in the matter, she was forced into prostitution. Yamamuro also mentions an eighteen-year-old woman named Yagi Shinayo of Kazusa, Shinohara in Nagasaki. Her father had been in the navy, but had died from an illness three years before her abduction. Shinayo had fled to Kobe to escape a marriage proposed by her mother, but when she got there a man approached her saying, "Let me introduce you to a place where you can find better employment." She got on a ship with him and was taken to Hong Kong. Likewise, when a twenty-year-old woman named Fukube Kuma of Katsumata, Mimasaki, was employed as a domestic servant in Kobe, two men who claimed to be brothers told her, "You can find employment with much higher wages in Sasebo," and talked her into boarding a ship with them. She was squeezed in between pieces of cargo, and after going for several days without either food or water, she was sold into prostitution in Hong Kong.

All of these women had been approached by "a certain man," in other words, a trafficker, and deceived by promises of better employment elsewhere. They had not the least inkling that they would be shipped off to mainland China or to Southeast Asia where they would be forced to sell their favors. It was precisely for this reason that a number of women, such as two sisters, one, seventeen years old, one nineteen years old, from Hiramura Village, Yoshiki County, Yamaguchi Prefecture, in extreme desperation chose to kill themselves as a last resort. These two sisters had been ordered to take customers from their first night on board ship. Commiserating over their bitter fate, they finally concluded, "Since our situation is hopeless, it would be better to die." The next morning very early, while the boss was still asleep, they ran outside barefoot, and desperately looked for some place they might kill themselves. They had just made it to the gangway and were about to throw themselves over when they were rescued by Yamamuro Gumpei.

As stowaways, the women encountered by Yamamuro Gumpei may have gone without food for a number of days until they were finally released onto dry land, but these were actually among the more fortunate, for there were many women who did not live until the ship reached port. One finds such ghastly tales in abundance in books such as *Sendo no nikki kara* (From a Mariner's Diary) and in *Madoros yabanashi* (Night Tales of a Sailor), two confessional works written by Kato Hisakatsu, a longtime ship captain of steamers plying the South China sea route.

According to Kato's account, one of the places frequently used by traffickers to hide their stowaways was the coal bunker in the bowels of the ship. Not only did the women find themselves in perpetual and absolute darkness, but they were exposed to natural gases emitted by the tightly packed coal. On steamers heading south they suffered from such extreme heat that they must have felt they were burning in hell itself. One of Kato's tales which takes place around 1911 describes the fate of two traffickers and some ten *karayuki-san* who had stowed away in the coal bunker of a cargo ship. The sailor who had been bribed to bring them food and water was suspected by another seaman and was unable to continue his trips down to the coal bunker. According to Kato's reconstruction of this incident, the women, whose lifeline had been severed, now found themselves suffering not only from the heat and coal gas, but from starvation and thirst. In addition they were overcome by the foul smell of decomposing excreta, until they could no longer endure their condition and began crying and screaming for help. However, their voices could not penetrate the iron walls of the bunker, and even if they had, there was no reason for anyone to come down into this part of the ship.

After some days went by there seemed to be a problem with the plumbing, for not a drop of fresh water would come out in the ship's cabins. Repairmen were ordered down to investigate the pump and distribution pipes, which necessitated entering the coal bunker. No sooner had they opened the door than, to their great surprise, they found themselves gazing at young women, their hair disheveled and their bodies smeared with coal dust and blood. When the horrified seamen searched the bunker, they found a number of women, their lips covered with blood, who had breathed their last while frantically biting at the water line. Buried in the coal were the bodies of two men, covered with bloody wounds from bites and scratches. The young women who were dying of thirst must have instinctively sensed the location of the water pipes and groped their way there through the darkness. Biting into the pipes with all their remaining strength, they apparently made enough holes for air to enter the pipes, causing the water to fall back into the tank. The two men must have received the brunt of their anger.

In addition to tragic tales about women in coal bunkers, there are also stories about women hidden as stowaways in water tanks. One such account tells of a number of women who hid in a tank that the trafficker and seamen involved assured them would remain empty.

However, through some human error the water was turned on and the tank began to fill. The terrified women broke their promise of silence, and begin beating on the metal sides of the tank and screaming. The water gradually rose to their ankles, then to their knees, and then up to their chests and continued to rise. After the ship had been under way for several days, a seaman turned on a faucet and began to drink, when he noticed a long hair come floating into his glass. Strange, foul-smelling bubbles rose up through the water. When crew members investigated the water tank, they found the bodies of women, so badly decomposed that they no longer retained their shape. In the high temperatures of this southern route, bacterial decomposition was a rapid process.

In addition to this, if you diligently investigate the literature on *karayuki-san* that I mention in chapter 1, you will find endless other examples of this nature, but even if the young women survived this stowaway hell and made it back to shore, the life of a *karayuki-san* was far from tranquil. Even if we overlook, for the time being, their nightly work of offering their flesh to one customer after another, the attitudes of both owners and clients were bad: the women were beaten if their earnings were low; they were looked upon coldly if they fell in love; and if they were to fall ill from sexually transmitted or local diseases, they could not expect even the most basic medical assistance.

In *Muraoka Iheiji jiden,* Iheiji writes about looking in on a brothel in Shanghai where he found a *karayuki-san* who had been sick in bed for a month. He did not know what she ailed from, but she was not permitted to see a doctor and was given only two pieces of *jintan* per day, a hard bitter candy popularly believed to have some medicinal value. Iheiji claims to have arranged her deliverance from the brothel owner. "Giving hard rice to an invalid like this—why, you treat her no better than a dog. This woman is a Japanese. Do you intend to starve her to death? I won't tolerate this any longer. If you have some objection, I'll deal with you later." Then, he writes, "Using her sash, I tied this woman in her soiled gown to my back, and took her to the hospital in a two-person rickshaw. . . . There I paid the hospital fees, rickshaw fare for someone to come look in on her, and food expenses for three months." Apparently, some *karayuki-san* were so pitiful that even a hardened trafficker could not overlook them.

The *karayuki-san* to whom Iheiji extended a helping hand was eighteen-year-old Mitaku Omatsu of Kumamoto, who managed to recover and met Iheiji again three years later in Singapore. However, there were many women who never again got up on their feet, suffering from syphilitic inflammations over their entire body, or contorted by the sharp pains that accompany the worsening of venereal disease. These women had no choice but to swallow their resentment and become transformed into the soil of a foreign land.

In 1917 Osada Shuto, scholar of French literature, nationalist in the spirit of Futabatei Shimei, and manager of a rubber plantation in Malaysia, published an account of his experiences in Southeast Asia. In this book, *Zunanroku* (A Record of Mapping the South) Osada says, "Just out of interest I decided to make the rounds of Japanese cemeteries throughout the world. Most of the grave markers I found, piled one upon the other, were those of seventeen- or eighteen-year-old *karayuki-san*. These remains cannot but bear the most bitter resentment. They deserve our utmost compassion. These women have no descendants to bow in respect before their bodies, placing on their graves the flowers and branches of the sacred anise tree. My condolences go to these bones, chilled by the winds and dew of a foreign land." Just hearing that seven or eight of every ten graves belonged to a *karayuki-san* is enough to send chills down my spine. Precisely because we get this information from someone such as Osada, who looked at Southeast Asia in such fine detail, and even more so because of the lyrical emotive power of his prose, we are convinced of its accuracy.

Compared to the extreme pain and sorrow experienced by these *karayuki-san,* we must say that, relatively speaking, Osaki's life was blessed. Unlike the young women whom Yamamuro Gumpei encountered, Osaki was from Amakusa, which historically produced the greatest number of *karayuki-san,* and it was not as if she had no knowledge at all about what it meant for a woman to work abroad. However vague, she understood to some extent what she was getting into, and went abroad of her own volition. She was not of an age when she might have attracted the attention of the police, but just a child when she went to Borneo, so there was no need for her to hide in a coal bunker or a water tank. In Sandakan, she worked for only one demon boss and later was fortunate to work for a kind madam such as Kinoshita Kuni. Then, in a relatively short time she attained the status of concubine to a Westerner, a much coveted position among *karayuki-san* of the time, marking their rise, as it were, in society. Ultimately Osaki was able to return to her country alive, escaping the fate shared by so many others of contracting an incurable disease or leaving her corpse exposed to the elements on foreign soil.

However, as I listened to fragments of Osaki's story day in and day out, her life as a *karayuki-san* weighed on me ever more heavily. Although she may have had some idea of what it meant for a woman to go work abroad, when Osaki was sold to the procurer Yoshinaka Tarozo she was only ten by Japanese count, just nine years old in actual years. Today, this would place her in the third grade of elementary school, making her about the same age as my own little girl, Mimi, waiting so anxiously for my return to Tokyo. As I listened to Osaki speak quietly, her back to the tattered shoji, in a room dimly lit by a thirty-watt bulb, I could not help but visualize my daughter's face superimposed upon Osaki's wrinkled flesh.

Who is to say which is the more tragic—for a small girl just growing out of childhood to be sold abroad without knowing anything about the occupation of a *karayuki-san,* or for her to offer to go of her own volition, knowing something of the fate that awaits her, in order to improve life for her relatives. Certainly we can say that they are both tragic, but if one must choose between the two scenarios, I find the latter all the more cruel.

Osaki's heartrending accounts of the manner in which business was conducted in the Sandakan brothels was beyond anything I had imagined. While there might not be many customers on a typical day, she said, if a ship came into port men were lined up at the brothel doors, ready to walk into a room as soon as the previous customer had finished. She said she had taken as many as thirty customers in one night. I thought that some of what she said might be random chatter, but she was consistent in repeating the same stories and figures day after day, in different places, and in the context of different questions or angles of approach. She was unwavering in the information she provided.

Because there is little information available about how many customers a *karayuki-san* would take each night, or how many times she was engaged in sexual intercourse, I was uncertain about how many customers, on average, she might entertain each evening. However, we can get some idea by looking at data from within Japan. In his book called *Hakusen no onna* [Women of the White Line], Nakamura Saburo, a researcher on the prostitution problem, has compiled business statistics for brothels in seventeen red-light districts of Tokyo during 1956–1957. Although he presents figures from after World

War II rather than from the Meiji or Taisho periods, taking them as a rough indicator we see that on average a prostitute received twenty-nine overnight customers and sixty-seven hourly customers per month. Sexual intercourse with overnight customers averaged 2.2 times per night, while that with hourly customers averaged 1.2 times. If we calculate the nightly average, we will see that a prostitute received one overnight customer and 2.2 hourly customers, engaging in sexual intercourse 4.8 times. Moreover, in his *Gaisho no shakaigaku kenkyu* [Sociological Research on Street Walkers] of 1950, one of the only books on prostitution written from a nonemotional, scientific standpoint, Watanabe Yozo writes, "If we calculate the average number of customers a streetwalker will entertain each day, we find that she receives a minimum of 1.1 and a maximum of 4.1, giving an average of 2.1 customers per day." "There are some prostitutes who receive as many as ten customers per day," he adds, "but this is unusual."

However, in Osaki's case, she took on average four or five customers per night, and in unusual cases she had as many as thirty. Though the fact of being a prostitute is unchanged regardless of the number of customers, and although it may be superfluous for me to even mention it, if one receives only two or three men, the couple would have the opportunity to exchange a few words, and although it might just be part of the business, there could be an exchange of smiles or laughter. Thus we cannot say that there was no room at all for some human engagement of the heart. Let her take thirty customers, however, in a short period of time, and it becomes physically impossible for any form of communication to take place at all. The women are used as "objects" by the men, and the women themselves feel as if they have been thoroughly "objectified." And yet, they cannot totally suppress their own feelings.

When a night of hell approached dawn and the last customer left her room, were there not times when a woman looked up into the dark blue southern sky and cried bitterly, unheard by anyone else? Why, when there are so many different countries on this earth where people are blessed, each in his own way, with some measure of happiness, she pleaded, beating her fists on ground shadowed by the fronds of coconut palms, did she and her sisters have to wander far from their homeland and endure such a tragic fate?

Of course, I also felt the weight of all I had learned about the tragic lives of *karayuki-san* from books and documents, but Osaki's life, which I shared under the same roof, weighed down upon me mercilessly. When I thought about the fact that every last detail she had shared with me was deeply engraved in her small frame, it made me want to cry out loud. I knew that if I did cry, Osaki would avoid telling me anything that might make me sad and would avoid the subject of Sandakan. Therefore I used all my willpower to suppress the sobs, but inside I felt that I would like to embrace that frail, bony body and cry my heart out.

How was I to dispel these feelings, driving away both the thought that I would like to embrace Osaki with tears, and the painful realization that I had to suppress this urge? The answer was clear. Since I had come to Amakusa to hear the voiceless voice of the *karayuki-san,* and since I had moved under Osaki's roof, I must learn about her life to the very last detail. And now that I had somehow heard her version of half a lifetime, the testimonies of those who had been close to her would help me understand her life all the more deeply.

I gradually concluded that I must visit a number of people mentioned by Osaki during her conversations with me and listen to what they had to say. According to Osaki, Ofumi, who had become a lifelong friend after they met at Brothel No. 8, was still alive in Oe. Osaki said that although Ofumi's friend Oshimo had died, the child she had raised for Ofumi, Matsuo, was still living in good health. If Osaki was not mistaken, the birthplace of the woman she so lovingly referred to as "Mother," Kinoshita Kuni, was Futae, and the trafficker who purchased Osaki, Yoshinaka Tarozo, was from Takahama. If I were to visit these places, the children or grandchildren of these people might still be there, and I might be able to get them to tell me something.

Thus it was that I decided to visit these people, beginning with Ofumi, who lived closest by in Oe. But first, I had to learn where exactly in Oe she lived, and then I needed to come up with a plausible reason for visiting. So, after mulling things over for a few days, I approached Osaki one evening.

—— 7 ——

Ofumi's Life

That evening, after we had finished our typically meager supper, I turned to Osaki and told her that I planned to go to Oe tomorrow to take care of some business. "So, if you have anything you'd like to say to Ofumi, I'd be happy to stop by her place," I added. As usual, Osaki did not question me at all about my motives for going to Oe, but simply responded, "I haven't seen Ofumi in a very long time. . . . Have you ever been to Oe before?" she asked.

When I replied vaguely that I hadn't, but that a friend of a friend lived there, Osaki paused to think for a moment, and then said, "It's not the kind of place you can visit easily by yourself, so if you have your heart set on going to Oe, maybe I'll just go with you. . . . Ofumi is not the kind of person who would talk to a stranger about her experiences abroad," she added softly, as if to herself. I felt that she had seen right through me and my heart started beating faster, but I responded that if she joined me, Ofumi would certainly be delighted to see her, and changed the subject.

Later that night I stretched out on the mattress of Borneo kapok, but had trouble falling asleep as usual. I was troubled by the fact that when I had mentioned going to Oe, hoping to be able to visit Ofumi, Osaki had suggested that she accompany me there. Why had she said, "Ofumi isn't the sort of person who would speak to a stranger about her experiences abroad." I thought Osaki had believed that I was a woman from the water trade who had come to stay for complex personal reasons, and that Osaki had allowed me to live with her out of compassion for someone who shared her lot in life. But perhaps she had figured out that this was not the case. Perhaps she realized that I was somewhat involved in academic affairs and that I was conducting research on women like herself who had gone abroad to make a living off their bodies.

I later learned that she had intuitively grasped my hidden motives, and that with this understanding she had determined to help me in my endeavors. But at that time Osaki's brief response stirred up my doubts and fears.

As there will be an opportunity to touch upon this later, let me turn to the events of the next day. From daybreak the weather was wonderfully clear and pleasant. Leaving the house around ten, we crossed the river and stopped at the general store—the one managed by Onami, who had also been a *karayuki-san*—to purchase a bag of sweets to take as a gift. Then we headed for Oe. From Osaki's village we hiked to Sakitsu. There was a bus that ran from Sakitsu to Oe, but as I mentioned earlier, Osaki was prone to motion sickness, so we decided to walk the whole way.

In spite of her small, thin frame, Osaki, who was accustomed to walking, moved right along without pause. Though of much larger build, I, on the other hand, found the distance almost unbearable. Finally we arrived in Sakitsu. From here I thought that she would follow the shoreline, but when we came to a fork in the path, Osaki called out "Tomoko, Tomoko. Let's take this mountain trail. It's a much shorter route," and she chose the path going off to the right. Although the Amakusa mountains are only three or four hundred meters above sea level at best, the trail upward took its toll. When we reached the pass and began to descend, however, I suddenly regained my spirits and energy. The sea of Amakusa, hidden from view as we climbed, spread out as far as the eye could see under the clear blue autumn sky.

As I walked along, exclaiming with joy at the beautiful view, Osaki kept her eye on me as she would a child of kindergarten age. When we had reached a certain spot, she stopped and pointed toward the foot of the mountain, saying, "Look, do you see that tiled roof and the red and white flag over there? That's Odaishisama of Ikusagaura." As I gazed at the banner, absorbed by this classic rural scene, she didn't forget to fold her hands next to her chest and offer a brief prayer.

When Osaki finished praying and we resumed walking, she said, "Whether it's about Yuji or my grandchildren, I make all my important requests to Odaishisama. I also pray on behalf of Ofumi." Broaching the subject in this way, she began to talk about Ofumi in bits and pieces. Ofumi is mentioned in Osaki's confession as well, but here I will write about what I learned on this occasion, trying to avoid repetition as much as possible.

***

Among my co-workers, Ofumi was my closest friend. Even if you live in the same village and see some one's face morning and night, there are people with whom you simply can't communicate. Then there are others who live far away, and with whom you may meet only once every three or five years, but who understand every nook and cranny of your feelings. Ofumi is this latter kind of friend.

Ofumi. I believe she said that her maiden name was Yoshimoto. Although I know she was born in Oe, I don't know what her father or mother did. I recall asking her once, but I've forgotten now. She was taken away by Boss Tarozo at age nine or ten, and crossed the ocean to Sandakan. She was thrown together with Oyae from Shimabara on the boat en route. When I arrived in Sandakan, Ofumi and Oyae were already neatly applying powder and lipstick each night and working as prostitutes. As I was also from the Amakusa Islands, Ofumi did her best to look out for me, and we have been friends now for some sixty years.

I was just a plain, worthless girl, but when she was young Ofumi was so beautiful, I wish you could have seen her. She could afford to be choosy about her customers. She'd let in Westerners like the English and Dutch, and she would see Japanese and Chinese, but you'd hardly ever see a local man enter her room. When Tarozo died of chronic asthma and his younger sister, Toshi, caused a big uproar by selling Brothel No. 3, Ofumi, who had already paid off her debt, and Oyae moved next door to Brothel No. 4. I was sold to Tawau, but I escaped and was taken into Okuni's Brothel No. 8. Since these buildings were on the same street, we could visit each other anytime.

It was around this time that Ofumi developed a close relationship with Yasutani Kiyoji. Ofumi had two children. The boy, Matsuo, was clearly Yasutani's child, but although she thought the girl was also his, she can't say for sure. Yasutani was a man with a vast coconut plantation, but because he had a wife and children at home, he couldn't take Ofumi to his house. Even if he hadn't had a legal wife, a man with such a big estate would be derided behind his back if he brought home someone from a brothel as a wife, so he probably wouldn't have wanted to do that.

Ofumi had to continue her work carrying an infant with her, but this would not do for a prostitute. During the day she kept the baby in her

Ofumi's sisters. Both went to Korea and Manchuria, in search of work.

own room and nursed it, but when evening fell she left it in the care of the proprietress, who lived below. Still, when the baby was upset and cried, Ofumi was beside herself with worry and couldn't relax with the customers. Pretty soon they were complaining about her, and she was forced into a corner. So, Ofumi came to an agreement with Oshimo to take care of her nursing baby Matsuo, in return for which Ofumi sent her some money each month. Oshimo of Shimoda had worked with Ofumi long before I met Ofumi. Oshimo worked out of Brothel No, 8, as I did, but eventually she married a Malay boat captain and went to live in Kozatoko. So, at the time of Matsuo's birth, she was no longer

Oyae and her English husband are on the left, in this photo taken on a sightseeing trip to the caves of Patopote. On the back of the photograph Oyae has written in phonetic script, "For Ofumi. This picture we had taken in a cave made me look like a wild monkey. Please look at it without laughing."

working as a prostitute. This was around the time the Taisho emperor passed away, and the present emperor took his place [1926].

However, not too long after that, when she gave birth to her second child—this time it was a girl—Ofumi really had problems. Even if she were to find someone to care for her, she just couldn't scrape together the money necessary to raise two children. What was her name? It was so long ago, I can't remember. So, Ofumi gave the child to Oyae. At that time Oyae had a Western husband, and because all Westerners were rich, she led a comfortable life. She was very sad, though, that she couldn't have children. Ofumi observed this and thought that because Oyae, whom she had known since they left Amakusa, was reliable and led a good lifestyle, it would be much better for the future of the child were she to be raised by Oyae than by Ofumi herself in the brothel. These must have been Ofumi's reasons for giving the child to Oyae.

Ofumi's little daughter stands in the middle. Sitting at the left is the wife of the brothel manager for whom Ofumi worked. Ofumi is standing next to her. Standing next to Ofumi and the little girl is Oyae. Oyae took in Ofumi's daughter. (The identity of the woman sitting at the right is not known.)

No one knows whether this daughter is still living or whether she died in the South Seas. Oyae is from Shimabara, so if you were to go there and talk to her you might learn something, but I can't recall her hometown. This conversation came up four years ago when I got together with Ofumi. "I haven't heard a bit of news about that girl," Ofumi said. "After all, I gave her away to another, so I can't hope to meet her again in this lifetime. Perhaps she's the wife of some Westerner right now, with two or three children of her own."

Her face was composed, but I think that deep inside she must have been crying and holding her hands in prayer. I understood how she must feel.

I don't remember exactly how long Ofumi continued her relationship with Yasutani, but I think it lasted three or four years. In the meantime I went back home for a visit, became mistress to Mr. Home, returned sick to Amakusa, got married, and in the end went all the way to Manchuria, so I'm not sure of the details of Ofumi's life. But I did catch some news carried on the wind that she was married two or three times.

When we met after the war and were talking about old times, I learned from Ofumi that Matsuo returned to Japan from the South Seas when he was ten. . . . Right, that would have been around 1935. Because he was, after all, her own child, Ofumi had gone to Oshimo's place to take him back, but Matsuo would not leave Oshimo's side. Even when she reached out to him with her hand and said, "Come now, I'm your real mother, so let's go back to Japan together," Matsuo just looked frightened, ran behind Oshimo's back, and wouldn't say anything. Since there was nothing else she could do, Ofumi thought, "If Matsuo thinks of Oshimo as his real mother and loves her so much, it would be best for their happiness if I leave him here," and she returned to Amakusa alone. You might say Ofumi is someone who was destined to be separated from her own children—don't you think so?

Unfortunately, two or three years after Ofumi returned to Amakusa, Oshimo's husband, the Malaysian, suddenly died of an illness. I had seen Oshimo's husband, and as might be expected of a boat captain, he was a fine man. Native men were proud to have Japanese women as their legal wives or concubines, and this Malaysian, too, offered Oshimo a life of luxury, dressing her in silk. Once he was dead, however, she had no further income, so she soon found herself struggling to make ends meet. She found jobs at rubber and coconut plantations and managed to feed herself and Matsuo. Matsuo himself left the English school he had been attending and started working at a coconut plantation. I can only imagine how difficult things were for them.

The Greater East Asia War began and Japanese soldiers went even to Borneo. I don't know whether any guns or cannons were shot there, but eventually Japan lost, and the war came to an end. Oshimo returned to Japan with Matsuo, and went to her hometown in Shimoda. But in addition to the fact that she had not a single relative there who could take her in, the black market price of rice and barley and potatoes was prohibitive, and she couldn't buy anything. So, even though she had managed to return to the place of her birth, in the end she hung herself from a rope tied to the branch of a willow tree and died. The night before she died, Oshimo called Matsuo to her and told him, "Since you're already twenty and you've made it back to Japan, I'm going to make a confession. I'm not your real mother. Your real mother is named Ofumi, and to the best of my knowledge she's in the village of Oe." We know then that she had planned in advance to hang herself. Only one month had passed since her return to Amakusa from many years in Borneo.

Once Oshimo was dead there were certainly not going to be any relations who would take in Matsuo, and, for his part, Matsuo couldn't bear to stay there any longer. As soon as the funeral was over, Matsuo went to Oe as Oshimo told him to do. He went around asking everyone, "Do you know Yoshimoto Ofumi?" or "Where might Yoshimoto Ofumi live?" but because he was born and raised in Borneo, he could only speak Malay and English. He knew only a few broken words of Japanese, so he must have experienced many hardships.

Yet, he somehow found Ofumi—how happy she must have been! And they've lived together ever since. At first he could hardly speak at all, so he decided that if he did manual labor it wouldn't matter if he could talk, and he signed up to be a laborer. He was still working as a laborer when I went to visit Ofumi four years ago. He had also gotten married. It seems his wife is the daughter of Ofumi's older sister who went to find work in Korea.

According to Ofumi, Matsuo treats her very well. However, although his wife is Ofumi's own relative, she treats Ofumi as a nuisance, and Ofumi is not able to like her daughter-in-law either. You'll see for yourself when we go to Oe today, but Matsuo's wife has lost her sight in one eye, and this seems to have made her very strong-willed. She's always railing at Matsuo, "How can you possibly call a woman 'Mother' who never even raised you yourself?" But, Matsuo is a fine person and always takes good care of her. Ofumi always says, with tears in her eyes, how grateful she is that this child who, despite being left in Oshimo's care as an infant and then relinquished to her entirely, should come back as a young man and take such good care of her just for being the woman who brought him into this world.

See, Tomoko, have a look over there. See all the houses over there now? That's the town of Oe. I remember that Ofumi's house was close

to the post office, but I've clean forgotten which street we should take
to the east, and where we should turn to the left.

***

Oe was a town in name alone, for if you cut off to the side from the
main street where the post office was located, you would find yourself
in narrow fish-smelling alleys. Houses pressed in on both sides, with
rocks weighting down the galvanized sheet iron roofing. It may be
because the beach was close by, but the alleys were paved with cement
only along the center, the path having caved in on each side in front of
the houses. This made for difficult walking. The eaves of the houses—
perhaps this was to ward off the coastal wind—were lower than my
shoulder height. Although the doors were all left wide open, every
house we passed was totally dark inside. Poverty seemed to hover over
the town like heat waves.

Osaki stopped some children at play and asked, "Where might
Ofumi's place be?" but the children just exchanged glances and she got
nowhere at all. Osaki then walked through one of the open doorways
and called out loudly, "Excuse me, I'm sure Ofumi's house was right
around here, but could you tell me which one it is?"

The woman who emerged from the back was about fifty, with
clearly defined features. "Ofumi's house is just right over there," she
said hesitantly, looking us over as if to ask who we were. Osaki, who
picked up on her feelings immediately, introduced herself saying, "I'm
Osaki, from ** Village. I used to work with Ofumi overseas." As soon
as she heard this, the woman relaxed her suspicious countenance and
replied, "My, my, so you're Osaki of ** Village. You don't know how
pleased Ofumi would have been to see you. But you know, Ofumi
came down with a dreadful illness three years ago and died."

Ofumi, who we had believed until just now was still alive and in
good health, had actually parted from this world some years ago. Feeling like we had been struck by lightning, Osaki and I just stood there
for a moment in shock.

The distance from Osaki's village to Oe is only about ten kilometers. For city residents this distance is no more than that between the
eye and the tip of the nose. Even people separated by one thousand
kilometers can easily share news by means of telephone or letter. However, in the world of the elderly *karayuki-san,* things are not so simple.

Even if she would like to write a letter, she lacks the ability. Even if she would like to speak on the telephone, she doesn't have one. Even if she would like to use public transportation to visit a friend, she lacks both the time and the money. For such women, a mere ten kilometers can be an infinite distance, and not only is it difficult to keep warm the embers of their friendship of some sixty years, but they cannot even reach each other for a final farewell. Even now I can feel within me the misery these women must have experienced.

Still grumbling about why we had waited to visit until it was too late, the fiftyish housewife led us to Ofumi's, in other words her son Matsuo's, home. Located in one section of a long, narrow fisherman's barracks, fronting onto the same alley, this home consisted of only a six-mat room and a tiny living room of three mats. An old-fashioned wood-burning stove punctuated the dark kitchen.

When the housewife called out, a tall laborer of about forty, sun-burned a rich chocolate color, appeared from the back. This was Matsuo, and he introduced us immediately to his wife. Exchanging a hasty greeting with Matsuo, Osaki suddenly crawled across the mats to the Buddhist altar, where she sat up sharply and folded her hands in prayer. Then, in a loud voice, as if she were addressing a living person, she said, "Ofumi. Why did you have to die so quickly? I was sure that you must be in the best of health. I came too late. Please forgive me!" She was trying to offer some incense, so I came up behind her to help her light it, and then I too offered a stick and held my hands in prayer. Together with a mortuary tablet of unfinished wood, the altar was decorated with a single photograph of a woman.

So this is Osaki's dear friend Ofumi, I thought. From the fact that she looked not quite thirty, I surmised that the photo must have been taken in North Borneo. Standing in a kimono, she presented a slim, graceful figure; her large, wide-open eyes had a cool, refreshing look, and the way she had tied her hair back was very becoming. She was indeed a beautiful woman who even today would invite second looks.

After we had paid our respects at the altar, I was introduced as usual as Osaki's daughter-in-law, and then Matsuo and Osaki, the neighboring housewife who had just returned from another errand, and Matsuo's wife and I had tea and talked about Ofumi. When Matsuo had returned to Japan at age twenty, he could speak only Malay and English, but now, some twenty years later, he spoke in fluent Amakusa dialect.

According to Matsuo, Ofumi had died three years ago—one day in February 1965. She was sixty-five. It was about two years after the end of the war that Ofumi and Matsuo had come to live in this place, and although she could point to no specific injury or ailment, from early spring the year before she died she had begun complaining frequently. "My head hurts," she would say. "There is so much pain in my head, I feel like I'm losing my mind." At about the same time an itching skin disease which began on her arms and legs began to spread over her entire body. No matter how much Matsuo spent at the local drugstore on fine medicines for her headaches and skin condition, none of them were effective, and finally, after indescribable suffering, Ofumi died. "After she was bedridden, it was I who took care of her, right down to bringing the bedpan, and she would keep telling me how grateful she was, so I have no regrets." This was Matsuo's conclusion about the last days of his birth mother.

Both Matsuo and his wife, and even Osaki who nodded her head and offered exclamations as they spoke, seemed to believe without any doubt that Ofumi's illness was no more than a headache and a skin ailment. But, as I listened, I could not suppress an upwelling of deep sorrow. This is because I believed that the illness that took Ofumi's life was not a simple headache or a skin ailment, but late syphilis. When she said, "There is so much pain in my head, I feel like I'm losing my mind," this must have been because the syphilis-causing spirochete *Treponema pallidum* had entered her brain. What people had interpreted as scabies or mange was most likely a result of spirochete affecting the skin. Indeed, when I returned to Tokyo and spoke with Dr. Nozue Etsuko, a gynecologist at Aiikukaifuzoku Aiiku Hospital, she said it was quite likely that Ofumi suffered from neurosyphilis as well as from the skin rashes and ulceration of tertiary syphilis.

I felt completely shattered. I had assumed that *karayuki-san* who had somehow made their way back home must be much better off than those who lost their lives while stowing away on a ship, or who had turned to soil in a foreign land. The reality seemed to be otherwise.

As the reader may know, there are few cases in which a person infected with syphilis will show symptoms of the disease right away. Rather, it tends to be a disease that lies concealed for ten to twenty years and then breaks out when one least expects it. If it infects the brain or spinal cord, it appears as if the victim has gone mad. She will blurt out anything and her actions are unpredictable. As the brain cells

Ofumi, in her later years, playing on the beach at Oe, Amakusa, with a neighborhood child. The photograph was taken around 1960.

are damaged, they die. If the disease breaks out on the skin, the entire body is tormented by boils, and the patient is in extreme pain until death. At present, with the development of antibiotics, unless the case is far advanced the patient can look forward to recovery. Still, it is a formidable disease.

If indeed Ofumi's death was due to syphilis, the bacteria must have been something she bore with her from her many years as a *karayuki-san*. According to Osaki, because she and her co-workers greatly feared becoming sick, they did not neglect to clean themselves with the disinfectant solutions given to them by the health inspectors. However, because spirochete can only be seen under a microscope, it's quite possible that these bacteria would penetrate the body before they would be noticed by the inspector. Therefore among those *karayuki-san* who did make their way through many trials and tribulations and were able to return to Japan, there must be countless numbers who experienced outbreaks of syphilis decades after they had contracted it abroad and were now dead or suffering. Not only this, but among *karayuki-san* who appear healthy today, spirochete might be present that could precipitate disease at any time. Osaki was not immune to this fate. For victims of the atomic bomb who do not know when radiation sickness might break out, even now, decades after the end of World War II, the war is not yet over. In this sense, *karayuki-san* as well have not yet been released from their lives as sex slaves.

That day, close to four o'clock, we took our leave from Matsuo's house and returned by foot to Osaki's place. After a day or two had passed, however, I felt that I must pay one more visit to Matsuo's home. Of course I wanted to hear what he might have to say about North Borneo, but more than this, I was interested in the large collection of photographs left by Ofumi of her *karayuki-san* days, of which Osaki had not a single one. After discussing this with Osaki, I sent a letter off to Matsuo, saying, "Mother would like to see some of the old photographs, and so we would like to drop by again in a few days." One afternoon a few days later I went to visit by myself.

When I arrived, Matsuo was away at his job as a day laborer and only his wife was at home. "He won't return until at least six," she said, so I asked if I could wait in the three-mat room. After she had served me a cup of tea, his wife moved about the small house doing this and that as I went to great pains to fill the time with social conversation. She appeared to keep a cautious eye on me the whole time, but perhaps my imagination is at play here, for her right eye was blind, and all I could see when she looked my way was the white of the eye.

Matsuo returned sometime after six. After he had washed his hands and feet, he stepped into the parlor and went right over to the closet. Taking out an old album, he handed it to me saying, "These are Mother's photographs. They were stashed away deep in the back, so it took quite a while to find them."

Compared to Osaki who had to flee her home in Manchuria and owned not a single photograph, let alone an album, Ofumi had quite a collection of photographs from her Sandakan days pasted in a large album. When I took the album from Matsuo a few loose photographs fell out, and when I picked them up I noticed that they were passport photographs with Ofumi's name on them. Putting them back where they had been, I turned the pages. There were photographs of the streets and port of Sandakan, group pictures of Ofumi with her co-workers, a photograph of a co-worker dressed in upper-class Western clothes and posing with a Western man, and a photograph that appeared to be a brothel entrance, though there was no indication of the number. As I looked at them very carefully, I found standing in one of the photographs a young *karayuki-san* who looked very much like she could have been Osaki. In another I saw the young, beautiful Ofumi sitting in a chair with a little boy of about one year. If Osaki had come with me, she could have told me which were Oyae and Oshimo of Shimabara. She could have pointed out the trafficker Yoshinaka Tarozo and Matsuo's real father, Yasutani Kiyoji.

When I took that heavy, old album in my hands, it felt heavier than its actual weight. When I considered that a glimpse of these women's lives in Sandakan appeared here in the concrete form of photographs, I could not help but feel some sort of piety. How I would love to have these pictures, I thought.

Telling them how much it would mean to Osaki, I succeeded in obtaining a single picture of Ofumi in her youth. Of course the best thing would have been to borrow the entire album, but I had only the shallowest relationship with Matsuo and his wife, having met them only two times, and I could not bring myself to make such a request.

The time had passed rapidly, and this was a remote area where the last bus came through very early. As soon as I had finished my business at Matsuo's I had planned to head on to Takahama, birthplace of the procurer Yoshinaka Tarozo. This no longer being possible, I accepted Matsuo's invitation to spend the night. After dinner was over and we had rested for a bit, Matsuo said, "I have some squid fishing business to take care of, so I've got to be off again." After that I was thoroughly interrogated by his wife and her cousin, who said she lived nearby. I didn't seem to be from Amakusa, they noted, so where was I from? What kind of lifestyle did Osaki lead? I somehow managed to break free of them by midnight, when I said I'd better go to my room and get some sleep. However, I kept thinking about the album, and sleep was slow to come.

This album, which had been tossed into the back of the closet and covered by all kinds of luggage and other objects, was something they had searched for only when I pretended that Osaki wanted to see it.

Pages from two of Ofumi's passports. The passports contain writing in Dutch, Malay, and English. The photo on the left indicates that Ofumi is 32 years old and 151 centimeters in height.

When I left the next morning it would, no doubt, be tossed back into the storage closet, never again to see the light of day. For me, however, or rather for the sake of the history of overseas prostitution, and by extension a women's history of modern Japan, Ofumi's album was a valuable piece of testimony.

The photographs related to *karayuki-san* available to us at the present are limited to those included in *Muraoka Iheiji jiden* [The Autobiography of Muraoka Iheiji], and beyond these there is not a single one available. Didn't I have the obligation to make sure that this testimony did not remain buried, but was brought into the open?

As I tossed about in bed I made a very important decision—I decided to steal the album and the passports. I would be betraying their kindness in putting me up for the night, returning evil for good. If I were discovered, I might even be detained for theft by the Amakusa police, but that would just have to be the price I paid for bringing to light the truth of the historical existence of *karayuki-san*. Matsuo would return from his night job, squid fishing, at about 3 A.M., so I would sneak out of the house with the album before that, either camping out somewhere, or fleeing as far as I could along the night roads.

I wonder how much time had passed? Three sets of bedding had been spread out in the six-mat room, and I was at the farthest end. In the dim light I looked closely at Matsuo's wife, who was sleeping right next to me. Lying face up and snoring softly, my hostess appeared to be in a light sleep. I pulled my slacks and socks out from under my pillow and put them on under the blankets. "Now—it's got to be now!" I thought to myself, trying to bolster my courage.

But no matter how many times I silently said these words, trying to move myself into action, I just couldn't bring myself to stand up and grab the album from the corner of the room where it had been left. As I said before, Matsuo's wife was blind in her right eye, and she couldn't quite close it completely. When she was sleeping it was half open, just as when she was awake, and the lamplight reflected off the white of her eye. Although I was quite certain that she was sound asleep, I couldn't help feeling that she was staring at me with that half-open eye.

Now I come to the part which is the most difficult to confess, but write it I must. When at last that miserable night was over, I seized my opportunity. When Matsuo's wife went into the kitchen to make breakfast and Matsuo was standing at the sink shaving, I pretended to be looking through the album as I took out a number of photographs which I desperately wanted. Lining them up neatly with the two passports, I tucked them under my clothing, close to my breast. On this trip I was traveling in a pair of slacks and my husband's old sweater, and so I somehow stuffed them up under the sweater.

I had been told that the bus bound for Takahama and Shimoda left at some minutes after eight, so I began to get my things ready to leave, but at that moment something happened that almost froze my blood. Matsuo picked up the album, saying, "Well, I'd better put this away." Then he added, "Mother isn't with us anymore, and there's no reason to look at it now," with which he began flipping through the pages. It was clear that old photographs had been removed here and there, and the two passports were no longer inside. "The photographs . . . and the passports . . ." Matsuo blurted out, raising his eyes and looking at me. Trying to slow my racing heart, I looked at Matsuo, but that was all I could manage. Not a word would come out.

Matsuo was also speechless, and after a few seconds, which seemed more like an eternity, his wife appeared from the kitchen. "What's wrong, dear? What's happened?" Wiping her hands on her apron, she entered the room with that same suspicious look. I couldn't conceal things any longer. I had just resigned myself to being beaten and handed over to the police, when Matsuo unexpectedly answered his wife, "Oh, it's nothing." Then, he grabbed a sheet of newspaper, casually wrapped it about the album and, sliding open the closet door, he tossed it in.

After I had bowed my head deeply and thanked Matsuo and his wife for their hospitality, I hurried to the bus stop without looking back. The photographs and passports jiggled back and forth against my chest, and the corners poked into me, but a much deeper pain filled my chest than this—the sensation that I had committed a crime. There was about a fifteen-minute wait before the bus was scheduled to arrive, so I sat down on the hard bench, and it was only then that I realized that not only my hands and feet, but my entire body was trembling.

Finally the bus arrived, but when I stood up to get on, someone came running up from behind calling my name. When I turned my head, it was Matsuo. Dressed for his day labor job in a jacket and workman's *tabi,* he called out, "Please take care!" and hurried off toward the beach.

As I think back on it now, I am certain that Matsuo knew I had taken a number of photographs as well as the passports. But, nevertheless, he had covered up for me in his home, and he hadn't referred to the incident at all when we met at the bus stop. Why would he take this course of action?

I can think of only one reason. Although Matsuo was aware of my unjust actions, he was willing to forgive me. Since I had not spoken a word about my real motives, concealed within my heart, Matsuo could not be expected to understand why I would want those photographs of Sandakan so much. Nevertheless, he seemed to understand my ultimate purpose and therefore forgave my actions. Born himself to a *karayuki-san* mother, and having tasted suffering each day of his life to no less an extent than his mother, Matsuo may have intuitively acknowledged my feelings—my desire to grasp the true form of the *karayuki-san* as testimony to the nature of the modern history of Japan.

The small bus I rode along the western shore of Amakusa–Shimo Island progressed steadily northward. The sky, not especially clear in the morning, became more and more clouded as we went on. I felt that the landscape outside had been submerged in a shadowy gloom. However, even though I had established my own justifications, as the perpetrator of a crime I found this gloomy sky far more appropriate than the clear sky of an Indian summer day which brought everything into clear focus. As I sat there immersed in such thoughts, the bus rolled into the rutted streets of Takahama, hometown of Yoshinaka Tarozo, the trafficker who took overseas not only Osaki and Ofumi, but a great many other daughters of Amakusa as well.

—— 8 ——

Oshimo's Grave

Like Oe, Takahama was a poor town, with a persistent odor of fish. Once I had stepped off the bus, I found myself at a loss as to what to do next. I was already upset, and, unlike my visit to Ofumi's place where I went with introductions, I had not the slightest clue about Tarozo. The only information I had was that Tarozo was born in this town. I hadn't the least idea whether he had any surviving relatives, and if he did whether they might still be living in Takahama.

I was grasping at straws, but as luck would have it, the right straw presented itself. I stepped inside a drugstore in front of the bus stop and made a small purchase, asking, "Would you happen to know anything about the family of someone named Yoshinaka Tarozo who went to the South Seas?" The pharmacist's wife, a woman at the upper end of middle age, thought about this for a minute, but didn't seem to come up with anything. In the end, the most she could tell me was, "Just down the road is the Snowy Egret Inn. If you inquire in there, they might know something. The innkeeper's father went to the South Seas, and she was born over there."

I stopped by the Snowy Egret Inn as I had been told, but although the building was in good shape, it was certainly an inn in name alone, for now it might be called more accurately a lodging house for teachers on temporary assignment to this town or for unmarried postal clerks, and the like. The person who stepped out to greet me was a well-mannered old woman of over seventy. When I explained my reason for coming, she responded, "I don't know anyone like that, but one of the neighbors might. Well, it won't do to talk standing here," she added, inviting me into the sitting room. As she made tea, she asked why I was searching for this Tarozo, to which I replied that he was a distant relation and so I wanted to learn something about him. She nodded, as if satisfied with this explanation. Then, without even being asked, she began to tell her own story. "To tell you the truth, I've been to the South Seas also."

When she said she had lived in Singapore, I thought for a moment that she must have been a *karayuki-san*. This was not the case, however, for when I heard her out, I learned that her name was Asaka, and that she was the oldest daughter of Ryu Naojiro. Her father, who actually went by the name of Kasada Naoyoshi, managed a rubber plantation in Singapore and is described in the documents of this period as a pioneer of the Japanese community in this region. Asaka's name and that of her father, Ryu Naojiro, appear in chapter 1, and I have run across her father's name time and time again as I have pursued *karayuki-san* through the available literature, such as *Nan'yo no gojunen* [Fifty Years in the South Seas (focusing on the activities of Japanese in Singapore)] published by Nanyo and Nihonjinsha, and Nishimura Takeshiro's *Zainan sanjugonen* [Thirty-five Years in the South Seas]. That I now should be hearing this name from his daughter herself filled my heart with deep emotion.

According to Asaka, her father Naojiro, who had been very successful in Singapore, began to yearn for his hometown as he grew older, and finally returned to Takahama. He built a house with fine hardwood he had shipped home with him, and lived here many more years until his death. In that case, through this building too, which looked to the passing traveler like no more than an old inn, flickered the shadows of Amakusa residents who had drifted off to Southeast Asia.

Be that as it may, Asaka stood up and asked me to wait a short while. It appeared she was calling out to a neighbor, and shortly she returned with an elderly woman who said she was eighty-nine. According to Asaka, this woman had been the wife of a fisherman, who was in turn a childhood friend of Yoshinaka Tarozo, and was the only person left alive who had known Tarozo. I quickly recovered my spirits, hoping to learn what little detail I could. However, this woman, who claimed she was eighty-nine, whether it was because she had really forgotten or because she held my character in suspicion, would do no more than repeat, "It was such a long time ago that I've quite forgotten everything," and I couldn't draw a thing out of her. Posing questions one way, and then another, with much difficulty I at last drew forth a significant clue. Close to the city hall there was a fishmonger named Hayashi, she told me. Apparently this was a relative of

Michiyo, the child born to Tarozo's niece, Toshiko, and her husband, a Kilin man of Borneo.

After we had chatted for some time, I took my leave of the Snowy Egret Inn, pressing my hostess to accept a humble gift. I located the city hall and stopped by the nearby fish shop. No matter how you looked at it, it was a country store through and through. A woman, apparently the proprietor, stood in front, but if you focused on her face alone, she seemed not to belong in such a setting. She was, perhaps, thirty-one years old. It appeared that there had just been a delivery, for this browned-eyed woman of large build and prominent facial features was moving about the shop, trimming and filleting fish with her kitchen knife. Her appearance did not surprise me, for I had already been told by the two elderly women at the Snowy Egret Inn that the fishmonger's wife was the daughter of Caucasian and Japanese parents. In this child of mixed blood one could see another aspect of the face of Amakusa, island of *karayuki-san*.

When I explained my reason for coming, that is, that I would be grateful to learn even the most trifling bits of information about Tarozo and his niece, Michiyo, she responded without fully looking at me or setting down her knife. "Since I came to this house as a bride, I haven't heard much about the past. My husband has gone off on a long trip, and even if he were here I doubt that he could tell you much. . . . There certainly is someone in my husband's family called Aunt Michiyo, but I've only met her once."

Judging from her words, it seemed that Michiyo, the child of the Kilin native in Borneo, had returned to Japan and possibly was still alive and well. Somehow I had to learn more about her circumstances. If the course of Matsuo's life, described in the previous chapter, represented a tragedy born of the phenomenon of *karayuki-san*, then could I not expect Michiyo, daughter of a man from Southeast Asia, to have faced an equally tragic existence? However, the more earnestly I questioned her, the more vague were the replies offered by the fishmonger's brown-eyed wife. I felt that her reluctance was due less to the possibility that she held my quest in suspicion than to the fact that she really knew very little about Tarozo, was not in the least bit interested in his affairs, and wanted to be freed from my questioning as soon as possible.

Realizing that I needed to pursue some other course, I changed the direction of my questions, asking her, "Do Tarozo and Michiyo have relatives anywhere else besides here at your place?" To this she responded, "Well, there are any number of households related to them, but, like me, they're unlikely to know about such distant events." Then, as if she had just recalled something, she muttered, "Come to think of it, we used to have a picture of Aunt Michiyo when she was a little girl. Tarozo was in it, too." After rummaging about near the cash box for a while she found a single photograph and held it out to me. "Here it is."

As I took the old photograph from her fishy hands, I shuddered involuntarily. So this was the trafficker who cajoled Osaki, Ofumi, and innumerable other young women from Amakusa into going to North Borneo and turned them into *karayuki-san.* Two medals prominently decorated his chest. Undoubtedly both were bestowed by the Japanese government, but what achievements could they possibly represent? And this must be Michiyo, child of a Kilin man, dressed in Japanese kimono, looking straight toward the camera with one tiny hand resting on Tarozo's knee. Although she bore a strong resemblance to him, there was something about the eyes, nose, and mouth which suggested the features of a native of Southeast Asia. I felt that I absolutely must have this photo to go with the ones from Ofumi's collection.

"I'd like to show this photograph to my mother," I said. "Might I possibly borrow it?" But before I had even finished speaking, the fishmonger's wife interjected, "Fine, fine. You needn't borrow it. I'll give it to you. It's of no use here." With this she terminated the conversation simply, never once pausing to lay down her knife.

Thanking her profusely, I walked away from the fish shop, beset by complex thoughts and feelings. I still felt uncomfortable about the incident at Matsuo's house, and although I was delighted to have in my possession a photograph of the procurer Tarozo, for the fishmonger's wife to have relinquished the photograph so readily indicated that for his relatives Tarozo had become a thing of the past. I felt that the trail of clues I had followed so far would produce no further results.

It must have been about two o'clock in the afternoon already. Although I should have been famished, I had no appetite. I looked up at the sky to check the weather. Low, heavy clouds threatened rain. I became ever more gloomy, not knowing what to think about anything, or how or where to go next. Clearly the best thing would be to return to Osaki's house, but that would mean passing through Oe. Matsuo had certainly forgiven me, but what if his wife later found out about the

Yoshinaka Tarozo with his niece Michiyo. She later became his adopted daughter. Her bracelets and necklace indicate that her father is Kilin, one of the native peoples of Borneo.

incident and was waiting at the bus stop for that moment when I would again pass through? With such thoughts running through my mind I couldn't bring myself to return to Osaki's by way of Oe. Fortunately the bus for Fukuoka pulled up, headed in the opposite direction of Oe and Sakitsu. So, telling myself, "I'll go to Shimoda; I'll go to Shimoda and visit Oshimo's grave," I hurried on board.

When the small bus arrived at Shimoda, the only hot springs town in Amakusa, a fine drizzle began falling from the dark sky. According to Matsuo, the grave of his adoptive mother, Mita Oshimo, was right near the bus stop on the top of a small hill overlooking the sea. When I stopped a passerby to verify this, however, I learned that graves bearing this description could be found on the north and south sides of Shimotsu Fukae River. I decided first to check out the cemetery on the north side, which was closest to the bus stop. With my hair covered only by a large handkerchief, I climbed uphill along the wet road.

On the hilltop were two or three hundred graves of all shapes and sizes. I expected to see only the usual upright stone monuments with their Buddhist mortuary tablets, but there were also flat graves engraved with crosses, apparently belonging to followers of Christianity, and there were quite a number of graves marked only by wooden Buddhist mortuary tablets, belonging to households unable to afford stone monuments. What moved me the most was that whether the wooden tablets had already rotted, or had never been present in the first place, there were a number of graves on the riverside marked only by natural stones. About one-fourth of the graves were of this type.

Although there was no one else present this evening in this cemetery drenched by autumn rain, I felt neither fear nor loneliness. Rather, as I walked up reading each inscription on stone monuments and wooden markers, brushing aside moss and fallen leaves to see if I might find the words "Mita Shimo," I felt very close to the deceased.

After perhaps an hour, though it could have been much longer, I suddenly heard a voice call out from behind, "Hello. What are you looking for?" I turned around to find a woman over forty, tanned by the salty winds, standing at the cemetery entrance staring at me with a questioning, but not accusatory, look.

When I explained my presence to her, the woman told me, "I don't know if she's Oshimo's relative or not, but once every three days or so a woman by the name of Mita comes here to visit one of the graves. This Mita has a house over there on the next hill—do you see it? He's an electrician who moved here from Osaka." She also reported that in the town of Shimoda there were only two families named Mita, one being the electrician, and the other a household at the bottom of the hill near the ocean. "I'm glad I had no need to worry," she added with great relief. "I can tell you I was pretty concerned when I saw you up there all alone in the rain, without even holding an umbrella, going up to each grave with that brooding expression on your face and showing no sign of leaving."

Forcing a smile at having been found a potential suicide, I thanked her for her concern and decided to give up reading grave markers for the time being and head for the Mita residence located at the foot of this hill along the beach. The Mita family upon which Oshimo had relied had been so poor that she felt compelled to take her own life, so it could not possibly be the pretty little house visible on the next hillside. Moreover, the woman had said that this Mita family just moved from Osaka, and so they were unlikely to have any connection to Oshimo. I decided therefore that the object of my search must be the seaside Mitas.

The Mita house, located next to the sea right below the cemetery, was a dilapidated self-built structure of wooden siding and galvanized sheet iron. Although I called out, there was no response, and when I looked inside it was pitch black. All I could see were a pair of children's canvas shoes in disarray on the dirt floor of the dimly lit entryway. It was still raining and soon evening would fall. Even though I had just found Oshimo's house, I decided I had better leave.

That night I stayed at Fukumotoya Inn, reputed to be the oldest inn in Shimoda Hot Springs. According to the young woman who brought tea, Fukumotoya was managed by a woman who was very knowledgeable about the affairs of Shimoda. Seizing the opportunity, I decided to ask her about the Mita family connection to Oshimo. The innkeeper responded that there was a woman much older than herself who knew a great deal about the past and that she would inquire for me the next morning. When I woke around nine, it had already been established that it was the electrician's family that was related to Oshimo.

The autumn drizzle of the previous evening continued through the next day. Borrowing a large umbrella with the name of the inn written across the top, I climbed the slippery road up the hill to the electrician's house. Shige, Oshimo's niece, had stepped out before I came, but her husband, a very plump gentleman named Takichi was at home. I introduced myself as the daughter of one of Oshimo's co-workers. Although he excused himself saying, "I'm afraid there isn't much we can tell you," Takichi went on to speak openly about all he knew regarding Oshimo and Matsuo.

***

I'm originally not from this Mita family. I was born in ** County in ** Prefecture, to a family called Satomi. In 1934 I came into Shige's family as an adopted son-in-law and assumed the Mita name. Oshimo would be an aunt to my wife, Shige. Shige's father was named Mita Ichiro. Oshimo was his third-youngest sister.

I had heard of Oshimo, but because she was in Borneo, I had never met her. At some point I forgot all about her. But then one year after the war—I don't remember if it was in July or in August—Oshimo suddenly returned to Shimoda. She took us completely by surprise. Not only that, she didn't come alone but brought with her Matsuo, a boy who couldn't speak a word of Japanese. They must not have been given much to eat on board ship, because when they arrived they were nothing but skin and bones. The clothes on their backs were in shreds.

I understand that Oshimo left Shimoda when she was thirteen or fourteen, and returned forty or forty-five years later. She must have been close to sixty when she came back. Her parents would have died long ago, and she had lost her siblings as well, so the only people she could rely on were a nephew and niece she had never set eyes on, and their children. We Mitas got together and discussed what we could do. It was a difficult time for everyone, so not a single person offered to take her in. Finally it was decided that since I was the head of the main branch of the Mita family, I would take in Oshimo and her son and look after them.

I thought our lives were really miserable with the additional burden of Oshimo and Matsuo, but we would have been miserable even without them. At that time I worked at an electric power station far up the river. Although I say power station, it was just a tiny generating plant, and my family lived in the same building in that river valley. I wasn't yet forty, and my pay was very low. I had five children, Kayo at the top, and a little boy just born that spring. The price of a single sweet potato back then would make your eyeballs pop out, and there were even people who said they wouldn't sell to you if you didn't bring them clothes and tobacco. I'm amazed we didn't starve to death. Because we were living like this, there wasn't much we could do for Oshimo.

Did you know that Matsuo was not Oshimo's son? At first we didn't know anything, and we simply thought he was Oshimo's son, but after they had been with us for a number of days, she told us that he was actually the son of someone in Oe. Yes, yes, just as you mentioned, I'm sure she said it was Ofumi of Oe. You certainly have this all figured out. After she revealed this to us, Oshimo muttered, "But after all this time she really has no obligation to come take him back."

We had Oshimo and Matsuo help us with child care and farm work. Oshimo spoke Japanese, but although Matsuo was fluent in English and Malay, his Japanese was no better than a baby's. Since he couldn't go outside to work, we had him take care of three-year-old Yoko and our newborn, Namio, as well as do farm work. Three-year-old Yoko got along very well with twenty-year-old Matsuo, even though he couldn't name a single plant, and I think that relationship did wonders for improving Matsuo's Japanese.

As for the farm work, well, I'm almost embarrassed to call it farm work because we didn't even have what you could call a field, but because there was a food shortage after the war, we plowed up the ground around the power station and made it into fields and paddies. We had Oshimo and Matsuo help us to apply night soil and to weed these tiny plots.

Oshimo was with us for only about one month. I'll never forget that morning of September 10. Matsuo asked us in the broken language of a small child, "My mother isn't here; where is she?" Thinking she must have gone out to weed or pick flowers, I didn't think anything of it, but at breakfast time she still hadn't returned. Since this had never happened before, we thought something was odd, and we all went off in different directions to look for her. It was Matsuo who found her.

She had hung herself from a branch on a tree just a little below the power station. Around the power station there were many cherry trees—probably planted around the time the power station was built. In spring they blossomed beautifully, and people would come from Shimoda with their picnic lunches to admire the flowers. However, the tree from which Oshimo hung her rope was not a cherry but a huge willow.

The police came and took Oshimo away in a bicycle-drawn cart. After looking at the body they determined that she must have hung herself at about eleven o'clock the previous night. I don't know what made her lose all hope, but don't you think she acted too rashly? Matsuo believed that Oshimo was his real mother, and although our lifestyle at that time was really terrible, if she had just kept living better days would have come.

Soon after the funeral Matsuo informed us that Oshimo had told him, "Go to Oe and visit someone named Ofumi." So, he got on a charcoal-powered bus belching black smoke and went off to Oe. I don't know how he managed to ask about Ofumi with that broken

Japanese of his, but eventually he found his way to his real mother. After that he returned just once to collect his belongings, such as they were, bundle them up in a large bandanna, and return to Oe. About two years later he came by to visit Oshimo's grave, but I haven't seen him now in over twenty years. . . . Is that right? So Matsuo is fine and is still living in Oe?

Some years after that I was transferred to the Kansai district and I retired only two or three years ago. I used my retirement pay to return to Shimoda and build a house. When there was a shortage of electricity following the war, even the little generating station that I worked at was operating at full capacity, but nowadays the company has no need for such a small station. It's been abandoned now for over ten years, becoming rather like a haunted house. I haven't been to see the place in some time, but I imagine that the old cherry trees and that huge willow from which Oshimo hung herself are still growing there, as before.

***

After I heard his tale, I asked Takichi if he would sketch a brief map for me indicating the location of Oshimo's grave, and I set off for the cemetery following the same road I had climbed yesterday. Just as Takichi's map indicated, Oshimo's grave had been erected on a slightly high spot right in the middle of the cemetery, overlooking the Sea of Amakusa. The nondescript gravestone had carved into it only the words "Mita Family Grave," and I don't think I ever would have found it on my own. Here rested Oshimo, together with others of the Mita family. Holding my borrowed umbrella off to the side, I circled around to the back where several more lines had been carved into the stone. The very last line read, "Buddhist name, Myoraku. Common name, Mita Shimo. Passed away September 10, 1946, at age 60."

In the autumn drizzle I clasped my hands together before the grave and spoke softly to Oshimo. Though I had never met her, she seemed as familiar to me as Osaki. "Please rest in peace, knowing that Matsuo, the child you loved and raised from infancy, is living a peaceful life in Oe. And, you will be happy to know that one of your close friends from North Borneo, Osaki—Osaki, who is kind enough to regard me as her own daughter-in-law—is still living in good health, albeit in the greatest poverty."

The flower vase in front of the Mita gravestone held two kinds of wildflowers—one type was a gentian, but I wasn't familiar with the other, a kind of yellow flower. All were as fresh and colorful as if they had just been offered. As I gazed at the flowers I suddenly recalled the words spoken to me by the woman here yesterday. "I don't know if she's Oshimo's relative or not, but once every three days or so a woman by the name of Mita comes here to visit the grave." I felt an icy lump, harbored deep in my heart, melting away.

No one had died in the Mita Takichi family following Oshimo's death. If that were the case, then the wildflowers that Mita Shige brought here once every three days must not be for her parents, who had died long ago, but for the repose of Oshimo's soul. In this act of offering flowers, which she did of her own free will and not at anyone's request, I saw reflected both the hostility of the Mita family which had driven Oshimo to her death, and also a faint glow of repentance as now, some twenty years later, blessed with material well-being, the Mitas began to look back on their earlier attitude.

Returning to the Fukumotoya Inn from the hilltop cemetery, I paid my bill and said farewell. I took a bus headed upstream along the Shimotsu Fukae River and asked to be let off at the stop near the former electric plant. This was because I wanted to see for myself that spot where Oshimo had brought an end to her life.

In front of the bus stop sign there was nothing but a kind of hut. There was not a human residence in sight. To the left was a mountain, the side of which had been dug out, leaving a high cliff. The Shimotsu Fukae River Valley dropped off steeply to my right. As I walked downstream from the bus stop I began to catch glimpses of a tiled roof and electric poles through leafy branches, just beginning to turn color. This would have to be the electrical plant of which Mita Takichi had spoken. I looked for a path leading down to it, but couldn't find anything. As I gazed down I noticed that a tiny section of the river valley had been terraced into rice paddies, where the rice had ripened into yellow ears. Thinking that there really must be a footpath down to the valley, I renewed my search and finally discovered a trail nearly buried under the tall understory. The rain had stopped and the sky was brightening, but raindrops still hung heavily from each blade of grass, and I was soon drenched, from my slacks up to my sweater.

Eventually I made it down to the paddies, but from there I could proceed no further. Although I could see the tiled roof of the electric plant just twenty or thirty meters across the river, there was nothing left of the bridge at my feet, save some rusty iron pilings. At one time this must have been a very sturdy bridge, but when the electric plant was abandoned and there was no longer anyone to cross over it, it must have fallen to ruin and finally just rotted away. If the water had been low I could have waded across, but the river was turbid and swollen with yesterday's rain. Since it appeared to be quite deep, I gave up any thoughts of crossing it.

Standing at the water's edge, I focused my gaze on the roof of the electric plant, barely visible through the canopy of trees. I couldn't tell for sure, but some of them certainly looked like they could be cherry trees. However, I couldn't single out anything that looked like a willow with long branches trailing toward the ground.

Even if I couldn't see it myself, however, I knew that somewhere, not too far from that roof, there grew a single willow, and that one evening in early autumn, about twenty years ago, an elderly *karayuki-san* had gone out there alone, hung a rope over one of its branches, and ended her life. This distant event had now been forgotten by nearly everyone, with the exception of a few members of the Mita family who laid flowers at Oshimo's grave at least every three days. Still, I could not help but wonder what sort of thoughts had passed through her head as she stood beneath that willow tree. The posthumous name carved into her tombstone was "Myoraku," meaning "wonderful comfort," but if we think about the many years she spent abroad as a prostitute and the suffering she faced until the end of her life, the words "wonderful comfort" have an empty ring.

If Ofumi, who died miserably from syphilis, represents one picture of the *karayuki-san* who was able to return to Japan, then Oshimo, who returned to Japan after forty-five years abroad and was compelled shortly thereafter to seek the solution to her difficulties in suicide, represents an alternative fate. I had but the briefest glimpse of only Ofumi and Oshimo. How many Ofumis and Oshimos, I wondered, lay hidden away in the many villages scattered across the hills of the Amakusa islands?

I don't know how long I stood there by the muddy water of the rapidly rising Shimotsu Fukae River, but gradually my thoughts returned to my present situation. I turned and scrambled up the steep path out of the river valley toward the bus stop. The misty rain soaked through me like Oshimo's endless tears, shed on that distant night when she ended her life.

—— 9 ——

Okuni's Birthplace

After making the rounds of Oe, Takahama, and Shimoda, reflecting with each step upon the thoughts and emotions that welled up within me, I was ready for two or three days of seclusion at Osaki's place. Although it had been a journey of only three days, after visiting so many unfamiliar people and places, even Osaki's house, little more than an abandoned hut, had the intimate familiarity of my own home. I had had enough, I resolved within my heart. I would not pay any more visits.

Nevertheless, when I showed Osaki the photographs I had been able to obtain and related to her the circumstances of all the people I had visited, this prompted her to reveal new episodes in their lives, and I found myself changing course. Although my information may not have been complete, I had pretty well pieced together the background of a number of people who had played a prominent role in her life, such as Ofumi, Oshimo, and the procurer, Tarozo. Would it be possible, I wondered, to go one step further, to collect as much information about and to try obtain photographs of that final person so important to Osaki's past—Kinoshita Okuni? It was clear that Okuni had fallen ill and passed away in Sandakan, but wasn't it likely that Okuni's adopted daughter, Osaku, and her daughter, Mineo, might still be living? I had heard that Okuni was born in Futae, on the northern tip of Amakusa–Shimo Island, within shouting distance of the Shimabara Peninsula, across Hayasaki Straits. If I were to go there I might very well come across some new clues, I thought, and even if I didn't, it would be nice just to have a look at Okuni's hometown. Day by day my desire to go grew stronger, and before long my resistance had dissolved, and I was on the road to Futae.

Because I didn't want to pass through Oe again, I boarded a bus at

Sakitsu and headed for Hondo City, passing through Ichimachida, where Amakusa Gakurin, an academy of higher learning, had stood during the Christian period. We then turned toward Shimoda Hot Springs, and from there headed north to Futae. Perhaps it was because I wasn't accustomed to this bus route, but somewhere along the way I transferred to the wrong bus, and by the time I reached Tomioka it was already dusk. I was told there would be another bus to Futae, but I didn't fancy searching in the dark for someone I didn't even know, so I decided to spend the night at Tomioka, which has some reputation as a resort town. When I asked the folks at the gift shop near the bus stop if they could direct me to the most historical lodgings in the town, they told me about the Okanoya Inn. Coincidentally, the well-known proletarian writer Hayashi Fumiko (1903–1951) had lodged here in 1950, using this experience as the basis for her short story, "Amakusa Nada" [The Open Sea of Amakusa]. It is due to this connection that a monument to Hayashi's literature has been erected next to the inn.

After I had finished my dinner at the Okanoya, the same blind proprietress who appears in Hayashi's story came to my room to greet me, and began a lengthy conversation. The room I was staying in was the very one Hayashi had used, she said, and the furnishings had been kept exactly as they were during Hayashi's stay. She spoke of her memories of Hayashi and the difficulties she had experienced in establishing the monument to Hayashi's literature. When at last this monologue seemed to have come to an end, she brought out a guest book and inkstone case. Pushing these toward me, she explained that she asked everyone who stayed here to write something. Even a picture would do.

She was not to be denied, so I took up the brush and, taking advantage of her poor sight, I wrote something like, "As I walk the stony soil of the Amakusa Islands, I begin to see these stones as the congealed tears of women sent off as *karayuki-san*." She picked up the book gratefully, bowing her head, and was off, but after a short time she returned to my room bringing some more hot tea. "I take it you are conducting research on *karayuki-san,* then?" She must have taken the guest book downstairs and asked someone to read what I had written.

I replied that I wasn't involved in any such difficult thing as a research project, but that there was someone close to me who had been a *karayuki-san.* I was quite interested in *karayuki-san,* I told her, and if she knew anyone like this I would very much like to meet them. So, she sat back down and began telling me about *karayuki-san,* and when she learned that I planned to go to Futae the next day to look for the surviving family of Kinoshita Okuni, she said, "The husband of one of my younger sisters used to teach at the elementary school in Futae. He mentioned that some of the girls he had taught went to the South Seas. After leaving his position as a teacher, he worked for some time in the Tourism Office at Tomioka City Hall. As he loves to dig into the past, he may know something about Okuni. I could him ask him about her tomorrow, if you like." Reassured by her kindness, the like of which I rarely experienced in Tokyo, I fell peacefully to sleep. When I awoke the next morning, I was told that the innkeeper's brother-in-law had already arrived and was waiting for me downstairs.

Terribly embarrassed, I rushed through breakfast, and after introductions had been made I set off for Futae with Sano Mitsuo, the innkeeper's elderly brother-in-law. No sooner had Mr. Sano stepped off the bus in Futae than he walked into a bedding supply store owned by one of his former students. After asking him about a number of things, Mr. Sano learned that a Mr. Mizukami Ryota, who was now a charcoal dealer, and a Mr. Yamaguchi Inokichi, now a fisherman, used to cultivate Manila hemp in North Borneo.

We visited Mr. Mizukami in high spirits, and sure enough, as soon as I mentioned the name Kinoshita Okuni, he looked at me as if he'd seen an apparition and said, "I owe more to Okuni than to my own parents. The very reason I went to Sandakan was because she told me what a nice place it was and encouraged me to go. . . . She has an adopted daughter," he added, but he couldn't seem to remember her name, so I said, "You must be referring to Osaku, right? Would you happen to know where this Osaku lives now?" "You're certainly well informed," said Mizukami, much impressed. "Osaku died some twenty years ago. Her daughter was here for a while, but she seems to have vanished somewhere." Mr. Yamaguchi, with whom I spoke next, wasn't able to add any new information.

After taking in these answers, Mr. Sano must have felt that if he couldn't provide more substantive news than this he would lose his reputation as a local guide, for he checked up on the names of a few other returnees from the South Seas, and was kind enough to take me to see them. However, we weren't able to learn anything more from these folks than we already knew. Although we had left Tomioka in the morning, it was already three in the afternoon, and I thought it was probably time to admit defeat.

Most people who went to live in the South Seas yearned to return to their hometowns, but according to Osaki, Okuni never showed any such inclination. It was only natural then that, differing from most others, she chose as her place of eternal rest not her hometown in Japan but a hilltop in Sandakan, where she built her own grave before she died. Was it not possible, however, that some remote suggestion for this act might be found right here in her birthplace? If I were to give free rein to my imagination, I could imagine that sometime in Okuni's youth, while she was still living in Futae, something must have happened that changed the course of her life; something that turned her toward Sandakan and led her to manage a brothel; and something that cultivated the kindness and warmth she showed to the prostitutes, in contrast to the extreme cruelty with which they were treated by their male bosses. While visiting this village of Futae, shouldn't it be possible to unravel some of these secrets?

Regardless of my inner thoughts, however, if Mr. Sano, a native of Amakusa, couldn't clarify these points even after exerting all this energy, how could I, a mere outsider, hope to do so? Perhaps not a single one of Okuni's successors was left in Futae. If that was the case, then, I would have to be satisfied simply with seeing the place Okuni had been born, just as I had resolved when leaving Osaki's house.

Explaining all this to Mr. Sano, I suggested that we return to Tomioka. "It's too bad, but I guess there's nothing else we can do," he said, but then asked me in an apologetic tone if I would just accompany him to the home of one more acquaintance. I had no reason to refuse, so we began walking along the beach, which we had been told was the shortest way. When we were about halfway to our destination, we ran into a woman of about fifty who had come to dump garbage along the beach. "Aren't you my teacher?" she called out.

Mr. Sano stared at the woman for a second with a puzzled expression on his face, and then he called back, "Oh, you must be Kimi, the class monitor."

"It was so many years ago, but you still remember," she replied, happily. We must come in for tea, she said, after such a chance reunion. Mr. Sano accepted her invitation at once, and we proceeded to her house. As might be expected, the conversation during tea revolved entirely around Mr. Sano's former students. Since I didn't know anyone being discussed, the conversation did not arouse my interest.

After the conversation had progressed for some time, the woman asked, "Mr. Sano, what brings you to Futae today, anyway?" Mr. Sano proceeded to explain my presence, that we were looking for Kinoshita Osaku and her daughter, Mineo, and that sadly we must leave without accomplishing our mission, for it seemed that both of these women must have died. At this the woman began to laugh, and as we looked questioningly at her face, she laughed even more. "Who on earth told you that Osaku and Mineo had died?" she asked. "Osaku is over eighty, but she's never once been sick, and Mineo is the very picture of health."

Although I hadn't fully understood her at first, as soon as her words sank in, I couldn't control the surge of heat that flashed through my body. Ofumi, who I had been absolutely certain was still living, had passed away, and now I was being told that Osaku and Mineo, who any number of people had told us had died, were still alive.

Mr. Sano, too, seemed to have doubts about this information. Looking back at me to confirm that I felt the same way, he said, "After being told by so many people that these women were dead, it's hard to be convinced right away that they're still alive." This brought on another peal of laughter, after which the woman said confidently, "OK, I'll take you to their place right now, then. They live just a few blocks from here!" Stepping into some straw sandals, she shuffled ahead quickly, leading the way.

Just as Mr. Sano's former student had said, Kinoshita Saku and her daughter, Mineo, were just fine. The house she led us to was a large farmhouse quite close to the spot where we had gotten off the bus. It was the home of the Kimuras, the family into which Mineo had married. Mineo's mother, Osaku, had also been taken in by the Kimura family.

Noticing the sign at the door which read "Kimura Ichiro," Mr. Sano said to himself, "Ho. This must be the home of Kimura-*sensei*!" Responding to our guide's voice calling him from the entryway, an old man of about sixty appeared at the door. As soon as he saw Mr. Sano, he exclaimed, "Well, what an honor . . ." Ichiro was devoting his retired life to farming, but before that he had taught social studies for many years at the same middle school at which Mr. Sano had taught. They were longtime acquaintances.

My visit had become the occasion for a reunion between Mr. Sano and Kimura Ichiro, and in no time beer bottles were being uncapped, but this was fine with me, for it put everyone at ease. Mr. Sano introduced me, and I explained to Ichiro's wife, Mineo, that I was someone close to Yamakawa Osaki. Because Osaki was prone to car sickness, I said, she couldn't come herself, so I had come to visit in her stead. At this, Mineo went out to fetch Osaku, who lived by herself in a building detached from the main house.

The old woman who came forward was of small build but of resolute attitude. Though her back was hunched over, she could walk without a cane. According to Mineo she was eighty-six, and other than the fact that she had suddenly become hard of hearing a few months before, she was the picture of health. She showed a certain refinement in the way she greeted me and in her choice of words, striking me as being a very dependable and proper person.

So this old woman was Osaku—the one and only descendent left in this world by Kinoshita Okuni, that "Okuni of the South Seas," who treated Osaki and other *karayuki-san* with such kindness. Except for this one woman, there was no one else still alive who could speak in detail about Okuni's life and character. I felt eternally grateful for whatever element of fate it was that had brought us together just when I was ready to give up, and for the assistance of Mr. Sano and so many other residents of Amakusa who had influenced this destiny.

I was eager to ask Osaku everything about Okuni, from beginning to end, but because Ichiro, with whom Mr. Sano was chatting away right next to us, was among the intelligentsia of Amakusa, and because Osaku herself was a woman of refinement, it would have reflected poorly upon me to jump right into the topic of Okuni's management of a brothel. So I limited myself to referring to this only in the most roundabout way, asking Osaku to share with me the details of Okuni's life, just as she recalled them. When I organized all my notes, this is the story that took form. Before I begin, however, I would like the reader to know that in talking about her mother, Osaku did not once use the term "brothel," *joroya*. Instead, she consistently used the word *cafe*.

***

. . . Osaki. Just hearing her name fills me with memories. Mother was more indebted to her than words can express. I'm most grateful for your visit. For years I have harbored in my heart the desire to express my thanks to Osaki. I had heard long ago from Mother that Osaki lived somewhere near Sakitsu, but I wasn't sure exactly where, and although I knew her first name, I didn't know her surname. This has been

Kinoshita Kuni, dressed up as a man, on the occasion of her sixtieth birthday.

weighing on my heart for some time. Now that you have kindly come to visit, representing her, I feel that a black cloud has been lifted from my mind, and my heart feels suddenly light and sunny.

Did you know my mother? Well, since she died in Borneo, I imagine that someone as young as yourself couldn't possibly have met her, but I suppose that Osaki must have a photograph of her, and that you are familiar with her from the picture.

You say that when Osaki returned from Manchuria after the war she was penniless? That she returned empty-handed without even a single photograph of herself from her younger days or of my mother? Is that right? Well then, please take a look at that photograph hanging above the lintel. It looks like a man, but it's really my mother, Kinoshita Okuni.

I don't remember exactly, but it must have been taken toward the end of the Meiji period, say around 1910. When she reached her sixtieth birthday, Mother said, "I'm sick of playing the role of a woman, and since I no longer have any feminine characteristics, I think I'll become a man." With that, she cut off all her hair and dressed up like a man. That photograph was taken in commemoration of this event. She put on the ceremonial cloak, *haori,* and loose pants, *hakama,* worn by men, and on her feet she wore white *tabi.* On the table next to her was placed a silk hat, and no matter from what angle you looked at her, she really looked like a man. Mother was someone who dared to give free play to her whims like this.

But Osaki probably knows far more about my mother than I do. You may have heard this from Osaki, but I'm not Mother's real child. I was adopted, and in Mother's later years we lived apart, so Osaki, who took care of my mother to the very end, can probably tell you more. If you want to know about Mother's life before she went to Sandakan, however, I may have heard more of the details than Osaki.

According to what Mother told me when I was still young, she was born in 1849. She said she was from a poor farming family who lived a little farther into the country from Futae. At any rate, I've been told that the year before Mother was born was a time of great turmoil. That was the year when all of the farmers in Amakusa rose up against the chief magistrate and began destroying government property. It was also around this time that ships from the American and British navies first entered the port of Nagasaki. I'm not exactly sure about the dates, but apparently when Mother was a little over ten she went by herself to Tokyo, which was at that time still called Edo. I don't know what the circumstances were that led her to go to Tokyo, or what she did when she got there. When she was fifteen she returned briefly to Futae and then went back to Tokyo, and this time it seems that she was taken in by an Englishman who lived in Yokohama. This man had come to show Japanese how to lay out a rail system for trains pulled by steam locomotives. I understand that he received an incredible salary from the government and lived the life of a millionaire, but around 1884 or '85, he completed his work in Japan and returned to his own country. I don't remember his name.

Mother says that while she was in the care of this Englishman she wanted for nothing. There were maidservants at the house, so she was waited on hand and foot. Since every bit of housework was done by someone else, she decided to fill her time with Japanese painting. The man who introduced her to this art was my real father.

My father's surname was Miyata. He used to be of the samurai class, but after being divested of his sword following the Meiji Restoration, he was no longer able to support his many children. In order to make a living, he decided to become a teacher of Japanese painting, an art he had studied while he was a samurai. I don't know how this came about, but his students were not Japanese, but Englishmen, Americans, and the like—all resident foreigners. Even if he had wanted to have live-in apprentices, our house was small and filled with children, so there was no place to spread out the glossed silk on which he painted. My father would walk from this house to that, giving private lessons.

I was born in 1882, so it must have been in 1885, when I was four by Japanese count: I'm not sure whether she dropped by to offer greetings upon the occasion of All Souls' Day in August, or whether it was at the end of the year, but it seems that Mother paid a visit to the Miyata residence. Seeing how impoverished the Miyata family were with all those children, whether out of pure sympathy, or because she was lonely after the Englishman's return to his own country, or perhaps because she was sad that by the age of thirty-five or thirty-six she still hadn't had a child of her own, she received a little girl from Miyata and adopted her. That little girl was me. My father, Miyata, had given me the name Mitsu, but Mother always called me Osaku. Now not even those very close to me are familiar with the name given me by my father.

I lived with Mother in Yokohama until I was nine. Even though I was small I still remember quite clearly that while in Yokohama we lived a lifestyle that spared no expense. All my kimono, from outerwear to underwear, were made of silk. It was quite as if we were making doll clothes out of the best dappled silk material. The reason we were able to live like that must be because the Englishman left behind a great deal of money when he went home.

However, when I was nine, my mother left me with her real family in Futae, and set off alone for the South Seas. If I was nine, that would make it 1889, and so Mother, who was born in 1849, would have been forty. I have no idea what Mother had in mind when she decided to go to the South Seas. As I piece things together in my mind now, I wonder if Mother hadn't been thinking it would be interesting to get involved with some type of trading business; after all, she had spent many years with an Englishman in Yokohama, and as a port town Yokohama carried on a flourishing business with foreign companies. Purchasing a large stock of dry goods, Mother first went to Singapore. However, she found that there was already a sizable Japanese community there, with both general stores and brothels, and so there didn't seem to be much room for her to set down roots. Then Mother heard about Sandakan in North Borneo. It was a location with few Japanese, but a place they were quite likely to develop later on, she was told, and so she went there right away.

On board the ship to Sandakan, Mother became acquainted with a Chinese man from Canton. "As soon as I get to Sandakan," she confided, "I'm going to sell off these dry goods and use the money to open a cafe." Because Mother had lived with an Englishman for so long, she had no trouble with English, and it's likely that this Cantonese spoke English as well. That's probably how they communicated. "I have a friend in Sandakan," he told her. "Please buy your liquor and coffee from him. I'll ask him to allow you to pay for it at the end of the month." He wrote Mother a letter of introduction, and this was how she opened shop with a cafe.

At that time there wasn't another Japanese in Sandakan. However, there were many Chinese, and as I just mentioned, if it was the Chinese who sold Mother her supplies, then it was also they who came to buy her empty bottles. They seemed grateful to have Mother's shop buy their wares and sell the empty bottles. The two Chinese who helped Mother get started became so wealthy that they eventually ranked among the ten richest men in the South Seas, but whenever they passed in front of Mother's shop they would stop by and ask, "Mama-san, how are you doing?" "Fine, thank you, kind sirs," she would reply. "We don't want to hear you calling us 'sir'," they would respond. "We are the ones who are indebted to you." The person who cooked meals at Mother's establishment for close to thirty years was also Chinese. If I recall correctly, his name was something like Ahen.

I don't know much about Mother's life in the early days of the cafe. It wasn't until I was fifteen that I left Futae and joined Mother in Sandakan. By that time the cafe was quite prosperous. As I said earlier, I was born in 1882, so this would have been 1897. Mother didn't come to get me herself. Rather, she asked a ship captain and customs inspector to help me out. I traveled alone from Nagasaki to Hong Kong, from Hong Kong to Manila, and from Manila to Sandakan by way of Mindanao. When we entered Sandakan harbor on board a ship that was half cargo, half passengers, we could see Mt. Kinabalu rising up dimly through the mist. I'll never forget that view.

In Sandakan there were not only tigers, wolves, and monkeys, but even orangutans and crocodiles. For someone who had just arrived from Japan, like myself, it was a most exotic place. There was only one water-supply pipe in Sandakan, but a Chinese man made the rounds selling rainwater, so we would buy ours from him. In Japan, December would be considered midwinter, but over there December and January were the rainy season. Rainwater was collected at this time and sold during the dry season. Their rice was called Siamese rice or purple rice. If we boiled this red rice in proportion with one-fifth glutinous rice, the stickiness came out just right. We relied mainly on charcoal, rather than kindling firewood; all of our cooking was done over hard charcoal.

Mother loved *mochi* and so she owned all her own equipment to make these rice cakes, including a steamer and a large wooden mortar and mallet, which she had ordered from Japan. Once a month without fail she would make *mochi*. If there wasn't a man around to help pound the steamed rice, she would do it herself. Since this was, after all, tropical Borneo, even after she'd gone to all the trouble of making it, the *mochi* wouldn't last more than three days, so Mother would have it delivered all over the neighborhood, sharing it with others. Mother loved to cook for people, and she treated them not only to *mochi,* but to all kinds of other dishes, such as curry, cooked with an entire chicken. She was very strict about the flavor, and it was really trying for those of us who worked in the kitchen. We were never short of green tea, all of which we had brought over from Japan. Our black tea came from Ceylon, and our coffee was grown right in Sandakan. Mother would roast the beans herself and grind them in a mill. Watermelons and melons were grown on Japanese coconut plantations so we could get them locally. The meat of the watermelons wasn't as red as those in Japan; it was more of a pink color.

Whereas most Japanese would celebrate New Year according to the new solar calendar, Mother tended to respect the old customs, and she always observed the New Year according to the old lunar calendar. She celebrated all the other holidays, as well, just as if she were still in Japan, and on occasions such as the Emperor's Birthday, she would fly the British flag and Japanese flag diagonally to each other and celebrate by uncorking a bottle of champagne.

There were about a hundred Japanese living in Sandakan when I arrived. A Japanese company was establishing plantations of coconut palms, and this attracted a large body of labor; others drifted into Sandakan simply to seek their fortune, trying this and that. There were seven or eight cafes run by Japanese with twenty-some women among them. There were four Japanese women who had married local men, and five or six who were concubines to Westerners.

You've probably heard this from Osaki, but the cafe Mother managed was called Brothel No. 8. Because Mother had the disposition of a man, and was the type who would give the clothes off her back to help another person, although she was a woman, she was ranked among the gentlemen of Sandakan. People called her "Okuni" with great respect. Among the other gentlemen were some whose greed led them to treat the women under contract and the Chinese and the locals very badly, but it wasn't in Mother's nature to behave this way. She was kind to everyone. In a travel guide to the South Seas published a long time ago—I've forgotten the title—Mother is described as a woman boss of great public spirit.

Not only did Mother take good care of the girls working at her cafe, but she was willing to lend a hand to every Japanese in Sandakan. Those who made it to the South Seas without even a passport would come to Mother begging, "Please, help me somehow," and she would help each one of them get on their feet and make their own way. When the southern fleet of the Japanese Navy entered the harbor, she fell over backwards to serve them all, from the commissioned officers down to the seamen. She went out of her way to help Chinese and local people as well. Every year the Governor-General of Taiwan sent her a box of shaddock. Mother would say, "They send the fruit because they haven't forgotten some trifling thing I did for them," but I never knew who it was in Taiwan that she had helped, or what she had done for them. The same travel guide to the South Seas I mentioned earlier said that no matter how many people Mother helped, she retained a great fortune But they didn't know what they were talking about. Mother used money so generously that we were always hard-pressed in the kitchen. After I arrived in Sandakan, when I found Mother spending her money so freely, I would reproach her, saying, "Mother, couldn't you spend only half as much?" Then everyone would gossip behind my back, saying, "Osaku is stingy."

I was in Sandakan for five years. At age twenty I returned to Japan with Mother, where a relative acted as a go-between and found me a husband. It seems that my husband-to-be had once been a samurai in Satsuma. At the time he lived in Koshikijima, so I went there to join him, but my mother-in-law was so strict, I couldn't endure it. I became pregnant and returned to Futae to have the child, but even after my baby was born I couldn't bring myself to go back to my husband, so that was the end of the relationship. The baby was a boy. I gave him up for adoption to a family in Jogawara. He was a smart child. He earned his way through college, graduating from Nihon University in Tokyo. After that he worked as a lawyer in Kobe, but he died very young.

Since I had put my child up for adoption and was all alone again, I returned to Sandakan and went back to work in Mother's kitchen. In the meantime I fell in love with a man from Nagasaki and gave birth to a girl. For certain reasons he was not able to stay with me. This baby was Mineo.

When Mineo was six the two of us returned to Japan for what I had intended to be a short visit. Osaki offered to look after Mother, and Mother felt that would be best, so I left her in Osaki's care. I entrusted Mineo to her father's older sister and went to work as a maid and baby-sitter in Shanghai, so I could send home money for Mineo's education. After that I continued to live in Shanghai, only returning home when Mineo entered Girls' School and when she married my son-in-law, who was a teacher.[1] Twenty years later, when Japan lost the war, I finally moved back, and today I am living a peaceful life, thanks to the kindness of my daughter and son-in-law.

But, back to Mother. Mother seemed to get along with Osaki much better than she did with me, and so she probably had no regrets about meeting her death attended by Osaki. For two or three years before she died, I wrote to her, saying, "Mother, you're getting on in years, so wouldn't it be best if you came back to Japan to be with me and Mineo?" But she would never agree. During New Year 1928, the year that Mother died, she finally wrote saying, "I'll come back in May." We were delighted, but then she passed away in February. Perhaps once someone decides to return to their place of birth they relax and die, or perhaps it was just that she knew her time of death was approaching, and she naturally began to yearn for the place she was born.

You've probably heard this from Osaki, but Mother's grave is in Sandakan. Saying it was for the sake of Japanese in Sandakan, Mother built a Japanese cemetery on top of a hill with a nice view of the sea.

She had a grave erected for herself there as well. It was a splendid grave made of marble brought just for that purpose from Hong Kong. The Japanese cemetery was usually a lonely place, but on All Souls' Day it became quite lively with thirty or forty lanterns moving up the hillside. They burned all night long, and it was truly a beautiful sight.

Buried in the hilltop grave she built for herself, Mother had realized a long-cherished ambition, but because we, who lived in Japan, could not visit her grave, we erected another grave for her here in Futae. . . . You say that if Mother has a grave here, you would like to pay a visit in Osaki's place? I'm sure that would make Mother very happy.

The days have grown short and it will be twilight in no time, so if you want to visit the grave, you'd better be off. But before you go, how about one more cup of tea. Just a minute, please . . . .

***

With Mineo—Osaku's daughter and Okuni's granddaughter—showing me the way, I visited Okuni's grave. Osaku would like to have taken me herself, but the cemetery was at the foot of the hills in back of the house, and it would soon be dark, so I felt uneasy about asking someone of her age to accompany me. Therefore I set off, with Mineo in the lead, carrying incense and a wooden bucket.

Okuni's grave in Sandakan was built on a hilltop commanding a fine view, and the grave here at her birthplace also stood by itself, looking out on the sea at Hayasaki Straits. In front of this grave, containing a portion of Okuni's bones and ashes brought over from Sandakan, I stood in Osaki's place to offer incense, clean the headstone with water poured from the wooden bucket, and pray quietly for the repose of Okuni's soul.[2]

After we returned from Okuni's grave, Mr. Sano, his aging cheeks lightly flushed from drinking beer, and I took our leave from the Kimura residence. As we were jostled about on the bus on the road home, I reflected absently on the day's events.

Although I had met with Osaku and Mineo, I still had not come close to the secrets that lay deep in the heart of Okuni, that unique brothel manager. Why had she left Futae when she was very young and gone to Tokyo? What did she experience before becoming the foreign wife of an English engineer? What led her at age forty to cross over to North Borneo and manage a brothel? What circumstances gave rise to the kindness with which she treated the *karayuki-san* in her employ? I had sought answers to all of these questions, but the most fundamental points remained obscure.

I felt that I had set out for a mountain of treasure and returned without the reward. It was true that I had not discovered the mechanism that ran Okuni's heart. On the one hand I felt defeated and humiliated, but on the other hand, Osaku and Mineo, daughter and granddaughter though they might be, were entirely different people than Okuni. The extent of their knowledge of Okuni's life history and her psychology might be limited. Moreover, I had to congratulate myself for learning as much as I did, given the respectable social position of a wife and mother-in-law of a middle-school teacher. After searching in all directions and almost giving up, through the good offices of one of Mr. Sano's former students whom we just happened to run into, I was able to meet with these two women. That alone should be considered an enormous harvest.

I learned from the woman bus driver that there was still another bus to Sakitsu, so I bid farewell to Mr. Sano in Tomioka, and headed toward Osaki's place. Mr. Sano had not only given me a precious day of his time, but had been willing to set out on a search that had no particular destination. I thanked him warmly, but when I tried to hand him some money wrapped in decorative handmade paper, Mr. Sano refused to take it, saying, "I did no more than any other Amakusa resident would have done for a guest from so far away. I should thank you for creating the opportunity for me to meet with my former student and with Mr. Kimura."

Then, after some ten days had passed, a letter written in ballpoint pen arrived at the home of illiterate Osaki. By this time I had already returned to Tokyo. The return address read "Kinoshita Saku, ** Town, Amakusa County." The entire text of the letter follows:

October 18

Dear Yamakawa Osaki,

Autumn has deepened. The other day a person by the name of Yamazaki Tomoko from Tokyo paid an unexpected visit. I heard that you were well and thought of you warmly as I spoke of events that happened decades ago. If I were a bit younger I should like to pay a visit to speak with you and thank you for taking such good care of Mother. However, I am old now and cannot go out anywhere. It's really too bad. I am still healthy, but my back is bent over. I thank you ever so warmly for your good care of Mother. Please do take good care of yourself. I regret that I cannot see you.

Sincerely,
Kinoshita Saku

Although Osaku's letter was written in the simple sentences of someone unaccustomed to writing letters, and although she knew Osaki could not read, it was a letter she felt she must send as one who had shared the same roof with Osaki in Sandakan. Read in this light, though it might seem quite ordinary on the surface, I felt that it contained the limitless love and sorrow of an eighty-six-year-old woman who realized that her remaining years were few.

Translator's Notes

1. In 1899 the Girls' Higher School Law was passed, requiring each prefecture to establish at least one middle school for girls. The few girls, such as Mineo, who continued their education beyond the elementary-school level attended such a middle school. This was generally the end of the educational track for girls in the public school system.

2. The burning of incense is an Indian practice that predates Buddhism. When the body of the historical Buddha was cremated, aromatic wood was used to offset the smell of burning flesh. It later came to be thought that incense aided in spiritual purification. Zen monks often burn incense during meditation. Today, it is the custom to offer a stick of incense before a gravesite or family altar, or before the image of a Buddha. It is also believed that deceased spirits can enjoy fragrances.

The practice of pouring water over graves is a later development in Buddhism. Early Buddhists ignored the power of water symbolism so important in Indian spirituality. In Indian thought water is the source of all things. In Japan, the emphasis on water cycles in agriculture, and the practice of external purification with water in Shinto rites, may have led to the use of water as a purifying agent in Japanese Buddhist practices. In Buddhism, however, the emphasis is not on external purification, but on the cleansing of the heart and mind from passions that bind us to this world. Hiro Sachiya, *Bukkyo to Shinto* (Tokyo: Shincho Sensho, 1987), pp. 73–76 and 81–82.

10

The Home of Gagnon Sana

The night I returned to Osaki's house from my visit to Okuni's hometown I had trouble falling asleep in spite of my fatigue. Toward dawn I had a very long dream. I forgot the chain of events, but it was about my daughter, Mimi. I awoke feeling depressed. I had kept a picture of her near at hand and looked at it from time to time, but now that I had seen her so vividly in my dream, I began worrying about how this little third-grader was getting along with just her father, and whether or not she might be ill, since she was prone to bronchitis. I had informed my husband of Osaki's address, but I had told him he mustn't send me anything. I, on the other hand, recorded everything Osaki and the others told me, sending letters and postcards home almost every day. Not hearing anything back could not help but be unsettling. Finally, for the first time since I began to live with Osaki, I felt that I must return to Tokyo. This feeling grew stronger each day.

If this had been all, I could have suppressed my longing for my husband and daughter and lived with Osaki for two or three weeks longer. Although I had heard Osaki's story and had learned all I could about Ofumi, Oshimo, and Okuni, I still felt that I didn't know enough, and I knew hardly anything at all about the procurer Yoshinaka Tarozo and his niece, Michiyo, let alone Osaki's childhood friends, Ohana and Tsugiyo.

However, my personal feelings aside, circumstances had developed to the point that I had to leave Osaki's village. The villagers had accepted my presence at Osaki's house because they assumed that if I were not Osaki's actual daughter-in-law, I must be a secret child or the child of some friend from her *karayuki-san* days. And, even if I weren't either of those, the villagers thought I might be someone seeking refuge from the water trade of drink and men. However, something

162

Osaki with the author, Yamazaki Tomoko. Amakusa, 1968.

had happened that made them suspend these beliefs. On a day when I was away from Osaki's house visiting Ofumi's birthplace, Mr. Yoshida Masuo, a high school teacher of social studies, came to visit me and Osaki at Osaki's house.

Osaki and I had met Mr. Yoshida several days earlier on our walk to Ofumi's village. Just before we took the shortcut through the hills to Oe, we had found a lumber pile on the side of the beach path, where we sat down to rest. Just then a man came along who appeared to be a little over thirty and was exactly one's image of a teacher. When I saw a camera dangling from his neck, I had a sudden idea.

I thought I would ask him if he would take a picture of me and Osaki together. It's not that I didn't own a camera, but I purposefully didn't bring one on this trip. I felt it was too bad that I couldn't take a picture of Osaki. But then, as if in answer to my prayers, someone had shown up with a camera. Assisted by the lightheartedness of one on a trip, I thought I would ask him if he would take just one photograph.

When I whispered my idea to Osaki, she replied, "What a good idea! I had my picture taken many times in Sandakan, but it's been decades now since I've been in one. I wonder if that young man will really take one for us." We quickly set ourselves to rights and I called out to the man, "Excuse me, but . . ." We didn't have a camera, I explained, so we would be grateful if he would take just one photograph of us together, and of course we would pay him for it. He agreed readily and lined us up together, pressing the shutter at least twice. Then he asked where to send the developed pictures.

I thought it wouldn't be good to tell him Osaki's address, and while I was stumbling for words, wondering what I should say, he introduced himself, saying that he was Yoshida, a teacher at the local high school. Pointing to a house by the road, he said it was the home of a student, and that when the photographs were ready he would send them there, so we should go pick them up. "In my student's garden are the remains of a tide-viewing tower dating from the Christian era. I came here to look at the site today because I'm conducting research on the history of Amakusa. If you're not in a hurry, won't you take five minutes to have a look?" Since he had been kind enough to take our picture, it would've been rude to refuse his invitation, so we accepted and followed him into the farmhouse garden to look at the stones that had been laid as the foundation for a tower used to observe the ebb and flow of the tide. During this interval he asked me a number of times who I was and how I came to be traveling with an old woman like Osaki.

As a high school teacher and a regional historian, he must have seen right through me, realizing that I was the type of person who would be interested in seeing such a relic of the Christian era. I was able to extract myself from the questions by being deliberately vague, but when I returned from Ofumi's town, Osaki pointed to two photographs of the two of us together, and said, "The teacher who took these pictures when we were on our way to see Ofumi stopped by today to deliver them, and he asked many questions about you." I didn't know how he had figured out where Osaki lived, and when I asked her she responded that while I was looking at the foundation stones of the tide-viewing platform, Mr. Yoshida had asked her directly where she lived and had delivered the photographs himself while I was in Futae.

In Tokyo a suit is the general form of apparel worn by men, regardless of class or occupation, but if one saw a person in a suit in the villages of the rural prefectures, particularly in a place like Amakusa, he had to be either a teacher or a government employee at the town hall. In this sense, the suit became a symbol of authority. If the man in the suit was a teacher—especially one of those teachers at the few high schools on Amakusa–Shimo Island—this person was not only a public servant but a celebrity. Hence Mr. Yoshida was known in Osaki's village as well, but to think that someone of his stature should visit such an impoverished shack as Osaki's home! The villagers, who seemed to have forgotten their suspicions regarding my identity, once again set their imaginations on fire. If Mr. Yoshida had paid a call at Osaki's house, then just what did that suggest about the woman staying with her, they whispered among one another.

Even so, if Mr. Yoshida had visited only that once, the villagers' doubts would have dissipated, and I might have been able to stay longer with Osaki. However, the day after I returned from Futae, a neighborhood girl who said she was a student at the high school dropped by to deliver a gift—a thousand-yen note and several bags of rice from Mr. Yoshida who had, apparently, been utterly shocked by the poverty in which Osaki lived. It seems that this girl let on that I would be returning soon, for two days later, Mr. Yoshida paid another visit. In addition to taking the photographs, he had also sent Osaki a gift, and so this time Mr. Yoshida presented himself, not as a mere passerby to whom we had no connections, but as someone who considered himself quite close to us. He told Osaki that although he had a wife and child to support and didn't live in luxury himself, if she found herself in any kind of trouble she should, by all means, let this be known to his student who would convey the message to him. Then, assuming an air of nonchalance, he confronted me with the following:

"I sensed from the first time I met you that you were not the old woman's daughter-in-law. The old woman pretty much confirmed this by the things she said to me on my last visit, so who are you, anyway? Are you a novelist or a historian investigating *karayuki-san*? If that's the case, since I fancy myself a local historian of the Amakusa region, I would begrudge you nothing in the manner of cooperation if you would simply tell the truth."

Mr. Yoshida was quite sincere, and although I appreciated his goodwill, to be perfectly honest I found myself in a real bind. It was precisely because I believed that Osaki and her acquaintances would never speak to someone from that class of people represented by the business suit that I had come to Amakusa in the guise of a woman who had just run away from home. Although I had sown the seeds myself, here was this man from the class of business suits who was about to tear apart my disguise.

When Osaki stepped outside for a minute, I took the opportunity to face Mr. Yoshida and answer him quickly and quietly. "Since you insist, I'll tell you who I am. I'm interested in pursuing women's history, and toward that end I moved in with Osaki so that I could hear what she had to say about *karayuki-san*. As a fellow historian, I'm sure you will understand my motives, but the greatest type of cooperation you could offer me right now is to stay away from me and Osaki."

As one would expect of a skilled local historian, Mr. Yoshida grasped my point immediately, and after chatting about this and that with Osaki, he took his leave. The villagers, however, were not as easy to satisfy. As an outsider, I could only grasp a fraction of what was felt in the community, but rumors were going about to the effect that even though Osaki and that other woman were acquainted with the high school teacher, that woman who was posing as Osaki's daughter-in-law was probably up to no good. Whatever her motives, they would certainly not bring honor to the community. This type of atmosphere hung heavily over the village. Whether it was the woman who owned the general store or familiar passersby, on the surface their faces were as congenial as ever, but as soon as we had cheerfully passed one another, they would turn around to take another look at me.

Though I pretended not to notice, these furtive looks actually pierced me to the core and left me trembling. My presence threatened to dislodge the veil the people of Amakusa had drawn over the existence of *karayuki-san* and to reveal this secret part of their history to outsiders. Those sideways glances cast by the villagers seemed to indicate that they had seen right through my true intent of moving in with Osaki in order to hear the voice of a *karayuki-san*. If this were the case, I could no longer expect to be treated kindly by the villagers. I might be ostracized, and, worse, I didn't know what kind of difficulties I would bring down upon Osaki.

As these thoughts ran through my mind, for the first time since I arrived in Amakusa I experienced a sense of fear. This fear, added to the anxiety I felt after dreaming about Mimi, increased my desire to return to Tokyo as soon as possible.

I knew that I needed to leave Osaki's house, but there was one more person I wanted to meet—Gagnon Sana. Sana was someone Osaki mentioned to me when she began relating her life story. Sana is also described by Mori Katsumi in his book, *Jinshin baibai* [The White Slave Trade (Tokyo: Shibundo, 1959):

> In ** Village, next to Oe, there was a woman named Gagnon Sana. When I met with her in 1950, she was sixty years old. She left home to escape an undesirable marriage that was being forced upon her by her parents. In 1920 she went to French Indo-China and married Marcel Gagnon, a government official at the provincial office in Phnom Penh. She returned to her hometown in 1927, after the death of her husband. I visited Sana one evening. While on the outside her home looked like a typical farmhouse, inside there was a splendid bed under mosquito netting and other things suggestive of someone who had returned from the South Seas. Sana had just returned home with firewood on her back. She had been totally transformed into a farm woman. She was of large build, and it seemed natural that she would be attracted to white men. She was a simple, unsophisticated woman, and she seemed embarrassed about having gone to the South Seas, as if she had done something bad.

According to Osaki, Gagnon Sana was a distant relative. She lived across the river, below Osaki's house, and her roof had become familiar to me as it was in constant view. The reason I had visited Oe, Shimoda, and Futae but had never stopped by Sana's home, just the distance from your eye to your nose, is because I didn't want the villagers to connect me with the image of *karayuki-san*.

But, if I was going to return to Tokyo anyway, I could throw caution to the wind. As long as I didn't do anything to drive Osaki into a difficult situation, visiting Sana and hearing her story was not only necessary for my research but had some practical significance. That is, heretofore I had focused on *karayuki-san* who primarily took Asians as their customers and had returned to Japan with almost nothing to their name. However, Gagnon Sana belonged to a completely different category of *karayuki-san*. She had married a European, a French official in a Southeast Asian colony. After his death, she inherited his fortune, and as one of the few wealthy people in the village, she lived a life of comfort and luxury.

The description of her in Mori Katsumi's book may have provided the stimulus, but whenever newspapers, magazines, television or radio wanted to get information about *karayuki-san,* they always came to visit Gagnon Sana. From a shallow contemporary perspective in which a person's worth is measured by their appearance in the media, Sana was universally acknowledged to be the most famous person in Amakusa. If I could hear her speak of the past, I would learn about the elite class of *karayuki-san,* and I might be able to learn how she viewed her life now.

When I said I would like to meet Sana, Osaki did not seem very enthusiastic about the proposal, but she put on her worn rubber thongs and led me there. From the outside, Sana's house looked like an ordinary farmhouse, but when I put just one foot into the entryway I set eyes on a huge white refrigerator, a rocking chair, and a splendid carpet of foreign design. Accustomed as I was to Osaki's house, this place was extravagant.

After Osaki had announced that we would like to speak with Sana, we waited for some time before an elderly woman of very large build and a round face came walking out calmly from the back of the house. I was sure I had seen this woman somewhere before, though I couldn't make the connection. In her left hand she held what one could see at a glance was a pack of foreign cigarettes. In her right hand she held a lighted cigarette from which she occasionally took a draw. Without saying a word she looked us over from head to toe as we stood waiting in the earthen entryway. Then, she blurted out, "You have some business with me?"

Osaki began to assume the attitude she takes before social superiors. She introduced me in a faltering voice, saying, "This is a relative who has been staying with me for the past half month. She said she'd like to meet you." I gave my usual speech, thanking her for being so kind to the elderly Osaki. Then I added, "This is my first visit to Osaki's place. She's been telling me about life overseas, and I found it so fascinating that I was hoping you would tell me something about life abroad as well." As she slowly exhaled cigarette smoke, Sana asked, "Will you be recording, or taking notes?"

For a second I couldn't figure out what she was talking about. Running it through my mind again, I realized what she had said, but it was totally unexpected. When I replied that I had come neither from a broadcasting station nor a magazine company, but simply as one of Osaki's relatives who would like to hear more about life abroad, Sana looked at me as if she did not care to be bothered further. "My nerves seem to be troubling me today," she said, clearly letting us know that she wouldn't see us.

It would have been rude to push the matter any further and would only have served to arouse her suspicions, so I merely nodded agreeably. I didn't want to give up entirely, so I said, "Perhaps we could drop by again tomorrow or the day after, when you're feeling better," and attempted to get her to allow another visit. Sana responded without once showing a smile. "This nerve problem is a complicated disease, and sometimes the pain doesn't go away for five or ten days at a stretch. Besides, although I went overseas, unlike Osaki I have nothing to say which would make for interesting conversation."

However indirectly, what she seemed to be saying was that she was of a different breed than Osaki and that for the likes of us to visit her twice would be a great breach of etiquette. Osaki must have felt sorry for me, because she tried to offer advice from the sidelines, but both her words and attitude seemed excessively timid. Osaki's helpless attitude, and Sana's air of contempt for Osaki and me, her relative, never changed until we gave up our mission and politely said good-bye.

I had failed miserably in my attempt to hear about life overseas from Gagnon Sana, but that evening as I petted one of the cats that had curled up next to me, I couldn't help but think about Sana's reasons for rejecting me.

When the media arrived in new cars and brought out cameras and tape recorders, she was more than willing to comply with their request and talk about her life in Southeast Asia. So, why had she so firmly rejected me? When I asked her if she would talk about her life, she had responded, "Will you be recording, or taking notes?" If I had been a journalist dangling a tape recorder from my hand who planned to print my interview in a newspaper or magazine, would she have happily complied with my request, inviting me into the parlor?

I will never know for sure, but I believe that Sana must have rejected me for the sole reason that I was someone closely related to Osaki. Although Sana may have gone overseas originally as a *karayuki-san,* she subsequently married a European, and enjoyed a life of luxury both during and after her husband's death. In this sense she may be considered the most successful form of *karayuki-san.* With Osaki, it was exactly the opposite, for she ranked among the lowest level of *karayuki-san.* Even today, in her old age, she lived a miserable existence from which she could have fallen no lower.

Within her own heart Sana, not surprisingly, had nurtured a consciousness of social status that clearly distinguished her, a woman who casually smoked the finest foreign tobacco, from the likes of someone who would scramble for and smoke old cigarette butts. For Osaki, this ruin of a *karayuki-san,* to now approach her as an old friend could only have deeply wounded Sana's pride. If Osaki had been alone, it might not have been so bad, but for her to drag along this nameless relative whom no one knew anything about and ask Sana to speak about her *karayuki-san* days cut the wound even deeper. This must have been her reason for holding us in such contempt that she did not smile even once as she dismissed us from her sight.

I was less concerned with my own sense of regret or discomfort, however, than with having subjected Osaki to such an unpleasant experience. Aside from this burden, which weighed on my heart, however, even though my visit to Sana's home had formally ended in failure, it was in another sense a great success. I had visited her because I wanted to learn something about the lifestyle and way of thinking of an upper-class *karayuki-san,* and though I didn't learn much about how she had lived, I was able to get a glimpse of how she viewed herself today.

As I have attempted to describe Sana's attitude in this chapter, I have come to the realization of what a truly splendid person Osaki is. Osaki was willing to put me up in her home for three weeks without knowing anything about my background. Would Sana have done the same? On the following evening, when I told Osaki that I would like to return to Tokyo, I felt the depth of her humanity even more keenly.

―― 11 ――

Farewell, Amakusa

The day after we visited Gagnon Sana, I took the bus to Hondo and purchased two plastic-weave floor mats, ten sheets of wrapping paper, replacement paper for the shoji, glue, and tacks. Before I returned to Tokyo, as a small token of my appreciation I wanted at least to cover the rotting, centipede-infested tatami with plastic-weave matting, to patch the holes in the earthen walls, and to change the soot-blackened paper on the shoji and fusuma. The reason I bought wrapping paper was that I couldn't find wallpaper anywhere.

The next morning, when I told Osaki, "Mother, we're going to make your house beautiful today," Osaki cheerfully followed my directions. First, we bound bunches of bamboo grass together with twine, using these to brush the soot from the walls. We tacked up the wrapping paper on the walls, then we laid out the new mats and, with some difficulty, fastened them onto the rotting tatami. We hauled the fusuma and shoji down to the stream below, where we went in barefoot and dipped the door frames right into the water. Using coiled-up sections of rough twine, we began scraping off the paper. The paper that covered the frames was for the most part movie posters and the like, and as the soot was washed away, I was surprised to see faces of well known actors.

Although it took us nearly until evening, when at last we were able to replace all the paper on the fusuma and shoji and put them back in place, our usual dim lightbulb seemed somehow to glow more brightly. Osaki frolicked about like a child. "How lovely," she exclaimed, happily. "It's just like a palace, and this is all thanks to you!" I could hardly bear to tell Osaki now that I planned to leave for Tokyo the next morning, but I couldn't very well not tell her either.

Dinner was the typical humble fare, though we ate a bit later that night due to our refinishing work. After we had eaten and spread out the bedding, there was nothing else to do but to go to sleep. The cats must have sensed this as well, for they had all gathered in the central room. I straightened my posture and said, "Mother." "What?" responded Osaki, looking up. "You've kindly taken care of me for many days now, but tomorrow I must return to Tokyo."

Appearing unable to understand a word I had said, Osaki repeated, "What?" When I said the same thing over again, the words seemed at last to sink in, for her face assumed a troubled expression. As I stared down at the design on the floor mats, I told her that three weeks had gone by since I arrived in Amakusa, that I was concerned that my daughter in Tokyo might have taken ill again, and that although I deeply regretted leaving, it was time for me to go home.

Perhaps it was to check her emotions, but Osaki lifted one of the cats onto her lap and stroked its back as I talked. When I stopped talking, she continued to stroke the cat for some time in silence, and then finally, letting the cat off her lap, said quietly, "I see. Yes, you'd better go home. You'd better go home right away. You may be worried about your daughter, but I'll bet Mimi is also sad to be separated from you." Then she added, "I knew you would have to leave some day, but I never dreamed you would be kind enough to stay in this kind of place for so long. I can't thank you enough. I came to believe over this last half month that you were really my daughter-in-law. I'll never forget you."

I was an intruder whose presence clearly strained an already miserable existence. On the other hand, I may have added at least some variety to an otherwise lonely and monotonous life, so I thought that Osaki might try to stop me from leaving. But by acknowledging that my daughter in Tokyo must be missing me, Osaki was forgiving my departure. Having been lured to the South Seas at age ten, where she experienced homesickness in full measure, she understood well the feeling of both mother and child, separated these three weeks, and so made no attempt to detain me.

I was grateful for her consideration, but when I thought about it, this was certainly not the only occasion on which she had shown so much empathy. From the time I intruded upon her home, with the flimsiest of excuses, until the present moment, the fact that I wasn't publicly denounced by the village, and that I was able to visit places closely connected to Ofumi, Oshimo, and Okuni and to hear their stories—all of these things were due to her deep concern for me. But, of the many

ways in which she expressed her consideration, I am most grateful for
the fact that she did not once ask me who I was.

In front of the villagers Osaki pretended that I was the wife of her
son, Yuji, but she, more clearly than anyone, knew this was not true.
Even to Osaki I had said no more than that I was from Tokyo and had
a daughter named Mimi. Of course she, more than any of the villagers,
must have wanted to learn my identity. Because she was providing me
with room and board, she certainly had the right to ask me about
myself, but she asked nothing.

When I first moved in with Osaki, I thought that if she asked,
"Tomoko, why did you come here?" I might answer that things
weren't going well with my husband and I'd left home, or that I'd
come to Amakusa thinking about suicide, and try to make my story
sound a bit real. But five days passed, then seven, then ten, by which
time I was so taken by Osaki's innate goodness, I lost any will at all to
lie to her. I concluded that if she did eventually ask about my identity, I
would simply have to tell her everything, at which point I would no
longer be able to hear her story. That I was able to stay with her and
learn as much as I did is precisely because she never questioned my
identity.

I felt that I had an obligation to open up to Osaki eventually and
reveal who I was and how I lived. There was no time left to do this
save this evening, but first I wanted to ask her why she had never
questioned me. "Mother, there's just one thing I'd like to ask you," I
said, approaching the issue, and I asked her why, although I was a
lodger in her house, she had never asked me who I was, or where I was
from. "Didn't you want to know anything about me?"

Placing a different cat on her lap and hugging it to her, Osaki replied
in a soft voice, "Of course I wanted to ask you. The villagers came up
with this theory and that, but I, more than any of them, wanted to know
who you were. . . . But," she continued gently, "everyone has their own
circumstances. If they want to explain themselves, they'll do so without being asked. If they don't say anything, there's a reason for their
silence. If you choose to be silent, how is it that another person has the
right to question you?"

When Osaki said this, her tiny frame suddenly seemed ten times
bigger. What mature words were these, these words just spoken by
Osaki!

Certainly a person will confide in another if they feel that in so doing they might find resolution to their problems, but if the burden of their distress or secret cannot be lessened by discussing it, they aren't about to open up to anyone. It often happens that when people of a rash, inconsiderate temperament see others who harbor some sort of distress, they will try to pry out these secrets, but a more thoughtful person will let the person who is suffering work things out for themselves. Since, for the time being, there is nothing they can do, they will simply look out for their friend from a distance, trying to lift some of that burden on their own shoulders. I understood this only too well, having once endured myself this type of anguish, which cannot be healed simply by speaking of it to others.

Earlier I mentioned that some twenty years ago I had been the victim of an incident which left scars on my face to this day and that this seemed to be an important factor in facilitating my approach to Osaki and the other villagers. While these wounds were still fresh, disfiguring my face in about ten places, I found myself in the depths of anguish. When I walked down the street, people would always turn and stare back at me, and my friends somehow became more distant. I had believed that a beautiful face was a woman's greatest attribute and was certainly her most important qualification for marriage. I had lost that qualification. The darkest despair filled my heart. Had I revealed this anguish, I would have received sympathy in return, but this sympathy would have done nothing to ease the pain.

I reached the point where I revealed my feelings to no one, and to me a considerate person was one who did not ask anything about the scars, and an inconsiderate person was someone who sought to offer sympathy and questioned me about how I got them. According to my definition, there were many people who showed consideration, but there were some of the highest learning and good sense who, nevertheless, would ask me how I came to have the scars and even count them with their fingers, pushing back my hair to see if there wasn't a larger wound concealed underneath.

Understood through these personal experiences, the weight of Osaki's words was almost painful. "If you choose to be silent, how is it that another person has the right to question you?" Some might absentmindedly let these words flow by, but to me it seemed that for a philosopher of life these words represented the pinnacle of thought.

And what sort of person was I compared to Osaki? Although she had enveloped me with such mature thinking, I had failed to notice it, and instead asked stupid questions like why she hadn't asked my identity. I was acutely aware of my pettiness, and felt that I had shrunk to the size of a mouse in embarrassment.

This was the time to reveal everything, I thought. At first I had thought this was my duty as Osaki's houseguest, but now I felt that I must confide everything to show my trust for this individual who had given so much to me.

After bowing my head for some time with my eyes closed, I looked right at Osaki and said, "Mother, I'm sorry I never told you who I am and why I am here." Then I let everything else pour out. That I had not only a child but a husband; that we got along quite well; that I was conducting research on women's history; that the reason I came to Amakusa was to do research on *karayuki-san*; that I had asked to stay at her house so I could learn about her life as a *karayuki-san*; that I hoped to write up the stories she and others had told me and to publish them; and so on. When I told her that to accept her kindness while hiding all of these circumstances was no more than the basest deception and begged her forgiveness, I broke down completely and began sobbing on the mats we had just laid out that noon.

Osaki remained absolutely quiet as I cried, but when I had cried myself out and somewhat regained my composure, she slid over close to me and begin to gently pat my back, saying, "There's no need to cry. At first I thought that you might be someone who had left home, but then I realized that you wanted to hear about my life overseas, and so I told you about it. There's nothing to worry about." Then, she added, "If you want to write about me and Ofumi, I don't mind at all if you are the one doing it—but I wouldn't feel comfortable about someone else. Everything I have told you, whether it be about my life overseas or about the village, is absolutely true. If you write only the truth, I don't think you'll cause trouble for anyone."

When I heard this I was not only surprised, but I felt that one riddle had been solved. When I said I wanted to visit Ofumi in Oe and Osaki had agreed to take me there, she had added, "After all, Ofumi is not one to talk about her experiences abroad with just anyone." Moreover, whenever I asked her to relate her experiences as a *karayuki-san,* I had always prefaced my questions with the explanation "because it's interesting to hear about life abroad." But, in spite of this weak excuse, she had been willing to talk about herself and her companions with great candor, and she had gone out of her way to facilitate my visit to the hometowns of Tarozo, Oshimo, and Okuni.

Osaki had taken me in not because she knew nothing of my purpose, but with full knowledge of what I was about. Knowing I was a woman in search of a secret no one from Amakusa wanted to reveal, she nevertheless helped me in every way possible.

Perhaps she treated me so kindly because, as she said earlier, "I came to believe over this last half month that you were really my daughter-in-law." It's possible that my own personality played a role in this, for I am quick to become intimate with others, but what encouraged this love the most was my sharing of her day-to-day life in this dilapidated cottage. As I mentioned before, the house looked like it could collapse at any moment, the rotting tatami was a haven for centipedes, and of the villagers, not one would step inside except the children. The fact that I slept and ate together with her every day bridged the psychological and spiritual distance between us, so that although she knew I was here to learn about her days as a *karayuki-san,* she was able to shower me with deep affection nonetheless.

Through the touch of her hand patting my back, I felt her love flow through my body. Restored by her calmness, I sat up. Osaki walked over and got my towel off a hook on the wall and wiped my face, as if I were a child. "Well, you'd better go to sleep now or you'll be exhausted on the train tomorrow," she said quietly, nodding toward the futon.

When I was a child and had been soundly scolded by my parents, only to have them come back and show me some kindness for fear they had treated me too sternly, I would get a strange, bittersweet feeling inside. I experienced the same feeling when Osaki had wiped away my tears. Suddenly feeling very submissive, I let Osaki assist me in getting ready for bed.

When I awoke the next morning, Osaki was preparing rice that looked whiter and tastier than usual, and she had even placed small slices of broiled mackerel on my tray, though I couldn't begin to guess how she had managed to pay for them. When we had finished our meal, clouded by the sadness of parting, I quickly finished my packing. Sitting up formally, I bowed to Osaki and thanked her again for her hospitality over such a long period of time. Then I offered her some money which I had set aside for this purpose. But Osaki said, "I didn't put you up in the hope of receiving money," and she refused to accept it.

I continued to press her, arguing that for the last three weeks I hadn't even paid for my own meals, and that if she wouldn't accept just that much, I would feel very uncomfortable. Finally, after much discussion Osaki said, "In that case, I'll take just enough to cover what you ate," and she accepted two thousand yen, but she wouldn't take any more than that.

There being no way to leave it, I was just putting away the remainder of the money when Osaki, as if she had been waiting for this very moment, timidly asked me, "I've already received money from you, but there's something else of yours I'd like to ask for." When I asked her what it was, she answered, "If you have more hand towels in Tokyo, would you mind giving me the hand towel you're using now?"

Trying to suppress the feelings welling up in me, I took the towel out of my Boston bag—the towel I had used every day for three weeks here in Amakusa, the towel Osaki had used last night to gently wipe away my tears. Accepting the towel with both hands, she said, "Thank you. Every time I use this towel it will remind me of you." She wore a happy smile that somehow also seemed sad.

At around 8 A.M., I dropped by the home of Osaki's sister-in-law, the old blind woman with blond hair, and spoke a few words of parting, just out of formality. Then I left Osaki's village. Osaki had said that she would like to see me off at least as far as Sakitsu, so we set off on foot. I decided that from there I would cross the islands on a bus bound for Kumamoto.

As we stood at the empty bus stop, Osaki took my hand in hers. Her face bore a strained expression as she told me over and over that she would like me to come again if I found the opportunity, and that she would be pleased if I would bring my husband and Mimi along too. Shortly the bus pulled up. I gave her slight shoulders a hug and then picked up my bag and climbed on board. At a signal from the young woman conductor, the bus started up, rocking back and forth. As I leaned out the window to wave, I noticed that Osaki's face was all distorted and that tears were rolling down her cheeks. My heart went out to her, but the bus had gathered speed, and her small frame soon vanished from my view.

The bus went from Ichimachida to Hondo, crossed the Hondo Seto Drawbridge to Amakusa–Kami Island, and then approached the Amakusa Pearl Line. Although I was going home to my husband and daughter, my spirits didn't lift. The rapidly shifting scenes outside my window—the dark blue sea, the islands, small fishing boats returning to port—were all very beautiful, but my thoughts could not settle on any of them. Instead, they were drawn back toward Osaki.

I wonder if Osaki has made it back to her own village? I wonder if she is talking to herself in the company of her cats, Pochi and Mii? What I thought about most, however, was how our conversation last night had so clearly revealed her fine character.

We generally consider intellectual and philosophical depth to be a state ultimately attainable by those with a solid cultural and academic background. That is, a person will read widely, thereby experiencing the truths harvested by others. She will systematize these truths and consider them in terms of their ethical value, and so on. Only then is it possible for her to attain a mature view of life.

But, if we look at Osaki from this viewpoint, she lacks all the conditions necessary to reach this philosophical height. She did not attend a single day of school, and cannot read a single letter or number. She has never encountered a piece of literature. And yet this very woman uttered words so sophisticated that they suggested a person of great philosophical depth. There can be no other interpretation than that she arrived at this state of mind through her life as a *karayuki-san*.

There may be no need to press my point, but in the life of a prostitute—a life given to permitting free play with one's flesh to many nameless men in return for money, but not for love—it is often the case that not only the flesh but also the spirit is despoiled. In a human society that has long upheld monogamy as the standard, prostitution violates established morals, and it is typical that women who have no recourse, save this occupation, find themselves the object of severe discrimination. Even if they should dream of an ordinary married life, their prayer is not granted. Instead, they are shunned by society, beset by scandalous diseases, and must continue to court poverty, with no end in sight. If they should then fall into decline out of spiritual despair, and head in a nonhuman, antisocial direction, who can blame them?

There are many people, however, who, though they may be sullied by the dirt of society, the more ugliness they encounter the more they learn from the experience, becoming ever more tolerant of and kind to others and continuing to mature as human beings. We can find a classic example in the character of the old pilgrim, Luka, from Maxim Gorky's play, *The Lower Depths.*

The setting for this play, written in 1902, is a sordid night lodging in nineteenth-century czarist Russia. The main characters include the greedy landlord and his lewd wife, a parasitic policeman, a sneak thief, an alcoholic actor, a locksmith, a streetwalker, porters, a heavy-drinking shoemaker, and so on—all people in the depths of despair. Living among these people, the old pilgrim, Luka, is equally kind to everyone, giving as much support as he can to all who need help. He consoles the locksmith's wife, Anna, who is on the verge of death. To her question, "Is it possible that I'll suffer in the other world as I did in this?" Luka replies, "Nothing of the sort! . . . You'll rest there . . . be patient." He encourages the alcoholic actor and the thief, Pepel, to change their outlook and start a new life. We know nothing about his past, but the reason that these people of the lower depths who believe in nothing at all are willing to listen to him is that his words are not based on cultural and academic education, but are the harvest of wisdom reaped from hardships piled upon hardships.

Although Osaki is not a man, I consider her Japan's "old Luka." Wandering to distant North Borneo, spending decades of her life in "the lower depths," selling her body to as many as thirty foreign men in one night, returning to her own country and struggling to keep herself alive in her old age on four thousand yen per month, looked upon by people with contempt, yet not becoming a cynic or indulging in antisocial behavior, Osaki's character was further refined. Moreover, while old Luka's kindness was based on Western humanism, taking only humans as its object, Osaki's kindness extended not only to people but also to the nine stray cats with whom she shared her food, saying, "They, too, are living creatures."

Most research on prostitution emphasizes the women's tragic circumstances and the sympathy of the researcher, but their "human worth" is completely ignored. Of course, in the final analysis, research on prostitution aims at the elimination of prostitutes from society and does not concern itself with character assessment. However, among the many types of prostitutes, including *karayuki-san,* while there are many who fall into despair as a result of having to sell their flesh to survive, there are others who rise out the filth to attain remarkable heights of philosophical discernment. This is a point unnoticed by research conducted to date. I felt compelled to write about it myself for the honor of those women surviving on the lowest rung of the social ladder through the sale of their most personal resource.

When I awoke from this reverie, the bus had just passed through Oyano Island and was approaching Tenmon Bridge. This bridge links

Oyano Island with Uto Peninsula. If you are coming from Kumamoto, it is the first of the five bridges that unite the Amakusa islands, and if you are leaving, it is the last.

The blue sea was as lovely as ever, but I knew that in crossing over this bridge I was leaving Amakusa behind. As I looked back in the distance toward Amakusa–Shimo Island, I silently spoke these words. "Farewell, Amakusa, good-bye, Osaki. And farewell to the graves of her friends Ofumi and Oshimo, and the grave of Okuni, who she loved as her own mother. Best wishes to all in Amakusa who helped me to learn about these women's lives."

As the small bus left Tenmon bridge, it rolled onto the soil of the Kyushu mainland.

—— 12 ——

Epilogue–*Karayuki-san* and Modern Japan

If the objective of my journey to Amakusa had been only to escape the clamor of the city, to gaze upon the green mountains and the sea, after but a year had passed my trip might have been reduced to a number of nostalgic scenes tucked away in the corner of my heart. However, my three-week sojourn on Amakusa-Shimo Island had quite the opposite effect, for the more time that passed, the more vivid the experience became, weighing heavily on my heart. Therefore, in order to be true to myself, I had to write about my trip to Amakusa, that is, my report on *karayuki-san*.

One of the reasons I remained stubbornly silent about Amakusa even while publishing articles on any number of other subjects was that I feared such exposure would not be in the best interest of Osaki and the other villagers, causing them embarrassment and inconvenience. Also, deep within, I wondered whether I had truly been able to capture the voiceless voice of the *karayuki-san*. There were certainly other methods of collecting materials than the one I employed, and there may have been another way to elicit her oral history. All I can say in my defense is that to the extent permitted by my own economic and family circumstances, and to the extent of my own sense of humanity, I did my very best.

Now, after two years, I have written at length about my journey to Amakusa. The one task that remains is to uncover some of the reasons why the *karayuki-san* phenomenon was concentrated in the Amakusa Islands of Kyushu. I defined the existence of the *karayuki-san* as the most elemental form of the lower-class woman, but if we are to examine this issue in context, the reasons behind the emergence of these women must be sought in the same phenomena that produced other women of the lowest rung of society.

If we are to sum up the major cause for the widespread appearance in this region of those overseas prostitutes called *karayuki-san,* it was, as we saw in Osaki's confession, none other than the backbreaking poverty of the Amakusa peasants. Osaki's childhood, even when she was still with her parents, was focused on day-to-day survival.

> There were days when I would have nothing to swallow but water from morning 'til night. When noon came around, or when the sun had set, I still hadn't had even the neck of a sweet potato to eat.

When her mother remarried, and the three children had to live by themselves, conditions became even harsher.

> By the time winter arrived, the barley box and potato tub were empty, and days would go by when not only was there no barley gruel, but we couldn't even sip on potato broth. Unlike the big house we lived in before, this little house didn't have anything like tatami. We were able to keep a fire going from dried twigs we gathered in the hills, but when the three of us would sit with empty stomachs on the wooden floor, we could think of nothing but food.

It will be acknowledged that "eating" is the minimum requirement for the sustenance of life, but Osaki and her siblings lived in such wretched circumstances that they did not even have sufficient food, let alone clothing and shelter. They were always on the brink of starvation. This was not true for Osaki and her family alone, however, but applied to every family who sent forth a daughter as a *karayuki-san,* and, indeed, even to the families of traffickers such as Muraoka Iheiji and Yoshinaka Tarozo.

But what was the source of this poverty, which was common to both the families of *karayuki-san* and procurers alike? Some explain that it stems from the inferiority of natural conditions on the islands, and has no other basis. Indeed, there are not a few persuasive points in this interpretation.

These people will tell you that the islands of Amakusa are large enough in terms of total land area that they should be able to sustain an independent local economy. However, they are made up of one mountain chain after another, and this is the source of the islands' poverty. In other words, though Amakusa does not have any particularly high peaks, the islands are mountainous throughout, and because the slopes are so steep, there are no large rivers. Flatland is scarce, and even if the people "plant all the way to heaven," creating terraced fields up the mountain slopes, the arable land thereby produced is insignificant. If the soil were fertile and produced an abundant harvest, that would be one thing, but the soil of Amakusa, consisting of ash deposits from the eruptions of Mt. Unzen soaring up to the north on the opposite shore of Shimabara, is extremely lean, capable of only low-level production.

Some might ask, if conditions on land are bad, why not establish one's livelihood by making use of the surrounding sea? With the exception of Ushibuka, however, Amakusa has not been blessed with good harbors, and due to the relationship of the tidal currents and other factors, there are few schools of fish that swim south of the Goto Islands, and so the establishment of a fishing industry would be difficult.

No one can deny that the inferiority of the natural resources on the Amakusa Islands has been a major cause of the poverty of its people. However, this is but one side of the coin. To get a glimpse of the other side, we must turn our gaze to the social conditions that have surrounded these people. In fact, it may be more accurate to say that it was not the natural conditions that existed before men moved onto these islands, but the various social conditions that developed after they moved there that are responsible for this poverty.

To begin with, in the Tokugawa period (1600–1868), the rate of taxation on crops in proportion to the yield was extremely high. According to *Amakusa kindai nenpu* [Modern Statistics of Amakusa] by Matsuda Tadao, and *Amakusa* by Yamaguchi Osamu, when Tokugawa Ieyasu became shogun in 1603, he bestowed upon Terasawa Hirotaka, lord of Karatsu Castle in Hizen, the two large islands of Amakusa as a reward for his performance in the Battle of Sekigahara. The first thing Terasawa did when he took possession of the islands was to have them surveyed. The total yield of all fields and paddies on the islands was determined to be the equivalent of thirty-seven thousand *koku,* one *koku* being the equivalent of 4.96 bushels. The sea was determined to yield the equivalent of five thousand *koku,* establishing the total value of the domain at forty-two thousand *koku.* Taxes against the peasants were levied accordingly. As you know, in the Tokugawa period taxes were paid in kind, generally in rice or barley. It was common for the rate of taxation to be set at 40–50 percent of the yield, so the peasants of Amakusa had to contribute between 15,000 and 18,500 *koku* each year.

If the soil had been productive, and if each household had been able to cultivate a sizable piece of land, the peasants probably could have paid this tax and still managed to survive. However, as previously mentioned, soil conditions in Amakusa were very poor, and there was very little arable land available for each household. Therefore, if the peasants put aside enough crops to equal the assessed value of the land, there was not enough left for minimum survival needs, let alone seed stock for replanting. Precisely because they faced such circumstances, the farmers of Amakusa cast their hopes for happiness not granted in this lifetime toward the Other Shore. Lending an ear to the Portuguese missionaries, who had just begun to propagate their faith, and to the words of the Christian daimyo, they too became Christians. In 1637–38, inflamed by the persecution of their faith as well as by the extreme poverty that had led them to embrace it, they bravely fought in what has come to be known as Shimabara–Amakusa Rebellion.

After this revolt against government policy, Amakusa was designated a part of the shogun's personal domain. Suzuki Saburokuro Shigenari was assigned the post of local magistrate, and his most significant accomplishment was to carry out a new land survey. He sent an appeal to the shogunate, requesting that the yield be assessed at about half the original amount, or twelve thousand *koku*. Such an appeal had no precedent and was rejected. As a last resort Shigenari resubmitted his appeal for reduced taxation to the shogunate and committed suicide through ritual disembowlment. The magistrate in a demesne of the shogun was expected to be the direct embodiment of the will of the shogunate. Nothing speaks more eloquently than Shigenari's appeals and his suicide to the fact that, magistrate though he was, he recognized that the fundamental cause of poverty among Amakusa's peasants lay in its disproportionately high taxation.

However, although these taxes caused inordinate hardship in themselves, it must be noted that Amakusa was burdened by yet another major problem. This problem, closely linked to the issue of taxation, was Amakusa's burgeoning population.

Whether you rely on records left by missionaries of the time, or look at documents left by the shogunate itself, it is clear that during the Shimabara–Amakusa Rebellion, shogunate forces exterminated Christians with a brutality that defies the imagination; in essence, they conducted a sweeping massacre of the peasantry. As a result, the population of Amakusa was reduced by half, and it is said that especially in the villages close to the Shimabara Peninsula, it was unusual to see smoke rising from a human dwelling or catch sight of the wild birds and mammals that used to inhabit the hills and fields. Thinking that it wouldn't do to leave things in this state, the year after the Rebellion was suppressed the shogunate instituted a resettlement policy, forcing people to move to Amakusa and to other domains in Kyushu. This went on for some fifty years.

Had there simply been a gradual increase in immigrants from other domains, things might not have been so bad, but from the middle of the Tokugawa period, Amakusa's population grew at an alarming rate. Designated a place of exile, Amakusa was forced to receive large numbers of prisoners from Kyoto and Edo. Moreover, because the surveillance of Christians was so strict, it was almost impossible for anyone to leave the islands. If we look at the statistical record, we see that population growth between 1863 and 1871 was especially pronounced, revealing a violent jump of 1,393 people per year, on average.

Had natural conditions been more hospitable, an increase in population would have meant an increase in labor power. Production would have risen accordingly, and poverty would not have been accelerated. But in resource-poor Amakusa an increase in population, far from bringing about an increase in productive power, only served to exacerbate the poverty of the entire island population. To elaborate the point, the soil of Amakusa's paddies and fields, lean as it was with its high concentration of fallen volcanic ash, could not be rendered more productive by increasing the labor force. A larger population had to exist on roughly the same yield, serving to push the islanders even deeper into poverty.

The peasants of Amakusa may well have expected that the Meiji Restoration of 1868, a major social upheaval restoring political power to the emperor and marking Japan's entry into the modern world, would serve to make their lives easier, but their hopes were not to be realized. Although the shogunal government had been toppled, the new Meiji government simply converted a tax in kind to a tax in currency and made no attempt to institute a policy that would lower the tax rate.

Naturally, then, the Amakusa peasant found himself struggling to survive in the same manner that he had during the period of Tokugawa feudalism. From the standpoint of the Amakusa peasants, however, one fundamental change did occur during the Meiji period (1868–1912). The ban against Christianity was lifted and the surveillance of religious sects abandoned. At last people could come to the islands and leave them as they pleased. Compared to life in the Tokugawa period when peasants had been forcibly bound to a land of low productivity, the freedom to travel at will certainly marked a step forward.

Absent change in the exploitive social structure, the only way the islanders could escape their grinding poverty was to leave the place of their birth, one by one, to find work outside. Peasants all over Amakusa employed this means to lessen the poverty of their family and relatives. The men found markets for their manual labor throughout Kyushu, and especially in Nagasaki. Some traveled abroad to work on plantations. Well, then, what did the women have to sell? There were some who pursued domestic positions as child care attendants and maids, but as domestic work has always been undervalued, the wages were very low. There were many women of Amakusa who accepted such jobs simply to reduce the number of mouths that had to be fed in their household, but there were also many coming from homes of such extreme poverty that they needed to be able to bring in a greater income than that available from domestic work. If we assume that these women, too, lacked any particular job skills or education, there was nothing they could sell but their own bodies.

In Meiji Japan we find migrant workers going ever farther abroad in increasingly large numbers. This was in part a reaction to the lifting of a longtime policy of isolation, and in truth it was easier to attain one's dreams of quick fortune abroad than at home. The Amakusa Islands were close both to the Chinese mainland and to Southeast Asia, and so when these islanders went overseas they did not suffer the same sense of separation experienced by those traveling away from the mainland of Honshu. So it was that the women of Amakusa who had determined to sell their own bodies, put their own country behind them, and set out for the Chinese mainland, or Siberia, or Southeast Asia. This was the birth of the *karayuki-san,* or overseas prostitute from Amakusa.

Thus, the advent of the *karayuki-san* may be attributed less to the natural conditions of the Amakusa Islands than to the social conditions prevailing in the Tokugawa feudal system and continuing into the early twentieth century. This being the case, the existence of *karayuki-san* is not an issue involving Amakusa alone, but is related to peasant life in many other regions of Japan and to women's issues that emanate from this peasant lifestyle. Or, it might be more accurate to say that the issue of *karayuki-san* is linked directly to problems surrounding the existence of all women in modern Japan. It is related, for example, to the existence of women working in the silk thread manufacturing and spinning industries of the Tohoku region, and to the existence of the Echigo geisha. In the Tohoku region of northeastern Honshu and the Hokuriku region opposite on the Japan Sea side, the land is buried under snow for nearly half the year, and so agricultural productivity is limited. However, the circumstances that pushed women into the textile industries or the life of a geisha were, more than anything, social in origin.

In the Tohoku region, during the Tokugawa period, low productivity combined with high taxes resulted in the spread of such vile practices as *mabiki,* the "thinning" of children at birth in an already crowded family, or the abandonment of older children.[1] Evidence of such practices may be found today in place names such as Warasugawara [Riverbed of Children]. During the Meiji period, while on the one hand the police kept an eye out for *mabiki* and child abandonment, on the other, textile industries began to flourish, resulting in a demand for factory girls. Now, girls of the Tohoku region who would have been subject to infanticide in the Tokugawa period were sent off to the cities as soon as they graduated from primary school and put to work in the factories. The picture presented by factory girl recruiters—in other words, procurers—that the girls would be able to continue their schooling and study flower arrangement and the tea ceremony and the like was far from the reality described in one factory worker song: "The factory is hell; the boss is a demon; the spinning wheels are wheels of fire." About life there the lyrics say, "Life in the dormitory is worse than being in prison, worse than being a caged bird."

In addition to the difficulties they experienced from heavy snow accumulation, the impoverished peasants of the Hokuriku region were inescapably ensnared by the landlord system. Moreover, ever since its propagation by Shinran, a religious leader of the thirteenth century, the Buddhist Pure Land faith, Jodo Shinshu, had set deep roots among these commoners. In other words, the land was monopolized by a small number of landlords, a system that forced the masses of peasants into poverty-level farming or tenant farming. The Pure Land faith, widespread among these peasants, set a high value on life, denouncing infanticide, which inevitably resulted in overpopulation of the region. In order to deal with the issue, some men left home to become professional quacks, selling snake oil in Toyoma, and some became apprentices to sake brewers or bathhouse attendants in Echigo. The women of this region were known for their snow-white skin, and those who did not go off to work in the textile industry became Echigo geisha.[2]

If we accept the fact that the appearance of this substratum of women in modern Japan—the *karayuki-san* of Amakusa, the textile factory girls, the Echigo geisha, and so on—was based more on social circumstances than on conditions arising from their natural environment, then it stands to reason that the government could have nipped these problems in the bud had it taken effective measures to do so. Because man cannot live in economic and spiritual isolation, society and the state are structures created by him for the basic purpose of guaranteeing his survival. Therefore, if there are people who are suffering for societal reasons, it is the obligation of that society to provide relief and to eradicate the problem at its very roots.

However, neither the Tokugawa government nor the modern Japanese state, built upon its collapse, made any attempt to help this substratum of Japanese women. Rather, it did quite the opposite. The Japanese government actually exploited these women in a most thorough and deliberate manner in order to invade other nations of Asia and thereby strengthen its sphere of influence.

Through its policy of seclusion, the Tokugawa shogunate had maintained peace in the country for close to 250 years. The modern Japanese state, on the other hand, which had been built in order to confront the military, political, and economic pressures exerted by the Western powers—nations that had already passed through the Industrial Revolution and instituted capitalist systems—established as its supreme goal the task of catching up with the advanced capitalist systems of the West.

Fukuzawa Yukichi, though long affiliated with the Opposition Party, was nonetheless one of the ideologues of the Meiji government. He wrote a treatise in 1885 called "Abandoning Asia" [*Datsua-ron*] in which he states that Japan should break its ties with Asia as soon as possible and align itself with the advanced capitalist nations. "Japan," he asserted, "should deal with China and Korea in the same way as Westerners do." Here we see a frank expression of the fundamental ideology espoused by the modern Japanese state. While Fukuzawa euphemistically says, "treat (Asia) in the same way as Westerners do," what he had in mind was the high-handed, merciless colonial rule instituted by the Western powers in Asia and Africa. Fukuzawa felt Japan should adopt this posture toward the rest of Asia.

By the middle of the Meiji period, toward the end of the 1880s, Japan was indeed making efforts to realize the slogan "rich nation, strong army," but there was as yet an insufficient accumulation of capital to achieve these goals. The country was weak economically and had little voice in the international arena. Japan could not readily advance its colonial rule in the rest of Asia without crossing swords with the Western powers, but she was not to be deterred. The Japanese state had one more scheme to advance her colonial rule: the exhaustive exploitation of women at the lowest level of society.

Muraoka Iheiji, the procurer mentioned in the first chapter, refers in his autobiography to *karayuki-san* and the traffickers under his command in the following manner.

> The women write letters home and send money each month. Their parents find some financial relief and earn a reputation in the neighborhood. Soon the village head has heard the news and imposes an income tax. One cannot overemphasize how much the country benefits from this. Not only does the brothel owner prosper, but the families of the girls do also. Moreover, no matter where you establish a brothel in the South Seas, soon a general store will appear. Shop clerks come from Japan. Companies open up branch offices. Even the master of a brothel will open up a business because he dislikes being referred to as a pimp. Within one year land developers are on the increase. Meanwhile Japanese ships begin to call. Gradually the place prospers.

No doubt this was something the trafficker Iheiji wrote in order to rationalize his immoral work. To some extent, however, he outlines a means for implementing the Japanese colonial policy advocated by Fukuzawa Yukichi. In other words, while the modern Japanese state was still too weak to advance on the Chinese mainland and the islands of Southeast Asia politically and militarily, it advanced economically in a way that required no capital outlay. It adopted a policy of sending out prostitutes, or *karayuki-san,* in large numbers, and using the foreign capital thus acquired to realize the slogan "rich nation, strong army." According to *Hojin kaigai hattenshi* [A History of Japanese

Overseas Development] by Irie Toraji, in 1900 Japanese emigrant workers in Siberia, primarily in Vladivostok, sent back to Japan about one million yen. Of this sum, 630,000 yen came from *karayuki-san.*

An article on *karayuki-san* entitled "A Land of Women," in the *Fukuoka nichinichi shimbun* [Fukuoka Daily News] dated September 9, 1926, also sheds light on this subject.

> These women . . . who traveled overseas from the four villages under the jurisdiction of the Kohama Government Seat [Shimabara] sent more than twelve thousand yen home to their families last year. If we calculate the total for the thirty villages and towns of the entire Shimabara Peninsula, the figure for last year exceeded three hundred thousand yen.

When the value of currency was high during the Meiji and Taisho periods, one can only imagine how much this foreign currency must have contributed to furthering the goal of "rich nation, strong army."

Seen from this perspective, the existence of *karayuki-san* was necessary to Japan until she could measure up to the Western powers politically, economically, and militarily. Therefore, regardless of repeated demands from Christians of conscience, from advocates of women's liberation—liberation in the broadest sense of the term—and from consuls stationed throughout Asia to rehabilitate the overseas prostitutes and control the traffickers, the government made no attempt to do anything. Naturally, the government did not give a thought to rehabilitating the *karayuki-san.* It made no move to curb the activities of the traffickers, who operated without restraint. Most importantly, the government did nothing to help the peasantry rise out of poverty, the womb from which all *karayuki-san* were born. It was only after Japanese capitalism was on stable ground at the end of the Meiji period, and after Japan had successfully fished the troubled waters of World War I, gaining enough political, economic, and military strength to compete, if only barely, with the Western powers, that the government issued an edict prohibiting overseas prostitution.

Moreover, this antiprostitution law was, in my opinion, so slipshod and so cruel, it makes you wonder how the government ever devised it. Let me explain. First of all, at the beginning of the Taisho period, around 1911–1912, owing to reports and pleas from consulates throughout Southeast Asia, the government was on the verge of strengthening its stance against overseas prostitution. But in 1915, when Japan presented China with its Twenty-One Demands, Chinese merchants throughout Southeast Asia protested by boycotting Japanese goods, and the Japanese government suspended its promulgation of the antiprostitution law. The Chinese boycott against Japanese goods was so effective that Japanese businesses throughout Southeast Asia began to collapse, one after another, and Japan faced a major crisis in the acquisition of foreign currency. The government quietly began to encourage the work of *karayuki-san,* and through their earnings were able to extricate themselves from a perilous position. However, to the Chinese, *karayuki-san* were no more than another form of Japanese merchandise, and so these women had to go to great efforts to increase their customers.

The stormy season of the boycott finally passed. Due to its alliance with the victorious nations in World War I, Japan's position in Southeast Asia stabilized, and so finally it took the step to abolish prostitution. However, the government did not take a single step to establish a rehabilitation policy to accompany its antiprostitution legislation. What the government did do was to round up *karayuki-san* from far and wide, force them on board Japanese ships, and dump them off in the vicinity of Nagasaki. And that was all. The government made no attempt to assist the women in beginning new lives or to help relatives back home who had depended on their earnings. Therefore these women, who still needed to send home substantial amounts of money, drifted off to undeveloped regions where they would be beyond the surveillance of Japanese officials and local Japanese associations. It is said that older *karayuki-san* who were unable to switch to other kinds of jobs had no recourse but to take their own lives. Such was the only "present" the Japanese government bequeathed to the *karayuki-san.* This was the reality of the legislation prohibiting overseas prostitution by Japanese women.

By now it should be clear that the *karayuki-san* was the pathetic victim of modern Japan's policy of aggression toward Asia. When we, as Japanese women, seek those who moan in suffering at the bottom rung of society, the more deeply and seriously we probe, we find that time and again what we run into is the modern Japanese state. It is our own government, which did not give the slightest thought to the people in general, let alone women, which we must confront head-on.

Half a century has passed since Japan issued, in the mid-Taisho period, a formal proclamation against overseas prostitution, and it has been a quarter of a century since Japan's defeat in World War II. The term *karayuki-san* is practically dead, and those women who worked as prostitutes on the Chinese mainland and in Southeast Asia are now in their seventies and eighties. One by one their lights are fading and going out. However, even when the last *karayuki-san* vanishes from the mountain recesses and coastal hamlets of Shimabara and Amakusa, the *karayuki-san* will not have left Japan for good.

This we know—that during World War II the Japanese Army invading China and the nations of Southeast Asia took with them Japanese and Korean women referred to as *ianfu,* or "comfort women." This we also know—that following Japan's defeat and her occupation by the Allied troops consisting mainly of Americans, "pan-pan girls" (*panpan gaaru*) sprang up like mushrooms after a rain to sell their favors. And further still, we know that although Japan should have become an independent nation upon signing the peace treaty, the grim reality is that American bases are still located throughout the country, most notably on Okinawa, and that around these bases swarm "special women" (*tokushu onna*) who sell themselves.

Although the clientele of comfort women serving the Japanese military were not foreigners, but fellow Japanese, from the standpoint that these women were forced to go overseas and sell their flesh, they were no different from the *karayuki-san* of the past. And, although the so-called "pan-pan girls" and "special women" of today do not have to go to distant destinations overseas, inasmuch as they take both black and white American customers, that is, from the standpoint that they serve foreigners, they are none other than present-day *karayuki-san.*

Among these present-day *karayuki-san* there is surely not a one who willingly took this path, imagining such a life to be ideal. If we take a look at these women one by one, we find a variety of reasons for their present circumstances: some fell into despair at having been betrayed by a lover; others lost all hope after being raped by strangers. However, there are few who entered prostitution for purely personal reasons; the majority entered upon this path for social reasons. And that it is poverty that lurks at the root of all such social reasons can be understood quite clearly upon reading the several volumes of memoirs published by prostitutes—for example, Okochi Masako's *Yoshiwara,* or Goto Tsutsumu's *Nihon no teiso* [Japan's Chastity].

If we then question the source of this poverty that compels women to take such steps, it lies not in the laziness of these women or their families, but in the policies of our modern Japanese government, which favors a few monopolistic enterprises and ignores laborers and farmers. If this is true, then the only way to get to the roots of the issue and cure our present-day *karayuki-san* problem once and for all is to eradicate the poverty that compels women to sell their flesh. We must change this government which has willfully neglected such poverty without once looking back. Yet this alone is insufficient. We must reform the political and social systems that made such poverty inevitable, and create a society that truly expresses the will of the people.

If we succeed in conquering poverty, not only will we have freed the last of present-day *karayuki-san,* such as those women who surround American military bases, particularly in Okinawa, but we will have liberated Japanese women as a whole. In his *Frau und der Sozialismus* [Woman Under Socialism], August Bebel (1840–1913) echoes Marx and Engels in saying that women's problems, including prostitution, are "only one of the aspects of the general Social Question, which is now filling all heads, which is setting all minds in motion and which, consequently, can find its final solution only in the abolition of the existing social contradictions, and of the evils which flow from them."[3]

Two years have passed since I returned from Amakusa. Though I very much wanted to write this manuscript, indeed felt obligated to do so, I hesitated to take up my pen. Now, as I rest my eyes, ready to bring this manuscript to a close, the image of Tenshudo Chapel in Sakitsu appears before me. Its dark gray steeple rises high above the flat roofs of the humble homes around it, the white cross at its peak mirrored in the quiet sea below. Inside, surrounded by panels of stained glass, an old farm woman, as still as a stone image, kneels before the altar.

I felt at that time that she was not praying for something as abstract as forgiveness of humankind for original sin, but for ultimate deliverance from her unending burden of poverty and hardship. It was in this sense, I wrote, that *karayuki-san* and elderly peasant women represent two branches of the same tree. When will these women, who have experienced bitter hardship in so many forms, be allowed, if not to know happiness, at least to partake of a way of life that fulfills basic needs for health and comfort? Until that day arrives, whenever I see the name "Amakusa," or hear the word *karayuki-san,* and whenever I speak of "women's liberation," I will inevitably see before me the old farm woman at her prayers in Tenshudo Chapel at Sakitsu.

Translator's Notes

1. For an extensive discussion of this topic, see William R. LaFleur, *Liquid Life, Abortion and Buddhism in Japan* (Princeton: Princeton University Press, 1992). LaFleur defines *mabiki* as "the culling of seedlings." "The agricultural analogy and its intention are patent: just as the growing of rice may yield a better crop if along the way certain weaker seedlings are removed, so too in human affairs the culling of some infants and fetuses may be desirable. Families, so the rationale undoubtedly went, needed thinning out as much as did rice fields glutted with more seedlings than could possibly survive," pp. 99–100. In the Amakusa region *mabiki* was not extensively practiced due to the influence of Christianity. Instead, family size was reduced by the selling of children. Mikiso Hane, *Peasants, Rebels and Outcastes* (New York: Pantheon Books, 1982), p. 218.

2. Echigo is the old name of Niigata Prefecture.

3. August Bebel, *Woman Under Socialism* (New York, Schocken Books, 1973), p. 1. Translated from the original German of the 33rd edition by Daniel De Leon.

In *Woman Under Socialism,* first published in 1879 and revised in 1891, Bebel, one of the principal leaders of German socialism, provided a platform for the socialist women's movement. Not only did he support all the feminist demands of his day, but he actually went further than did most feminists of his time. The passage quoted in Yamazaki's text continues: "Nevertheless, it is necessary to treat the so-called Woman Question separately. On the one hand the question, What was the former position of woman, what is it today, and what will it be in the future? concerns, in Europe at least, the larger section of society, seeing that here the female sex constitutes the larger part of the population. On the other hand, the prevailing notions, regarding the development that woman has undergone in the course of the centuries, correspond so little with the facts, that light upon the subject becomes a necessity for the understanding of the present and the future. Indeed, a good part of the prejudices with which the ever-growing movement is looked upon in various circles—and not last in the circle of woman herself—rests upon lack of knowledge and lack of understanding."

Author's Afterword to the First Edition (1972)

As I peruse the galley proofs in front of me, I find myself beset by a mixture of emotions; I am at once happy and sad, and a bit anxious as well. I am delighted to see my third book in print, but when I think that with the publication of this book I will have brought to a conclusion many years of research on *karayuki-san,* I cannot help but feel sad. Then, when I consider that the publication of this work may bring about some unexpected inconvenience to those who assisted me or of whom I wrote, I feel quite uneasy.

As I mentioned in chapter 1, it was in 1968 that I spent three weeks living in Amakusa with a former *karayuki-san.* It was two years later, in 1970, that I completed my manuscript describing this experience. There are probably few researchers who are not anxious to publish the results of their work. I had two reasons, however, for not revealing my work to anyone until now. I continued to wonder if I had been able to hear, as clearly as I might, the voice of the *karayuki-san.* In addition, I was concerned that the publication of my work would cause problems for the many residents of Amakusa who were so kind to me.

The reason I have decided now, two years later, to publish my work is that a number of conditions have changed.

First of all, it has become popular of late for the mass media to deal with issues about the lower classes. Journalism has turned its spotlight on *karayuki-san,* with the result that a number of people have come to me asking for materials or introductions. Some articles were written simply for the reader's amusement, and looking at this trend I began to question the wisdom of my reticence. With the hope that I could bring honor to the name of *karayuki-san,* I decided that I must publish a record of those life stories I had gone to such lengths to hear.

In the second place, the elderly *karayuki-san,* Osaki, who had shared her home with me, moved to another location, and it would now be more difficult for anyone to find her. Moreover, Osaki has grown very weak lately, and I would very much like to present her with this record of her life while she is still living.

Structurally, my work assumes the form of a travel account, but I intend it to be a research document. At first I thought I should minimize subjectivity and emotion, but due to the nature of the theme and my unique methods of collecting information, my writing took the form of a travelogue. With the exception of a few small fictional touches, the content is an accurate rendition of the facts. However, to avoid inconveniencing anyone, I have omitted village names and some other place names. The names of all people have been changed. The reader may say this negates the significance of entries from family registers, but it was a measure I had to take to protect the individuals concerned. In order to document Osaki's present lifestyle I made a third trip to Amakusa to see her, accompanied by artist Yamamoto Michiyo as photographer. However, in order to protect Osaki, these photographs will not be included in my book.

I would like to take this opportunity to thank many people, but especially the residents of Amakusa, for their kindhearted cooperation. Without their help, I could never have written this documentary. In that sense, this work should be considered co-authored by them. I borrowed many valuable photographs from the people of Amakusa, all of which have been returned to their owners.

Amakusa novelist Shima Kazuharu was kind enough to check the Amakusa dialect used in "Osaki's Story," and Miyaoka Kenji, the author of *Shofu-kaigai roruki* [Prostitutes—A Record of Overseas Journeys], mentioned earlier in the text, allowed me to read through thousands of travel accounts in his possession. I am grateful to critic Usui Yoshimi who, despite his failing eyesight, reviewed hundreds of pages of manuscript, and made this publication possible. Finally, I would like to express my appreciation for all the advice offered by my husband, Kami Shoichiro, a researcher of children's culture, as I revised my work.

In closing, I would like to introduce a letter sent to me by Osaki last autumn. Because Osaki cannot read or write a single letter, it has been the pattern for a neighbor to write thank-you notes on her behalf when I have sent her things from time to time over the past four years. Lately an elementary schoolgirl who lives next door has been writing for her, and I have received nearly fifty letters. Indeed, I receive not only letters. Even though Osaki has a very limited budget, she sends me presents as well—local products like seaweed and mountain greens. In the course of this four-year exchange, I have come to call her "Mother" from the depths of my heart.

This is the first letter written by the little elementary schoolgirl for Osaki. Of all the letters, I believe that this one expresses Osaki's feelings most directly.

September 19

Dear Yamazaki Tomoko,

Thank you for sending money, as always. I've become very weak from my asthma. I don't have a kotatsu in this house either, but please don't send one.¹ I'm not at my old place any more, but a little to the * * * of where I used to be.

I think of you as my daughter, and call you Tomoko, so please think of me as your mother.

I wake up at four every morning and pray for your well-being to Odaishisama and to other gods.

This is about all that I can do, but I'm praying with all my might. I imagine you must face many difficulties too, but please don't let anything get you down.

When are you coming to visit again? The next time you come, please bring your daughter.

I'll be waiting.

Please take care of yourself.

I'm Sachiko. Grandmother prays for you every day, Auntie.² Please come to Grandmother's house again.

From Yamakawa Saki
(Okada Sachiko)

As soon as this book has been printed, I plan to take a copy to Amakusa. So far I have experienced Amakusa only in the summer and fall. The next time I visit I will be able to see Amakusa at the end of spring. But my thoughts have already taken off ahead of me, reaching out toward the sea and hills and making their way to Osaki's side.

Translator's Notes

Sandakan hachiban shokan was first published in hardback by Chikuma Shobo in 1972. Bungei Shunju assumed rights for the paperback edition in 1975.

1. A low table with electric coils under the tabletop; a quilt hangs over it to keep in the warmth. One sits on the tatami, with one's feet underneath the quilt. In traditional homes, *kotatsu* was a hole in the floor where one placed a charcoal brazier. One sat at a low table placed over the hole, dangling one's feet down to keep them warm next to the brazier.

2. *Obaasan* "Grandmother," and *obasan*, "Auntie," are polite ways to refer to an older woman and a young to middle-aged woman, respectively, particularly by younger members of their own sex.

Translator's Afterword

Reader Response

Was the publication of *Sandakan Brothel No. 8* an invasion of Osaki's privacy? This question tormented Yamazaki, as she began to piece together Osaki's story. She submitted the manuscript to a large publishing house. The editor assigned to her work made so many changes that he had in effect rewritten the book. Some acquaintances encouraged Yamazaki to accept the changes just so that she could see the book in print. Acquiescing to their advice, she called the publisher. Then, her true feelings emerged. She was furious. Instead of giving the editor permission to print his version of her book, she demanded that he restore her manuscript to its original form, and return it. (Since this happened before home computers were available, the original manuscript and all changes were handwritten.) Perhaps it was best not to publish the manuscript after all, she decided.

Shortly after this incident, Yamazaki paid another visit to Osaki. "You told me you were going to write up my words in a book. Has it come out yet?" she asked. Yamazaki explained what had happened. In the sixteen years that she knew her, Yamazaki writes in a 1989 essay, this was the most forceful reaction she had elicited from the old woman. "Tomoko, what nonsense you are talking. Since I can't write, there is no way I can express myself. If you don't write the words for me, who else will reveal what is stored in my heart?"

"I felt like I had been struck by thunder," Yamazaki writes. "I realized that my pen was really her pen, and I finally got the courage to pursue publication of the manuscript."[1] Shortly afterward, Yamazaki met Usui Yoshimi, noted critic of cultural affairs and founder of the journal *Tenbo*. Usui read Yamazaki's manuscript and recommended it for publication, without editorial change, by Chikuma Shobo.

When *Sandakan hachiban shokan* appeared in 1972, the book met with overwhelming reader response. Ms. Yamazaki received letters from innumerable readers, ranging in age from a fourteen-year-old girl to a man in his nineties, and representing a broad spectrum of occupations, from university professors in foreign countries to local bar hostesses. Initially, a major sector of her audience consisted of young women in high school. Yamazaki read their letters with interest, wondering what would attract these girls to someone so far removed from their age and era. One girl wrote, "I felt both a sense of shock at the tragedy of Osaki's existence and a sense of humiliation, as if I myself had been violated."[2] Yamazaki realized that this sense of identification was possible because she had not written about *karayuki-san* as if they were part of the past, but as a category of person still living in the present. Osaki took her first customer when she was twelve or thirteen. These young teens could identify with Osaki's feelings as they learned about a new aspect of the history of women in their own country.

Older readers, on the other hand, were familiar with the former system of licensed prostitution, and a number of them had even heard about *karayuki-san*. Their letters did not express the element of surprise present in the high school girls' reaction. These older readers expressed a deep sympathy for the *karayuki-san*. Yet, the focus of their interest was not on these women's past but on their present. They saw in Osaki "the ideal image of the elderly person," someone with a giving nature who respected the privacy of others.[3] The disintegration of the family unit is one cost of Japan's rapid move into a high-growth industrial society. Hence, the people who experience the greatest sense of isolation and loneliness are the elderly, particularly women. This generation of women, explains Yamazaki, lived their lives for their fathers, their husbands, and their sons. Many of these elderly women could identify with Osaki, cast out in society, without psychological and economic support.

When she was working on her manuscript, Yamazaki relates, she did not imagine her audience to be the academic elite or people of money and leisure, but the average person on the street. A housewife with little to spare herself sent a small amount of money each month, with instructions for Yamazaki to pass it on to Osaki. A gambler wrote from prison with promises to reform and do better by his wife and children. In one location a number of bar hostesses met as a group to discuss their own lives in the context of Yamazaki's book. One day Yamazaki gave a lecture in Shikoku on changes in the status of Japanese women over the past hundred years. Afterward a man approached her with tears in his eyes. He said he was sixty-eight and that he had worked for some time during World War II as an accountant at a famous brothel in the Kansai district.[4] The most important part of his job, he related, was not keeping the books but keeping the girls in line. If a girl did not bring in much income, or was choosy about customers, or tried to escape, it was his job to take her into a room where bedding was stored and lash her with a whip. He said he could still hear their screams ringing in his ears, and that Yamazaki's book had made him reflect upon his own contribution to the misery of lower-class women.[5]

Another reader, a young sailor just out of high school, read Yamazaki's book while working on a route through Southeast Asia. He hadn't even imagined, he said, that there were women like Osaki who worked as prostitutes at Sandakan and other port towns. One evening, he wrote in a letter to Yamazaki, he was talking about her book with some shipmates when an old sailor who had been in the Japanese Imperial Army spoke up and told the group he had been in Sandakan during the war. "He said that since there weren't any battles to be fought, the soldiers decided it was their division's moral duty to stage a guerrilla mop-up. Soldiers went into a nearby village and raped the women. It would have been inconvenient for the noncommissioned officers, had they been discovered, so they killed the eyewitnesses. If there were soldiers who were too weak-hearted to shoot a person, an officer would order them to do the killing." For someone born after the war, such as this young sailor, such brutality was hard to imagine. When he read Yamazaki's book, he said, he was filled with anger and sorrow at the plight of the *karayuki-san*; but when he heard his senior shipmate talking about the war, he felt even sadder that Japanese had committed such atrocities. He had just read about the discovery of a *karayuki* cemetery in Sandakan, he said. He planned to pay a visit and scatter flowers.

The *karayuki* cemetery to which the young sailor referred was the cemetery established by Okuni, owner of Brothel No. 8. Yamazaki first learned that these graves had been uncovered on Obon, or All Souls' Day, in mid-August, when the Japanese believe that the spirits of their ancestors return to the home of their descendants. In the early morning hours Yamazaki was awakened by an excited voice, "We've found the grave of Kinoshita Kuni!"

One of Yamazaki's readers was a Japanese man in the business of importing hardwoods. He often went to Sandakan on business and had in fact lived there for seven years. After reading Yamazaki's book, this businessman had been curious about the *karayuki* gravesite and had searched the outskirts of the city in the vicinity of a cemetery built for Chinese residents and another that had been built for the Japanese military. One day, when he was clearing an old path, taken over by the tropical forest beyond the Chinese cemetery, he came upon a concrete box partway up the hill. Clearing away more vegetation, he discovered one grave after another, in a place commanding a fine view of Sandakan Bay. The largest grave was that of Kinoshita Kuni. He also located the grave of Yasutani Kiyoji, Ofumi's lover and Matsuo's father. The grave marker showed that Yasutani had died on August 21, 1941, at age sixty-one. He was from the Shimabara Peninsula, one of a few poor migrant workers who made his fortune in the South Seas. By the time he died he owned four hundred acres of coconut plantation.[6]

Upon hearing this news Yamazaki herself visited the site. In Sandakan she met an elderly local couple familiar with Yasutani. The man had worked on Yasutani's plantation, and it turned out that his wife had managed a coffee shop very close to Brothel No. 8 in the early '20s. She had known Okuni, she said—a thin woman, in her sixties at that time. There were seven or eight girls working at Okuni's place, the woman recalled. When customers wanted Malaysian food, Okuni would send them down to this coffee shop. The girls would come by on their own, as well, when they had free time at midday. Perhaps Osaki was among them.

More About Osaki

As soon as *Sandakan Brothel No. 8* came off the press, Yamazaki went to Amakusa and presented a copy to Osaki. She had been looking forward to giving a copy to Osaku, daughter of Kinoshita Kuni, and to Mr. Sano, who had accompanied her to Osaku's house, but both of these kind Amakusa residents had passed away. In response to reader interest and concern, Yamazaki wrote a number of essays about Osaki following the publication of *Sandakan Brothel No. 8*. Although she does not say so directly, it is clear that Yamazaki made use of income from her book and subsequent movie rights to look after Osaki's welfare.

We know from Yamazaki's Afterword that Osaki moved to a house not too far from her old one. After Yamazaki returned to Tokyo, she continued to correspond with Osaki about twice a month. Until Osaki moved, she would have the lady who owned the general store or the postman read and write letters for her. After the move, a fourth-grader, Sachiko, who lived nearby took over as letter writer. Fond of children, Osaki had helped take care of Sachiko when she was a baby, carrying her about on her back. Yamazaki relates that when she spent three weeks with Osaki, Sachiko would drop by almost every day to chat or run errands. When Sachiko wrote letters for Osaki, she would write down everything, just as Osaki had dictated. To thank Sachiko for her help, Yamazaki began sending her clothes that her daughter had outgrown, as well as new school supplies. When Yamazaki went to Amakusa to present Osaki with a copy of *Sandakan Brothel No. 8,* she again met Sachiko and her younger brother Yuichi.

"I was looking forward to seeing how they had grown, but brother and sister standing under the dim lightbulb were much shorter than I had expected they would be. While my own daughter was growing rapidly, Sachiko, only a year younger, appeared not to have grown at all. Her bony frame seemed about half my daughter's height.

"Noticing that I couldn't bring myself to utter the typical greeting, 'How big you've gotten,' Osaki spoke up from the sidelines, explaining the family circumstances. Three years ago the children's father had lost his sight and been hospitalized. He eventually returned home, but he couldn't work, so their mother had to go out to work as a day laborer in order to support a family of five. Sachiko and her two siblings would come home as soon as school was out to work in their vegetable garden. Besides doing gardening, Sachiko, as the oldest, had to care for the two younger children and do all the housework.

"As Sachiko clenched her large hands together, listening to Osaki's words, I couldn't help seeing superimposed on her the image of ten-year-old Osaki when she was sent overseas."[7]

Yamazaki relates that when adults had written letters for Osaki, they had made polite references to the weather, followed by formal thanks for money received, and so on. In Sachiko's case, however, she would always mention how Osaki's asthma was, how the nine cats were doing, and that Osaki had prayed to Odaishisama.

In the popular worship of Odaishisama we see a mixture of Shinto and Buddhist elements. Odaishisama is a term used to denote an extremely virtuous and highly revered monk. In Japan the term was applied especially to the Buddhist monk Kukai, or Kobo Daishi (774–

835), about whom legends are told throughout the country. In Shinto, which encompasses a variety of indigenous beliefs predating the introduction of Buddhism to Japan in the sixth century, one finds the worship of spirits and deities of nature as well as the spirits of ancestors, including wise men and saints. In this sense Odaishi may also be considered a Shinto deity.[8] Folk religions, such as the worship of Odaishisama, have been revived in many rural areas in response to the isolation of the individual in the process of modernization.

When Osaki wanted to communicate directly with Odaishisama, she would hike to a neighboring village where an everyday farm woman served as a medium, or *miko*,[9] between this deity and his supplicants. Osaki would find the farm woman out in the fields and let her know she had come to worship. The farm woman would walk back to the farmhouse with Osaki, chatting about the weather or the crops. At the farmhouse, the medium would serve her guest with tea and seasonal pickled vegetables, engaging her guest in conversation in order to learn what troubles or thanks the believer might want to express to her god. Eventually the medium would stand up and drape a shawl of white cloth about her shoulders. With her farm smock thus covered, she assumed a new persona, upon which she would sit down in front of the altar and begin to pray. The prayer was particular to each visitor, conveying those concerns they had just expressed over tea. The deity would then respond through the medium, assuring the believer that her prayers would be answered. Relieved to know that her message had been communicated, a believer such as Osaki would be able to return home with a lighter heart.[10]

The reader will recall that Osaki became an ardent believer in Odaishisama after a visit to this deity brought an end to the severe headaches that had assailed her following Okuni's death. In Osaki's old age Odaishisama continued to provide spiritual strength. Osaki's diet and asthmatic condition gave Yamazaki much cause for worry, however, and she made arrangements for two local residents to look after her Amakusa "mother." One of these residents was the woman who owned the little shaved-ice shop where Yamazaki first encountered Osaki. The owner's family were Catholics who had gone into hiding after the persecution of Christians in the early Tokugawa period, and she herself was a devout believer. Yamazaki paid the proprietress monthly to provide Osaki with a large meal whenever she stopped by, including fresh fruits and vegetables and her favorite drink, *shochu.*[11] On days when Osaki did not stop by the little restaurant, arrangements were made for the neighborhood children to deliver a box lunch, in which case a lunch for the child was included as well. In another village there was a retired doctor who continued to practice in Amakusa in order to offer services at no or very low cost to poor rural residents. Yamazaki made arrangements for this gentleman to check on Osaki regularly and to provide periodic medical exams.[12] Osaki continued to live modestly, but with further provisions for her health and comfort, and found new happiness through frequent contact with her "adopted daughter" Tomoko. Osaki died on April 30, 1984.

Translator's Notes

1. Yamazaki Tomoko, *Ikite ikite* [Living] (Tokyo: Kairyusha, 1992), pp. 51–53.
2. Yamazaki Tomoko, *Sandakan no haka* [The Graves of Sandakan] (Tokyo: Bungei Shunju, 1977) pp. 187–89.
3. Ibid., pp. 194–98.
4. The Kyoto–Osaka–Kobe region.
5. Ibid., pp. 226–30.
6. The discovery of the cemetery established by Kinoshita Okuni is described in *Sandakan no haka*, pp. 9–34.
7. Yamazaki writes about Sachiko and her family in an essay, "Little Letter Writers," included in *Sandakan no haka*, pp. 199–202.
8. Hiro Sachiya, *Bukkyo to Shinto* (Tokyo: Shincho Sensho, 1987), pp. 99–102.
9. *Miko* refers to a shamanic medium who acts as a mouthpiece for a *kami* (spiritual beings who are the principal objects of worship in Shinto), or an ancestor. This word is used today to designate women who assist in rituals in large Shinto shrines. For further information on *miko,* see Carmen Blacker, *The Catalpa Bow* (London: George Allen and Unwin, 1982).
10. Yamazaki, *Sandakan no haka*, pp. 211–14.
11. *Shochu* is a distilled spirit made from sweet potatoes, rice, buckwheat, or other ingredients. It is strong and relatively inexpensive. *Shochu* has been regarded traditionally as a low-class drink, but current research suggests that *shochu* drunk in moderation may be helpful in preventing heart problems and cerebral thrombosis. *Shochu*'s ability to prevent or dissolve blood clots is apparently most effective in liquor made from sweet potatoes, which is the type of *shochu* most readily available in the Amakusa region. *The Japan Times Weekly International Edition,* November 24–30, 1997; p. 17.
12. Yamazaki, *Sandakan no haka,* pp. 220–25.

Southeast Asia, c. 1900

British colonial territory	
Dutch colonial territory	
French colonial territory	

0   250   500 Miles

0   250   500 Kilometers

MONGOLIA

RUSSIA

MANCHURIA

KOREA

JAPAN

CHINA

Nagasaki

KYUSHU

Shanghai

RYUKYU
ISLANDS

INDIA

Canton   Amoy

TAIWAN
(FORMOSA)

BURMA

TONKIN

MACAO

LAOS   Hanoi

HONG
KONG

British
Sphere

SIAM   French Sphere

ANNAM

PHILIPPINES

Manila

CAMBODIA

SOUTH
CHINA
SEA

PACIFIC
OCEAN

Saigon

COCHIN
CHINA

British
Sphere

NORTH
BORNEO

Sandakan

Davao

Penang

MALAYA
(British
Protectorate)

BRUNEI

SARAWAK
(British Protectorate)

Mt. Kinabalu / 4101m

Tawau

SUMATRA

SINGAPORE

BORNEO

CELEBES

INDIAN
OCEAN

JAVA

DUTCH EAST INDIES

SCALE:
0 250 500 Miles
0 250 500 Kilometers

RUSSIA

MONGOLIA

MANCHURIA
(MANCHUKUO)

KOREA
(CHOSEN)

SAKHALIN
ISLAND

KURILE
ISLANDS

HOKKAIDO

SEA
OF
JAPAN

Amur River

Hwang Ho

CHINA

Yangtze River

Nagasaki

Shanghai

Tokyo JAPAN

HONSHU

SHIKOKU

KYUSHU

INSET
AREA

PACIFIC
OCEAN

RYUKYU
ISLANDS

BONIN
ISLANDS

VOLCANO
ISLANDS

Amoy

Swatow

Canton

HONG
KONG
(British)

TAIWAN
(FORMOSA)

Hanoi

FRENCH

THAILAND INDO-

CHINA

Saigon

SOUTH
CHINA
SEA

PHILIPPINES

MARIANA
ISLANDS

GUAM (U.S.)

JAPANESE
MANDATE

**Extent of Japanese Empire
in 1941**

Japanese territory

0 25 50 Miles
0 25 50 Kilometers

Shimabara
Peninsula

Nagasaki
Peninsula
Tachibana Bay
Hayasaki Straits
Shimo Island

AMAKUSA
NADA
SEA

Nagasaki Moji

Oniike

Shimoda

Sakitsu Hondo

Ushibuka

AMAKUSA
ISLANDS

Kami
Island

Minamata

207

Preparing for a press conference about the movie "Sandakan Brothel No. 8." From left to right: Kumai Kei, director; Yamazaki Tomoko, author; Takahashi Yoko, actor playing Osaki as a young woman; Kurihara Komaki, actor playing Yamazaki; and Tanaka Kinuyo, actor playing Osaki as an old woman. © TOHO CO. LTD.

From the movie: Tomoko spends three weeks with Osaki, learning about her past and present lives. © TOHO CO. LTD.

Index

About the Author
and Translator

Yamazaki Tomoko has published numerous books and articles documenting the modern history of lower-class Japanese women who have gone abroad and Asian women who have come to Japan. For three decades she has conducted a study group in Tokyo which provides a forum for research on women's history in the context of Japan's interaction with Asian countries.

Karen Colligan-Taylor is Professor of Japanese Studies and Women's Studies at the University of Alaska-Fairbanks. She earned her Ph.D. at Stanford University, focusing on the evolution of environmental literature in Japan. In her current research she continues to explore the environmental and human costs of rapid economic development.